Approaching Emily Dickinson

Studies in American Literature and Culture:
Literary Criticism in Perspective

Scott Peeples, Series Editor
(*Charleston, South Carolina*)

About *Literary Criticism in Perspective*

Books in the series *Literary Criticism in Perspective* trace literary scholarship and criticism on major and neglected writers alike, or on a single major work, a group of writers, a literary school or movement. In so doing the authors — authorities on the topic in question who are also well-versed in the principles and history of literary criticism — address a readership consisting of scholars, students of literature at the graduate and undergraduate level, and the general reader. One of the primary purposes of the series is to illuminate the nature of literary criticism itself, to gauge the influence of social and historic currents on aesthetic judgments once thought objective and normative.

Approaching Emily Dickinson
Critical Currents and Crosscurrents since 1960

Fred D. White

CAMDEN HOUSE
Rochester, New York

Copyright © 2008 Fred D. White

All Rights Reserved. Except as permitted under current legislation, no part of this work may be photocopied, stored in a retrieval system, published, performed in public, adapted, broadcast, transmitted, recorded, or reproduced in any form or by any means, without the prior permission of the copyright owner.

First published 2008 by Camden House
Reprinted in paperback and transferred to digital printing 2010

Camden House is an imprint of Boydell & Brewer Inc.
668 Mt. Hope Avenue, Rochester, NY 14620, USA
www.camden-house.com
and of Boydell & Brewer Limited
PO Box 9, Woodbridge, Suffolk IP12 3DF, UK
www.boydellandbrewer.com

Paperback ISBN-13: 978-1-57113-477-6
Paperback ISBN-10: 1-57113-477-8
Hardback ISBN-13: 978-1-57113-316-8
Hardback ISBN-10: 1-57113-316-X

Library of Congress Cataloging-in-Publication Data

White, Fred D., 1943–
    Approaching Emily Dickinson: critical currents and crosscurrents since 1960 / Fred D. White.
       p. cm. — (Studies in American literature and culture. Literary criticism in perspective)
    Includes bibliographical references and index.
    ISBN-13: 978-1-57113-316-8 (hardcover : alk. paper)
    ISBN-10: 1-57113-316-X (hardcover : alk. paper)
    1. Dickinson, Emily, 1830–1886 — Criticism and interpretation — History.   I. Title. II. Series.

PS1541.Z5W53 2008
811'.4—dc22

2008008291

A catalogue record for this title is available from the British Library.

This publication is printed on acid-free paper.

Cover: Oil painting of Emily Dickinson © 2006 by Nicole DeClerck Murray.
www.declerckgallery.com

For Therese, with love

Contents

Acknowledgments		ix
Note on References		x
Introduction		1
1:	Approaching Dickinson's Rhetoric, Poetics, and Stylistics	12
2:	Trends in Dickinson Biography and Biographical/ Psychoanalytic Criticism	40
3:	The Feminist Revolution in Dickinson Criticism	64
4:	The Manuscripts of a Non-Print Poet	85
5:	Dickinson in Cultural Context: Principal Critical Insights	106
6:	Dickinson's Poetic Spirituality	125
7:	Scholarship on Archetypal and Philosophical Themes in Dickinson's Poetry	146
8:	Reassessing Dickinson's Poetic Project: A Postmodern Perspective	162
9:	Emily Dickinson in Belles Lettres, Music, and Art	176
10:	Concluding Reflections	187
Selected Editions of Emily Dickinson's Poems and Letters		193
Works Cited		195
Index		215
Index of First Lines		225

Acknowledgments

I WISH TO THANK Atom Yee, Dean of the College of Arts and Sciences at Santa Clara University, together with my colleagues in the English Department, especially Professors Phyllis Brown, Diane Dreher, Cory Wade, Eileen Elrod, and John Hawley (who is also department chair), for their ongoing encouragement during the three and a half years that I have been working on this project. I am especially indebted to Professor Scott Peeples, College of Charleston, editor of the Studies in American Literature and Culture: Literary Criticism in Perspective series, for his valuable comments on an early draft of the manuscript, to Jane Best and Tracey Engel, my production editors, and to James Walker, editorial director of Camden House, for his keen eye and wise counsel at every stage of the project. I would also like to thank Harvard University Press for permission to reprint the following:

- *The Poems of Emily Dickinson: Varorium Edition*, edited by Ralph W. Franklin: Reprinted by permission of the publishers and the trustees of Amherst College from *The Poems of Emily Dickinson: Varorium Edition*, Ralph W. Franklin, ed., Cambridge, Mass.: The Belknap Press of Harvard University Press, Copyright © 1998 by the President and Fellows of Harvard College. Copyright © 1951, 1955, 1979, 1983 by the President and Fellows of Harvard College.
- *The Letters of Emily Dickinson*, edited by Thomas H. Johnson: Reprinted by permission of the publishers from *The Letters of Emily Dickinson*, Thomas H. Johnson, ed., Cambridge Mass.: The Belknap Press of Harvard University Press, Copyright © 1958, 1986, The President and Fellows of Harvard College; 1914, 1924, 1932, 1942 by Martha Dickinson Bianchi; 1952 by Alfred Leete Hampson; 1960 by Mary L. Hampson.

I also wish to thank Barbara F. Lefkowitz for permission to reprint lines from "Emily Dickinson's Sestina for Molly Bloom," and W. W. Norton & Co. for permission to reprint lines from "Emily Dickinson" by Linda Pastan: Copyright © 1971 by Linda Pastan, from *PM/AM: New and Selected Poems* by Linda Pastan. Used by permission of W. W. Norton & Company, Inc. Finally, to my wife, Therese, whose own fascination with Emily Dickinson has led to many a fruitful conversation about the poet, I express my deepest gratitude.

Fred D. White
January 2008, Santa Clara, CA

Note on References

For the sake of consistency all citations of Emily Dickinson's poems follow the texts reproduced in *The Poems of Emily Dickinson* (3 vols.), ed. R. W. Franklin (1998), even if the scholar quoting the poems in question used a pre-Johnson or pre-Franklin version. In cases where more than one manuscript exists, I choose either the fascicle text or the text cited by the scholar being discussed, and indicate this text with the letter used by Franklin. Thus "Musicians Wrestle Everywhere" is Fr229B. To facilitate ease of reference for readers who do not have easy access to the Franklin variorum I also include in every case the Johnson number (J157 for the above poem). For poems that exist only in one manuscript version, I reproduce the Franklin number only, not the letter A, as is Franklin's practice.

In reproducing the texts of the poems, I include Dickinson's manuscript variants (indicated by a +), if any. If more than one variant is indicated for a given word or phrase, I separate the variants with an asterisk (*). I also reproduce her possessive *it's* as *its* and regularize her spelling of *opon* as *upon*.

Citations of Dickinson's letters are indicated by their Johnson/Ward numbers (L1, L2, etc.), and follow the text as reproduced in *The Letters of Emily Dickinson*, 3 vols., ed. Thomas H. Johnson and Theodora Ward (Cambridge, MA: Belknap Press, 1958).

Introduction

> *A Rapture as of Legacies —*
> *Of introspective Mines —*
> (Fr1689; J1700)

IN THE FORTY YEARS SINCE Klaus Lubbers published his bibliographic survey *Emily Dickinson: The Critical Revolution* (1968), the number of academic studies of Dickinson and of literary and artistic creations inspired by her life and work has greatly exceeded that of the hundred-year period (1862–1962) covered by Lubbers, thus creating an urgent need for a new survey.

What has contributed to such a proliferation of Dickinson criticism and belletristic writing? I see three major factors. The first and most obvious is the steadily growing appreciation of Emily Dickinson's extraordinarily brilliant, innovative, complex artistry — an artistry that both extends and dismantles established notions of poetic possibility, genre boundaries, and even of the way language constructs meaning. The second is the availability of a number of reference tools published since 1955, without which contemporary Dickinson criticism could not have flourished. (See under the heading "Major Reference Tools Published since 1955," below.) And the third and most pervasive influence on Dickinson scholarship has been feminist criticism, which arose in the mid-1970s and flourished in the 1980s and early 90s. Feminist criticism, of course, is multi-faceted; it engages other methods of critical inquiry — such as formalism, cultural criticism, psychoanalytic and textual criticism — and in so doing redefines the aims of those earlier or concurrent methods. Chapter 3 examines the spectrum of feminist critical approaches to Emily Dickinson.

The Aim of This Book

Approaching Emily Dickinson aims to provide new and veteran students of the poet with a detailed and up-to-date map of the scholarly terrain and to trace lines of inquiry that have evolved during the past half century — that is, since Thomas H. Johnson made the complete poems available to the public. A good bibliographic survey, however, should do more than simply report what's out there; it should also provide readers with a sense of the most valuable studies within a particular area of inquiry. This does not mean ignoring or disparaging "lesser" studies — but it does mean suggesting which ones merit primary attention. Finally, a survey of this nature should be readable and (dare I say it?) engaging — daunting objectives indeed when one is navigating a vast sea of scholarly and artistic works.

Dickinson scholarship today cannot be neatly categorized into discrete schools. A cultural or feminist critic may well employ psychological, textual, archetypal, rhetorical, structuralist or poststructuralist methodologies. Textual scholars, working with R. W. Franklin's assembled fascicles, or with the penciled drafts archived at Amherst College's Robert Frost Library, have not only illuminated our understanding of Dickinson's methods of poetic composition; they have also made connections between those methods and the masculinist editorial and publishing conventions of her day, which she subverted by violating traditional lineation, capitalization, and punctuation, and by refusing to title her poems. For example, Susan Howe, in her 1993 book *The Birth-Mark*, sees Dickinson's editorial transgressions as representing "a contradiction to canonical social power" (1), while Cristanne Miller, in her *Emily Dickinson: A Poet's Grammar* (1987), uses stylistic and grammatical analyses to show how Dickinson exercised her own authority over male-constructed language norms. Like a set of Chinese boxes, a given study might contain a strict formalist reading of a poem within a framework of a psychoanalytic approach that purports to advance a cultural-studies perspective on Emily Dickinson's oeuvre. Thus, rather than attempt to classify Dickinson scholarship by "schools," I have opted to examine it by "approaches," a term I hope will emphasize the distinctive intentions of individual scholars.

Major Reference Tools Published since 1955

This survey begins approximately where Klaus Lubbers leaves off; but I have found it necessary on occasion to re-examine, from the vantage point of half a century, a few of the earlier (pre-1960) Dickinson studies that Lubbers includes in his survey — studies insufficiently examined by him or requiring discussion in a new context. *Approaching Emily Dickinson* also builds upon several of the relatively recent short critical surveys: James Woodress's "Emily Dickinson," from his *Fifteen American Authors before 1900* (1971), and the following bibliographic essays from *The Emily Dickinson Handbook*, edited by Gudrun Grabher, Roland Hagenbüchle, and Cristanne Miller (1998):Martha Ackmann's "Biographical Studies of Dickinson"; Margaret Dickie's "Feminist Conceptions of Dickinson"; Jonnie Guerra's "Dickinson Adaptations in the Arts and the Theater"; Roland Hagenbüchle's "Dickinson and Literary Theory"; and Marietta Messmer's "Dickinson's Critical Reception." Mary Lynn Cooper Polk's unpublished doctoral dissertation, "Emily Dickinson: A Survey of the

Criticism and Selective Annotated Bibliography" (1984) also served as an important resource.

Thomas H. Johnson's three-volume variorum *Poems of Emily Dickinson* (1955) in effect opened the door to modern Dickinson studies. Before 1955 no single complete edition of the poems was available, and many of the poems were heavily edited and organized into vague categories, such as "Life," "Nature," "Love," "Time and Eternity" in the Bianchi/Hampson volumes. Johnson was the first editor to reproduce more-or-less accurately the poems as Dickinson had written them. Then in 1998, R. W. Franklin published a second variorum edition in three volumes, *The Poems of Emily Dickinson*. Unlike Johnson's variorum edition, Franklin's prints every known extant manuscript of every poem, each with its own set of variants. Thus, for the 1,789 poems by Franklin's reckoning,[1] there are 2,500 separate texts, including transcriptions of the lost manuscripts.

In 1958 Johnson, together with Theodora Ward, published the three-volume *Letters of Emily Dickinson*. As with the poems, Johnson and Ward based their reproduction of the letters on the existing manuscripts, presenting them in chronological order insofar as dates could be ascertained.

Franklin's reconstruction of the forty fascicles and fifteen sets comprise *The Manuscript Books of Emily Dickinson,* published in two volumes in 1981. Included here are holographic reproductions of all the poems that Dickinson had sewn into forty booklets (fascicles) of approximately twenty poems each. Franklin has restored their original sequences by matching up watermarks, paper imperfections, pinhole variations, ink stains and the like. This is an indispensable reference tool for Dickinson scholars. As Franklin explains in his introduction, "the manuscripts of this poet resist translation into the conventions of print. Formal features like her unusual punctuation and capitalization, line and stanza divisions, and display of alternate readings are a source of continuing critical concern" (ix).

With the poems finally in print, scholars needed a concordance to navigate through them, a gap that was filled in 1964 with S. P. Rosenbaum's publication of his *Concordance to the Poems of Emily Dickinson*. This complete concordance even includes variant words, reproduces every line from every poem in which a given word appears, and identifies the poems by

---

[1] As compared with 1,775 poems in the Johnson variorum edition. Franklin excludes five poems on grounds that they "exhibit characteristics of verse without being so written" (1998), 1577. Franklin also includes seventeen poems not in Johnson's variorum; these formed parts of letters and in Franklin's judgment were intended as verse. Franklin prints separately twelve poems that Johnson combines; and Johnson prints separately five poems that Franklin combines. See Franklin's appendices 9 and 13.

their Johnson numbers, that is, the numbers Thomas Johnson assigned to them in his 1955 variorum edition.

Two richly documented biographies of the poet, Richard Sewall's two-volume *The Life of Emily Dickinson* (1974) and Alfred Habegger's *My Wars Are Laid Away in Books: The Life of Emily Dickinson* (2001), supersede earlier biographies, which were highly speculative. Sewall and Habegger base their inferences on documents from the Dickinson family and a plethora of civic, institutional, and literary materials.

Existing Surveys of Dickinson Criticism

Klaus Lubbers, in the only other book-length discussion of Dickinson's critical reception, identifies three critical phases in Dickinson criticism: (1) the discovery phase (1862–97), during which individuals who corresponded with the poet during her lifetime, and, shortly after her death, became aware of the scope and quality of her production and saw to publication of the first volumes; (2) the rediscovery phase (1897–1930), during which Martha Dickinson Bianchi nurtured Dickinson's reputation by publishing the first twentieth-century collection of Dickinson's poems, *The Single Hound* (1914); and (3) the "consolidation" phase (1930–62) during which academic criticism of Dickinson first flourished. In his concluding chapter Lubbers provides additional insights into each of the critical periods covered. He also includes a brief appendix summarizing the "noncritical acceptance" of Dickinson — her appearance in textbook anthologies, in stage dramatizations such as Frederick J. Pohl's *Brittle Heaven* (1935), and the setting of her poems to music. Lubbers's first chapter focuses on the reception by private readers: Dickinson's personal and epistolary interaction with her sister-in-law Susan Gilbert Dickinson, with Samuel Bowles (the co-editor with Josiah Holland of the *Springfield Republican*), with Helen Hunt Jackson (a childhood friend who in later years became the first to recognize that Dickinson was "a great poet"[2]), and with Thomas Wentworth Higginson, with whom Dickinson initiated a correspondence that lasted twenty-four years, from 1862 until the end of her life. The first public critical reception of Dickinson's work is marked by the publication of Higginson's "preview" article, "An Open Portfolio," in the September 1890 *Christian Union,* two months before the Roberts Brothers publication of *Poems* edited by Higginson and Mabel Loomis Todd. This was followed by a flurry of reviews in periodicals

---

[2] In one of her few surviving letters to Dickinson, Jackson wrote, "I have a little manuscript volume with a few of your verses in it — and I read them very often — You are a great poet — and it is a wrong to the day you live in, that you will not sing aloud" (L444a; ca. 1875).

throughout the 1890s — a flurry kindled on by the publication of the two additional Roberts Brothers volumes, *Poems, Second Series* (1891), edited by Todd and Higginson; and *Poems, Third Series* (1896), edited by Todd alone.

The other existing surveys of Dickinson criticism are anthologies. In *The Recognition of Emily Dickinson: Selected Criticism since 1890* (1968) Caesar R. Blake and Carleton F. Wells include short journalistic pieces, magazine articles, and book prefaces from 1890 through 1900 (16 items); from 1901 through 1930 (14 items) and from 1931 through 1960 (15 items). Among the selections included are Higginson's article "An Open Portfolio" (mentioned above); reviews of the inaugural volume by Arlo Bates, William Dean Howells, and Maurice Thompson; Mary Augusta Jordan's review of the first publication of Dickinson's letters (by Mabel Loomis Todd in 1894); Martha Hale Shackford's important early essay on Dickinson's poetry in the *Atlantic Monthly* (January 1913); and articles by the most important of the "academic" essayists writing between 1920 and 1950, among them Conrad Aiken, George F. Whicher, A. C. Ward, Allen Tate, R. P. Blackmur, and Austin Warren.

Ann Lilliedahl divides her bibliographic survey *Emily Dickinson in Europe: Her Literary Reputation in Selected Countries* (1981) into four sections: Dickinson's reputation in Sweden (and Swedish-speaking Finland), in Norway and Denmark, in France (and French-speaking Switzerland), and in Germany. The first foreign language in which Dickinson criticism appeared was German: a two-part article, mainly on Dickinson's letters, appeared in a German-American newspaper published in Chicago, *Der Westen*, on June 12, 1898 (Lilliedahl 132). As for the other European countries Lilliedahl surveys, Dickinson did not enter the critical literature until the 1940s.

Mary Lynn Cooper Polk's dissertation "Emily Dickinson: A Survey of the Criticism and Selective Annotated Bibliography" is organized into four chapters: Early Criticism; Critical Trends, 1955–1968; Recent Critical Commentary, 1969–1981; and A Critical Overview and Projected Needs. Several of the projected needs Polk identifies, such as an up-to-date edition of Duchac's *Annotated Guide* and "a study of the relationship of the poems in their respective fascicles," have since been filled. Another project recommended by Polk, "a more complete record of foreign scholarship of Dickinson," has not yet been carried out.

In *Emily Dickinson's Reception in the 1890s: A Documentary History* (1989) Willis J. Buckingham reprints a complete set of reviews — more than 560 pages worth — of the three volumes of Dickinson's poems published in the United States and in England during the last decade of the nineteenth century, a valuable resource for the critical history of Emily Dickinson's initial reception. "These documents," Buckingham states, "illustrate the interaction between readers, texts, and norms of valuation by which literary meaning is established and disestablished" (xii) — an eloquent justification, I wish to stress, for bringing together critical voices of very different perspectives between two covers.

Finally, most recently, Graham Clarke's four-volume *Emily Dickinson: Critical Assessments* (2002) gathers biographical studies, such as the complete texts of Genevieve Taggard's and Josephine Pollitt's 1930 biographies; early reviews (also included in Buckingham's *Reception*), and modern literary criticism of the poet. Despite the apparent comprehensiveness of this collection, however, there are, according to Daniel Lombardo in his review of this reference work (*EDIS Bulletin*, Nov.–Dec. 2003), several "inexplicable omissions" such as commentary by Martha Dickinson Bianchi and George F. Whicher.

Reference Tools for Dickinson Scholarship

In addition to the works described above, the following reference tools important to Dickinson studies have been published since 1968:

Willis J. Buckingham's *Emily Dickinson: An Annotated Bibliography: Writings, Scholarship, Criticism, and Ana, 1850–1968* (1970). This splendid bibliography contains over 2,000 entries, including bibliographies and concordances, books and articles about Emily Dickinson; foreign language studies (Italian, French, German and Dutch, Spanish and Portuguese, Japanese, and other languages); theses; creative tributes; recordings, films; commemorations and exhibitions; miscellanea such as Dickinson family materials; and unpublished materials such as papers delivered at scholarly conferences.

Joseph Duchac's *The Poems of Emily Dickinson: An Annotated Guide to Commentary Published in English;* vol. 1, 1890–1977; vol. 2, 1978–89 (1979; 1993). This valuable reference guide includes synopses of commentaries on individual poems, drawn from monographs, biographies, and articles. Organization is by Johnson numbers, together with first lines. This reference is especially valuable because it not only provides students and scholars with a rapid means of locating the full text of a given commentary, but also allows them to compare and contrast the commentaries, many of which differ radically in interpretation.

Jeanetta Boswell's *Emily Dickinson: A Bibliography of Secondary Sources, with Selective Annotations, 1890 through 1987* (1989). Boswell's annotations, including those of doctoral dissertations, are generally well-detailed.

Sheila T. Clendenning's *Emily Dickinson: A Bibliography: 1850–1966* (1968), which is still useful as a reference to articles published through 1966. Clendenning's entries are well-annotated and her introduction succinctly describes the changing emphases in Dickinson criticism during the period she covers.

An Emily Dickinson Encyclopedia (1998), edited by Jane Donahue Eberwein. This compact and very useful reference work includes entries on people, places, and institutions of importance to Emily Dickinson; entries on the editing history of her poems and letters and the reception of her work around the world; and entries relating to Dickinson scholarship.

The Emily Dickinson Handbook (1998), edited by Gudrun Grabher, Roland Hagenbüchle, and Cristanne Miller. The twenty-two essays in this volume are organized under the following headings: Biography, Historical Context, Manuscripts, Letters, Poetics, Reception and Influence, and New Directions in Dickinson Scholarship. In his introductory essay for the volume, "The Continuing Presence of Emily Dickinson," Richard B. Sewall remarks how Dickinson's poems, like Shakespeare's *Hamlet*, "will never let us rest . . . from each we learn a little more about *what it means to be alive*" (6–7; emphasis Sewall's).

Joel Myerson's *Emily Dickinson: A Descriptive Bibliography* (1984). Myerson's bibliography precisely describes all editions of Dickinson's writings published since 1890. It does not include publications about Dickinson or her work. Many facsimile illustrations of title and copyright pages are included.

A Historical Guide to Emily Dickinson (2004), edited by Vivian R. Pollak. This book provides five essays situating the poet in her cultural milieu. Along with an illustrated chronology and brief biography, topics include politics, faith in an age of upheavals, and other women poets of the nineteenth century. For a more detailed discussion of this work see chapter 6 of this book.

Cynthia MacKenzie's *A Concordance to the Letters of Emily Dickinson* (2000). Emulating Rosenbaum's concordance to the poems, MacKenzie's concordance locates every word in Dickinson's extant letters.

A biographical reference work published in 1960, one that Lubbers mentions (166), but which deserves further attention, is Jay Leyda's two-volume *The Years and Hours of Emily Dickinson* (1960). "The tiniest scraps of biographical fact," writes Leyda in his introduction, "might be the very detail needed to help grasp a cluster of associations, the missing piece of the puzzle that makes plain a series of relationships in the life that in turn reveals a major theme or continuity in the poems" (xix). Leyda understands that Dickinson, contrary to the notion that her reclusive way of life disconnected her from the world, was keenly aware of worldly affairs, read widely and deeply, and shared her thoughts with many through her correspondence (a small fraction of which, while voluminous in its own right, has survived). In excerpting passages from local newspaper stories, announcements, sermons, lectures, and such, Leyda has produced an extraordinary body of source material that has repeatedly proven useful in shedding light on the historical and cultural context of Dickinson's work as well as what he famously refers to as the "omitted center" in Dickinson's poetry:

> The riddle, the circumstance too well known to be repeated to the initiate, the deliberate skirting of the obvious — this was the means she used to increase the privacy of her communication; it has also increased our problems in piercing that privacy. With so much background detail coming constantly to light, her poems and letters take on unexpectedly deep roots in national and community life, in family crises, and in her daily reading. (xxi)

Leyda's survey covers the years 1828–86, from two years before Dickinson's birth to two weeks following her death. Leyda also includes a supplement consisting of materials that would not fit into a chronological reconstruction; namely reminiscences, anecdotes, and remarks by friends and relatives. Perhaps most importantly, Leyda does not include or exclude material on the basis of "relevance." The most seemingly insignificant, gossipy tidbit has the potential to shed important light on some aspect of the poet's life and work — but distinguishing such revelatory connections from insignificant details are the responsibility of the scholar-critic, not the scholar-compiler.

Introductory Volumes on Emily Dickinson

Concise introductions to the poet serve beginning and advanced students well in their ability to identify major themes and historical contexts. The most useful of these include the following:

Donna Dickenson's *Emily Dickinson* (1985). Dickenson discusses the richness and complexity of Emily Dickinson's poetry, how it generates a virtually inexhaustible stream of meaning.

Paul J. Ferlazzo's *Emily Dickinson* (1976). One of the Twayne's United States Authors Series volumes. Ferlazzo's introduction is admirable for its concise and insightful commentary on key poems, categorized in a more or less conventional manner: faith, mortality, love, nature.

Bettina L. Knapp's *Emily Dickinson* (1989). Similar in design to Ferlazzo's volume, Knapp's book provides insights into some of Dickinson's more mysterious poems. Knapp's prose becomes purple at times, however ("Dickinson, who had eaten of the forbidden fruit of the Tree of Knowledge, questioned always"; 81).

Joan Kirkby's *Emily Dickinson* (1991). Kirkby manages to capture facets of Dickinson's genius overlooked by others; for instance, how the poet regarded intellect ("the 'Native Land' and 'the only Bone whose Expanse we woo" [L888]). Dickinson, Kirkby writes, "was fascinated with the way the mind locates itself in the world through language" (20).

Sharon Leiter's *Critical Companion to Emily Dickinson* (2007). Leiter includes critiques of 150 poems in this comprehensive introduction.

Helen McNeil's *Emily Dickinson* (1986). McNeil's study is one of the most insightful of the short introductions in print. See chapters 1, 3, and elsewhere in this book for commentary on McNeil's work.

John Robinson's *Emily Dickinson: Looking to Canaan* (1986). Robinson examines Dickinson's poetic ideas, such as her conception of history, with uncommon insight and lucidity.

Photographic Guides to Dickinson's World

Polly Longsworth's *The World of Emily Dickinson* (1990) contains numerous images of people and places relating to Emily Dickinson. Many of these images are familiar, such as photographs of Emily Dickinson's brother Austin and sister Lavinia, T. W. Higginson, Charles Wadsworth, Samuel Bowles, and Otis Lord. Others, such as a photograph of the poet's mother (Emily Norcross Dickinson), or Mary Lyon, the founder of the Mt. Holyoke Seminary for Women, are less familiar.

Another important photographic collection is *The Dickinsons of Amherst* (2001), Jerome Liebling's intimate photographs of Dickinson domestic artifacts, interiors of the Homestead and the Evergreens (including the long sealed-off room of Gilbert Dickinson, Emily's nephew, who died from typhus at the age of eight). Essays by Christopher Benfey, Polly Longsworth, and Barton Levi St. Armand accompany the photographs.

The Emily Dickinson Electronic Archives

A work in progress, the Dickinson Electronic Archives (www.emilydickinson.org), produced by the Dickinson Editing Collective spearheaded by Martha Nell Smith, includes the following:

- Writings by the Dickinson family, including commentary on the "letter-poem" as a distinct Dickinson genre, as well as Dickinson's cartoons and collages
- Responses to Dickinson's writing
- Emily Dickinson International Society Conference proceedings
- Scholarly articles
- Guides to teaching Emily Dickinson
- Displays of many of Dickinson's manuscripts
- An open forum for commentary, review, and critical analysis

The Emily Dickinson International Society

According to Jonnie Guerra in her "Reflections on EDIS — Past, Present, and Future" (1998), the idea of an Emily Dickinson society was suggested by Margaret Freeman while standing in line with "a bunch of [Dickinson] enthusiasts in a Dayton, Ohio restaurant" in October 1986 (16). From such an inauspicious conception, the suggestion became a reality with the inauguration and incorporation of the Emily Dickinson International Society on May 24, 1988. With its two periodicals, *The Emily Dickinson Journal* and *The EDIS Bulletin*, the society has lived up to its name from the very beginning, having members from seventeen countries around the world, and holding international conferences — among the venues thus far: Washington, DC; Innsbruck, Austria; South Hadley, Massachusetts (Mt. Holyoke College); Trondheim, Norway; Hilo, Hawaii, and Kyoto, Japan. The society has launched a Scholar in Amherst Program to foster research in Dickinson studies.

The *EDIS Bulletin* provides detailed information on the society's domestic and international conferences, along with profiles of or tributes to noteworthy Dickinson scholars,[3] reviews of scholarly works (including scholarship published in other countries), Dickinson miscellanea of all sorts, such as a history of the poet's white dresses,[4] as well as exhibits and performances related to the poet.

Teachers' Guides to Emily Dickinson

Robin Riley Fast and Christine Mack Gordon's *Approaches to Teaching Dickinson's Poetry* (1989) is a valuable collection of twenty essays on teaching Dickinson at the undergraduate level. Topics include appreciating the poet's love of paradox, complexity, and semantic ambiguities; determining a principle of poem selection; and suggestions for designing assignments around the poems. The collection begins with Richard B. Sewall's "Teaching Dickinson: Testimony of a Veteran," which calls attention to "the *disunity* of the canon, the disparity of the parts," and the fact that

---

[3] For example: Polly Longsworth, "Millicent Todd Bingham, 1880–1968" (6.2; Nov./Dec. 1994: 4–5; 17); Gudrun M. Grabher, "A Portrait of Roland Hagenbüchle" (8.2; Nov./Dec. 1996: 1–2, 19); Takao Furukawa, "A Portrait of Toshikazu Niikura" (9.1; May/June 1997: 3, 5); Benjamin Lease, "The Magic Circle of Charles Roberts Anderson" (9.2; Nov./Dec. 1997: 14, 27); Mary Elizabeth Kromer Bernhard, "Alfred Habegger: An Original Dickinsonian (15.1; May/June 2003; 1–2, 21); Judith Farr, "A Tribute to Richard Sewall" [d. 2003] (15.1; Nov./Dec. 2003, 10–11, 33).

[4] Cindy Dickinson, "The New White Dress," 12.1 (May/June 2000): 10, 12.

"we hear many voices — joy, sorrow, pleasure, pain, faith, doubt, the voice of innocence, the voice of experience" (32; emphasis Sewall's). He also suggests that teachers use *The Complete Poems* because "[a]nthologies take the fun away" (31). One of the most useful essays in the collection is Cristanne Miller's "Dickinson's Language: Interpreting Truth Told Slant." "Understanding the patterns of her language use," Miller explains, "may, in turn, clarify the direction of Dickinson's intent in individual poems" (78). Miller then lays out the syntactic elements of Dickinson's poems, such as compression and nonrecoverable deletion, elements that Miller examines in greater depth in her monograph, *Emily Dickinson: A Poet's Grammar,* which I discuss in chapter 1. The editors include an appendix containing several classroom assignments for different levels of instruction.

The *Emily Dickinson International Society Bulletin* occasionally publishes articles on approaches to teaching the poet. For example, in "'The Distance would not haunt me so —': Teaching Dickinson's Poetry through Distance Education" (2002) Connie Ann Kirk discusses her strategies for teaching Dickinson's poetry online, making use of the Dickinson Electronic Archives. And Jed Deppman, the 2005 recipient of the Emily Dickinson International Society's Scholar in Amherst Award, discusses, in "To Own the Art within the Soul: Emily Dickinson and Creative Writing" (2005) ways of using Emily Dickinson's poetry to teach poetic skills to creative writing students.

Conference issues of *The Emily Dickinson Journal* (also published by EDIS) occasionally include papers on pedagogy. For example, the issue containing selected papers from the August 1999 conference at Mount Holyoke College includes a delightful and useful essay, "'Goblin with a Gauge': Teaching Emily Dickinson" (2000), by Jay Ladin, who describes his experience teaching seminars on Dickinson's poetry to the community at large at the Dickinson Homestead. His challenge was how to respond to widely (even wildly) differing interpretations of various poems, in particular "'Twas like a Maelstrom, with a notch" (Fr425; J414). "One student," Ladin writes, ". . . explained the poem as an idiosyncratic portrayal of Christ's ordeal on the cross. Another student vehemently disagreed. Having found that Dickinson studied German in school, he was certain that 'Maelstrom' should be punningly interpreted as 'male stream'" — and so on (33). Because Ladin "found the all the readings too convincing to dismiss and too disparate to harmonize," he decided to apply Stanley Fish's reader-response method, encouraging the students "to focus not on what Dickinson's poems mean but on what happens in our minds as we read them, to see them as experiences to be lived through rather than statements to be 'gotten'" (34).

1: Approaching Dickinson's Rhetoric, Poetics, and Stylistics

> "Speech" — *is a prank of Parliament*
> "Tears" — *a trick of the* nerve —
>
> (Fr193A; J688)
>
> *Being the most subjective and confidential of poetic genres, the lyric nevertheless exists as much to communicate with others as does verse narrative and drama.*
> — Willis J. Buckingham, "Emily Dickinson and the Reading Life"
>
> *Dickinson's use of her poems in letters suggests one way in which she may have intended them to be read: they are private messages universalized by a double release from private circumstance.... [First,] their audience is limited; their addressee is "the World," although she would speak to its members one by one under the ambiguity of the pronoun "you." Second, the speaker in the poems is more a dramatic than a personal "I."*
> — Cristanne Miller, *Emily Dickinson: A Poet's Grammar*

ALTHOUGH EMILY DICKINSON left us with no *ars poetica* per se, many of her poems can be regarded as "dramatic speeches" in Aristotle's sense of the term.[1] Archibald MacLeish notes that more than 150 of her poems begin with the word "I,"[2] which he calls "the talker's word," adding that "few poets ... have written more *dramatically* than Emily Dickinson, more in the live locutions of dramatic speech, words born living on the

---

[1] In Section 19 of the *Poetics* Aristotle calls attention to the interplay of the rhetorical and the poetic in the context of artistic discourse. "Dramatic incidents must be treated from the same points of view as the dramatic speeches, when the object is to evoke the sense of pity, fear, importance, or probability. The only difference is that the incidents should speak for themselves without verbal exposition, while the effects aimed at in a speech should be produced by the speaker, and as a result of the speech (93).

[2] According to Brita Lindberg-Seyersted, the exact number is 158, including the contractions "I'd," "I'll," "I'm," and "I've." (*The Voice of the Poet* 32).

tongue, written as though spoken" (103–4; emphasis MacLeish's). But is Emily Dickinson engaging in oratory? Helen McNeil, for one, says no. Unlike Whitman, who seems to be "returning poetry to its authentic basis in human speech, Dickinson reverses these priorities" (83). In fact, McNeil argues, "Dickinson associates speech with falsehood," whereas truth "must be sought out *inside* language" (85; emphasis added) — and extracting the truth can only be undertaken through writing, ironically through the deployment of rhetorical strategies.

A Rhetorical Poet

Dickinson lived in an age that valued the art of oratory as well as the art of conversation. It was also an age in which "literature was meant to be read rhetorically" (McNeil 76). Belletristic rhetoric had been imported from Scotland and taken root in New England schools. Scottish rhetoric, developed in the eighteenth century by Hugh Blair, George Campbell, Lord Kames, and others, influenced American rhetoricians such as Samuel P. Newman, whose *Practical System of Rhetoric* (1834) became a standard textbook.[3] This new rhetoric, drawing from the empirical philosophy of Hume and Kant, overtook the more logic-driven, pragmatic rhetoric of Aristotle, Quintilian, and Cicero. Writing in 1996, Bryan C. Short explains that, "Scottish enlightenment rhetoric adapts the shape and style of discourse to the innate faculties of the mind . . . stressing parallels between rhetorical and cognitive processes" (263). What constitutes "evidence" in the context of the new rhetoric, according to Short, should conjure up memory patterns that the audience can use to reproduce internally an argument's movement toward conclusion. Any distinction between what is rhetorical and what is not disappears. Most importantly, as we consider Dickinson's rhetorical education, the audience for a discourse is no longer thought of as a group but rather as individuals. Distinctions between public and private genres are de-emphasized (263–64).

According to Short, Emily Dickinson adheres to the principles of the Scottish New Rhetoric "by presenting forms of experiencing, remembering and judging oriented toward exercising — and thus improving — the mind's fundamental epistemological processes. She establishes an intellectual bridge between persona . . . and audience, an effect she masters in her letters and carries over into her verse" (265). This leads us to pose a basic question: What, exactly, comprises the rhetorical elements of a poem?

---

[3] As Carlton Lowenberg has shown in his bibliography, *Emily Dickinson's Textbooks* (1986), Dickinson learned rhetoric from Newman's text as well as from Lord Kames's *Elements of Criticism* (1833; new edition, 1849), and Ebenezer Porter's *Rhetorical Reader* (1832; new edition 1841).

"Macro" rhetorical elements may include definition, example, arrangement, paragraph (or stanza) pattern and progression, and voice. "Micro" rhetorical elements are what are usually designated *stylistic* elements: diction, syntactic structures, punctuation, inflection, sound, rhyme, meter, and rhythm. Taken together, these macro and micro rhetorical elements transform the text from a static, self-contained objet d'art, as mainstream formalists would have it, to a dynamic interactive relation involving the writer, the text, and the reader.

Clark Griffith, by contrast, in his 1964 book *The Long Shadow: Emily Dickinson's Tragic Poetry*, calls attention to Dickinson's "deliberate effort to *suppress* rhetorical forms" (emphasis added) by preferring "austere, laconic, carefully guarded utterances" such as "plainness in diction, a hesitant and hence involuted syntax, a studious avoidance of ornamentation, a cautiously subdued tone" (61–62). Griffith explains that "in lyric poetry, where the speaking voice is likely to be that of the poet himself, rhetoric is the language of involvement.... On the whole ... Miss Dickinson shied away from rhetorical devices because most forms of the rhetorical were totally at odds with her ironic pattern of thought" (62).

It seems to me that Griffith has in mind rhetoric-as-ornamentation or rhetoric-as-sophistry instead of rhetoric as the art of conveying ideas through discourse, regardless of genre. One could argue that Dickinson's effort to avoid or suppress rhetorical devices, assuming such an effort to be the case, is itself a rhetorical act. Griffith himself makes this apparent when he compares Dickinson to John Donne. Donne, like Dickinson, uses "verbal incongruities, the strained and convoluted syntax" to serve as "reflectors of his philosophical position" (63). Moreover, both Donne and Dickinson attempt "to record the treacheries of experience by the blunt antitheses, the guttural expression, the abrupt break in meaning, the barbarous lapse from rhyme" (64) — examples of suppressing rhetoric-as-ornament indeed, but this suggests, I would argue, a subtler, more *artistic* use of rhetorical strategies.

In *Rhetorical Analyses of Literary Works* (1969), Edward P. J. Corbett distinguishes between traditional literary criticism and rhetorical criticism by asserting that the latter "regards the work not so much as an object of aesthetic contemplation but as an artistically structured instrument for communication. It is more interested in a literary work for what it does than for what it is" (xxii). A Dickinson poem, however, will perform a rhetorical function by seemingly presenting itself as *a*rhetorical — for instance, by being inserted into a letter (or by accompanying a letter), without overt prefatory or explanatory commentary — on the contrary, teasing the recipient to discover rhetorical interplay between the poem and the surrounding (or accompanying) prose text. By placing lyric poetry into a discursive field and epistolary discourse into a poetic field, Dickinson is enlarging the rhetorical power of both genres.[4]

It is sometimes difficult for us to envision Emily Dickinson, the quintessentially and fiercely individualistic private poet (as she has often been characterized), writing for an *audience*. But Dickinson had a "persistent lifelong quest for an audience," argues Dolores Dyer Lucas in *Emily Dickinson and Riddle* (1969: 26). Lucas sees Dickinson assuming a specific speaking voice (say that of a child) in order to communicate her obsession with the great riddles of existence and death, with both a proximate audience (her circle of correspondents), and a wider audience ("the World" of "This is my letter to the World" [Fr519; J441]; Lucas 106). Through the use of poetic riddle the child speaker heightens the mystery of death and at the same time exposes the internal ambiguities and contradictions of the supposedly unambiguous Christian view. In "She lay as if at play" (Fr412; J369) the childlike riddle-posing "What am I" leads to a shocking disclosure in that "what this poem details is not so much the death of a child as it is the description of a dead child, a corpse" (67):

> She lay as if at play
> Her life had leaped away —
> Intending to return —
> But not so soon —
>
> Her merry Arms, half dropt —
> As if for lull of sport —
> An instant had forgot
> The Trick to start —
>
> Her dancing Eyes — ajar —
> As if their Owner were
> Still sparkling through
> For fun — at you —
> . . .

But if Dickinson's wider audience is the world, Lucas wonders, what is the general sensibility of that world? "How . . . can it be made to listen? And . . . what should be the voice of the speaker who speaks to the audience 'who never spoke to me?'" Dickinson's answer seems to be that the poetry determines its audience: if it captivates, if it can scalp the reader's naked soul with bolts of melody, then it will succeed; and yet, as Lucas notes, "so much depended on the recipient" (110). As Dickinson ex-

---

[4] See Marietta Messmer, *A Vice for Voices: Reading Emily Dickinson's Correspondence* (2001).

claims to Higginson in 1885, "What a Hazard a Letter is!" (L1007). One way to keep the audience listening is to keep it guessing: "The Riddle that we guess / We speedily despise —" (Fr1180A; J1222). Dickinson's riddling poetry becomes a mirror of riddling existence.

Besides being fond of the riddle, Emily Dickinson was also fond of the proverb, as Daniel Barnes demonstrates in his article, "Telling it Slant: Emily Dickinson and the Proverb" (1979). Beginning with Kenneth Burke's assertion in *The Philosophy of Literary Form* (296) that proverbs are "strategies for dealing with situations," Barnes observes how Dickinson, who "from an early age . . . displayed a fondness for proverbial lore" (221), uses the proverb ironically as a way of confronting traditional authority — in other words, citing a proverb only to deny its validity, as she does in the following poem (Fr1526; J1485):

> Love is done when Love's begun,
> Sages say —
> But have Sages known?
> Truth adjourn your Boon
> Without Day.

Here, Barnes explains, "she clearly implies that to accept the truth of the Sages would be tantamount to dismissing even the possibility of the gift of love (a gift which Sages appear never to have known) before it can see the light of day" (228). Barnes goes on to explore Dickinson's "tendency to simulate the proverb in both form and function" (232).

One of the most ambitious efforts to establish a solid interconnection between rhetoric and poetics is achieved by Mutlu Konuk Blasing in *American Poetry: The Rhetoric of Its Forms* (1987). Blasing first posits a fourfold "typology of generic rhetorics" (2), each of which represents a particular rhetorical strategy applied poetically. The first type or strategy is *allegory*. Poe is an allegorical poet because he "maintains an irreducible difference between experience and representation . . . [which] reaffirms the barrier between the mind and nature, the soul and the body, the spirit and the letter of language" (7–8). In contrast to the allegorical poet is the analogical poet — Emerson being representative because of the way in which "he regards language as representing our perceptions of correspondences between the mind and nature" (8). The third type is *anagogy*, which "proposes a coincidence of textual and existential experience, figurative and literal language, poetic and natural form" (9) — the representative anagogical poet being Whitman. And finally, we have the strategy of *irony*, best represented by the poetry of Emily Dickinson. "Dickinson's rhetoric of irony, Blasing notes, "emphasizes the differentiation of the very categories of subjective and objective realms, mental and natural experience, of the signifier from its referent, and thus dismantles the rhetoric of the Logos, the identity of word and thing that anagogy upholds. She recognizes only an articulating and disarticulating syntax — the process whereby letters, syllables, words, and sentences add up to a mind and a world" (9). Blasing captures Dickinson's rhetoric of irony even more succinctly in her chapter on "Dickinson's Untitled Discourse" by noting how the poet overturns traditional efforts to use symbolism to capture the transcendent, as in the first stanza of "Those — dying then" (Fr1581; J1551):

> Those — dying then,
> Knew where they went —
> They went to God's Right Hand —
> That Hand is amputated now
> And God cannot be found —

Blasing explains that "the violent juxtaposition of the metaphoric 'hand' with a surgical term like 'amputated' reduces the metaphoric to the literal and thus disarticulates the whole anthropomorphic myth of God, for the reduction of the metaphoric to the literal is in effect a loss of faith. Any system of belief rests upon the symbolic function of language" (181). In my opinion, however, Blasing does not go far enough in her rhetorical analysis. For example, the second stanza presents us with a very different perspective on what is taking place rhetorically in the last stanza of "Those — dying then" (Fr1581; J1551):

> The abdication of Belief
> Makes the Behavior small —
> Better an ignis fatuus
> Than no illume at all —

As James McIntosh asserts in *Nimble Believing: Dickinson and the Unknown* (2000) this poem "works as a dialectical qualification to the confident assertion of 'On subjects of which we know nothing.' ... Her transcriptions of Christian ideas and her reworkings of Christian texts are not dogmatic but experimental, heuristic, and in their own way pastoral; she is trying to create a newly religious language" (3).[5] By presenting us with dialectic, Emily Dickinson shifts focus from the subject-matter being argued (the nature of our connectedness to God), to the dialectic itself — to the

---

[5] Another example of Dickinson's reworking of Christian texts is her appropriation of hymnal meter. See Martha Winburn England and John Sparrow, *Hymns Unbidden* (1966), 113–48; Cynthia Griffin Wolff, *Emily Dickinson* (1986), 185–86; and Shira Wolosky, "Rhetoric or Not: Hymnal Tropes in Emily Dickinson and Isaac Watts" (1988), 214–22.

fact that such issues of "faith alone" become problematic through poetic scrutiny. Roland Hagenbüchle remarks in "Emily Dickinson's Poetic Covenant" (1993) that "Dickinson's refusal to choose between alternative possibilities — in individual poems a well as in her poetic sequence as a whole — is itself an all-important decision" (16) — a rhetorical decision, I would stress, that enables her audience to perceive, instead of a transcendent reality, a linguistically contingent one.

Some of Dickinson's poems also appear to support "an aesthetic of silence," as E. Miller Budick notes in *Emily Dickinson and the Life of Language* (1985: 163), especially when we consider poems like "The Definition of Beauty is / That Definition is none —" (Fr797B; J988). Although in one sense Dickinson "is anything but silent," the speaker is aware that "language may distort meaning . . . It is just possible that silence is simply the absence of meaning, the ultimate cosmic default" (165). Budick cites as an illustration "Death's Waylaying not the sharpest / Of the Thefts of Time — / There marauds a sorer Robber — / Silence — his name —" (Fr1315; J1296).

Is Dickinson being "Janus-faced" as Budick asserts (166)? I would say no if we regard her poems as a kind of ongoing dialectic — dramas of argument the roots of which go back to Plato — that generate deep understanding through grappling with conflicting ideas. "Death's Waylaying" also points to a different kind of rhetorical context, a biographical one. Dickinson incorporated this poem into a note to her aunt Catherine Sweetser upon hearing the news that her husband Joseph had disappeared after leaving the house. Dickinson's note begins, "Saying nothing, my Aunt Katie, sometimes says the most." In this context, "Death's Waylaying" can be regarded as a poem with its own intrinsic qualities while simultaneously serving as a more-or-less conventional transaction, in this case as a poem that offers solace.

In *The Rhetoric of American Romance* (1985) Evan Carton examines another facet of the dialectical nature of Dickinson's poetry. Just as in "The Poet" Emerson calls attention to the capacity of language to dismantle the very meanings it constructs ("[The poet] recognizes that 'all symbols are fluxional'" [Carton 82]), Dickinson appears to be exploiting language's capacity for paradox in many poems. Taking as an example Fr1404; J1382 ("In many and reportless places / We feel a Joy — / Reportless, also, but sincere as Nature / Or Deity —"), Carton sees this poem not as an example of "unnaming" as Robert Weisbuch saw it (1975: 68–69; Carton 83), but as paradoxically capturing what cannot be captured: "Dickinson's language," Carton explains, "exercises its power as it seems to announce its impotence; and, most importantly, it intricately involves itself with its object while ostensibly opposing itself to it. The repeated stress on the word 'reportless' in the first stanza underscores the fact that the poem is itself a report" (83).

Let us take a closer look at the extent to which Emily Dickinson "wrote rhetorically" (McNeil 7) despite having distanced herself from public discourse. Dickinson "uses her art to break open received certitudes. She is ... a poet of investigation.... Her poetry experiences and argues and questions." And with what does Dickinson wish to argue, asks McNeil? "Received certitudes," she answers, adding that the poet does so by confronting "a frightening abstraction and evolv[ing] its attributes from experience, not tradition" (10). The poems, McNeil points out, "typically begin with a declaration or definition in the first line and proceed to a metaphorical breaking-open of the original premise" (11). For example, she begins with declarations such as "The Fact that Earth is Heaven — / Whether Heaven is Heaven or not" (Fr1435; J1408), or "More than the Grave is closed to me —" (Fr1532; J1503). But then, McNeil explains, "the poem veers, often unexpectedly, into surmise, renewed rhetorical inquiry, or an open closure. The dash that ends so many Dickinson poems is a graphic indication that the debate does not finish with the poem" (11). The poem that embodies this rhetorical strategy most memorably is "I know that He exists. / Somewhere — in silence — / He has hid his rare life / From our gross eyes...." (Fr365; J338). McNeil writes that "[d]espite its blunt opening ... this is a poem of desire and doubt. The delicate, disappearing God seems to be playing a game of celestial hide-and-seek" (13).

As for the role of the speaker — the "I" of the poems that has befuddled critics of all stripes, McNeil provides a compelling insight by first reflecting on what Dickinson *does not* do with the speaker: "She never uses the 'I' to presume an intimacy with an audience which is then meant to take her side, as Sylvia Plath can do. She doesn't rework her intimate history in public, as John Berryman and Robert Lowell do, to lay bare what went wrong" (12). McNeil then brings her rhetorical perspective into alignment with her feminist one when she suggests what Dickinson *does* do with the speaker: "Dickinson has the direct access to emotion which is ... characteristic of much women's poetry. She doesn't, however, soften those emotions into acceptability or use poetry as an escape ..." (12). The poet embodied as a woman of her time will use her art to pluck not literal berries but metaphorical ones — entire Earths — dropping them into a basket large enough to hold entire "firmaments," as she proclaims in Fr358; J352, from summer 1862:

> Perhaps I asked too large —
> I take — no less than skies —
> For Earths, grow thick as
> Berries, in my native Town —

> My Basket holds — just — Firmaments —
> Those — dangle easy — on my arm,
> But smaller bundles — Cram.

When Mabel Loomis Todd and Millicent Todd Bingham published this poem for the first time in *Bolts of Melody* (1945: 306) they grouped it in the section designated "Poems Incomplete or Unfinished" (presumably because the second stanza contains only three lines). But this is most assuredly a finished poem — not only because it appears in a fair copy among Dickinson's fascicles (#17), but because the deliberately truncated second stanza, along with the truncated last line, plays off the notion that a literal woman's berry-picking basket is too confining for her (see McNeil 16).

Dickinson's sophisticated use of metaphor, syntactic compression, indirections, discontinuities, ambiguities, and other rhetorical strategies must take place in *written* discourse, not oral. As McNeil puts it, "Dickinson associates speech with falsehood, and writing with truth. The falsity of speech is not just found in unpleasant instances. It is innate."[6]

It seems necessary also to emphasize that Dickinson's idea of writing differs from that of Emerson, for whom writing provided a direct channel from the Over-Soul through the individual poet and, in turn, to society. For Dickinson "'slant' or metaphorical writing is the only way to write accurately," McNeil explains, "because the truth is never obvious. It must be sought inside language" (85).

From Martin Orzeck's and Robert Weisbuch's perspective, audience awareness not only formed part of Emily Dickinson's poetic consciousness, it did so in three ways: in a theoretical sense, an epistolary sense, and a public-historical sense. These are the categories investigated by twelve scholars in their collected volume *Dickinson and Audience*. But for a poet who "praises silence over all utterance" (2), I wonder, how can we even assume that her audience, as we commonly think of it in discourse theory, mattered to Dickinson, apart from the obvious and superficial sense of addressing a letter or a poem to particular recipient?

The way in which Dickinson closes the gap between self and other in her poetry is suggested by Weisbuch in his article, "Nobody's Business: Dickinson's Dissolving Audience." "All of Dickinson's poems," he asserts, "offer the reader a fill-in-the-blanks test, and, once you get the pattern right, the number of correct specific answers is infinite" (69). Weisbuch elaborates as follows:

---

[6] McNeil quotes from Fr540B; J407 to illustrate: "If what we — could — were what we would — / Criterion — be small — / It is the Ultimate of Talk — / The Impotence to Tell —".

That is, her reader, freed from a particular subject to bring any number of her or his experiences that fit the pattern to participate in the poem's design, experiences an intimacy without egotism. The poems are, in a sense, an autobiography not of Dickinson but of the reader, and yet, finally, this reader is remade beyond the limits of personal experience, the bounds of ego. (69)

Weisbuch illustrates this by detailing the thoughts and impressions he himself experienced when reading "Did the Harebell loose her girdle / To the lover Bee" (Fr134; J213). He begins with a conventional enough explication: "We move from a backyard garden to the Garden, Eden, via a medieval moat, which is also a feminine yielding. The fear that the bee will no longer honor or value the flower once it consummates its desire becomes in the second stanza a fear that reaching paradise, intimacy with the Godhead, might similarly reduce its value" (70).

There are other ways to think about Dickinson's "writerly" poetic texts, which are nonetheless "readerly" or audience-directed. In her contribution to the Orzeck and Weisbuch volume, "Dickinson's Figure of Address," Virginia Jackson sees Dickinson using writing to generate an intersubjective intimacy with the reader. "In the illusion peculiar to written address," Jackson explains, "the condition of your absence (the condition of my writing) conjures a presence more intimate than the whisper — more intimate, that is, than the metaphor of the voice, of a speaking presence, would allow" (82). Dickinson's poetry, paradoxically, represents a privacy made public, in which "I" represents "you," and in which the poet's solitude represents the reader's solitude (79). For example, "I cannot live with You" (Fr706; J640) dramatizes an encounter that the speaker does not want fulfilled, "because seeing the other's face would mean turning 'You' into a fiction. That fiction would allow address to transcend the material circumstances of separation, as the abrupt and seamless transition from physical death to life after death insists. . . . But by not imagining its own apostrophe as transcendent, the poem does not give a 'Face' to *You;* what it does, instead, is to tally the consequences if it were to do so" (91). The collapsing of speaker and audience in this poem, then, illustrates the role that audience plays in Dickinson's idea of lyric poetry. A conventional transaction between self and other is replaced by a subsuming of the latter by the former.

Dickinson's Style as Poetic Communication

What does Emily Dickinson's style contribute to her idea of poetry, and of communicating via poetry? Attempting to answer these questions is the job of literary scholars trained in linguistics and rhetoric, and describes what Brita Lindberg-Seyersted and Cristanne Miller accomplish in their respective monographs, *The Voice of the Poet: Aspects of Style in the Poetry of Emily Dickinson* (1968), and *Emily Dickinson: A Poet's Grammar* (1987).

Lindberg-Seyersted begins her stylistic analysis holistically, by considering the nature of Dickinson's poetic voice, which she describes as "feminine," and as conveying "feminine identity." But Lindberg-Seyersted's idea of feminine identity seems quaint with thirty years of feminist literary criticism behind us. What she designates as the "Wife" poems (e.g., "I'm 'wife' — I've finished that —"; Fr225; J199) she interprets as the speaker's having "left her girlhood behind" (37). She also notes how a great many of Dickinson's poems project a child's point of view, which may account for some critics' perception that many of the poems are marred (38). Dickinson's love poems also appear to be marred by the childish voice becoming "sentimentally coy and bashful" (39) — here Lindberg-Seyersted uses Fr734; J704 ("No matter — now — Sweet —"); and Fr382; J425 ("Good Morning — Midnight —") as examples. She next examines Dickinson's colloquial diction, first alluding to William Howard's useful study of the topical range of her vocabulary ("Dickinson's Poetic Vocabulary," 1957), and concluding that Dickinson strives for "a colloquialism embodied in a vocabulary of everyday life played off against the literary, the solemn, and the foreign" (61). In "The Robin's my Criterion for Tune —" (Fr256; J285), Lindberg-Seyersted sees Dickinson indicating "a conscious program of viewpoint and selection of material" in her poems: "The Robin's my Criterion for Tune — / Because I grow — where Robins do — / But, were I Cuckoo born — / I'd swear by him — . . ." Criteria for tune, in other words, are relative to whatever environment a poet finds herself part of — a simple enough truism, but readers often miss the extent of Dickinson's regionalisms. Lindberg-Seyersted closely examines easily overlooked words like "thill" (a rural expression for a buggy's shafts [Fr758; J647, and Fr1288; J1254]); "parlor" (a preferred room for formal occasions [Fr684; J457 and Fr1784; J1743]); "brook" — a word Dickinson uses frequently (as in Fr94; J136 and in Fr1588; J1558), and even the word "bucket" (as opposed to "pail"), an old New England term that Dickinson uses in poems like Fr598; J632 as a metaphor for the brain.

Scholars have long debated which edition of Noah Webster's *American Dictionary of the English Language* (First Edition, 1828) Dickinson used. Lindberg-Seyersted believes it is the edition "of 1847 [that] she studied so assiduously" (63) — but her only evidence is Dickinson's famous statement in her second letter to Higginson, that after her "Tutor" (Benjamin Newton) died, "for several years, my Lexicon — was my only companion —" (L261). According to Willis J. Buckingham, however ("Emily Dickinson's Dictionary," 1977), the correct edition is an 1841 reprint of the 1828 edition, for that is the one that is among the volumes owned by the

Dickinson family. Richard Benvenuto, in his essay, "Words within Words: Dickinson's Use of the Dictionary" (1983), concurs, noting that because of the creative ways in which she used her dictionary, it is very important that we know exactly which edition she relied on.

In her examination of Dickinson's prosody and rhetorical patterns that occupies the second half of her study, Lindberg-Seyersted identifies those elements that work together to blur the boundaries between speech and literature — a blurring that Dickinson deliberately maintained through her variations of traditional hymnody, her combination of "questions, exclamations, and vocatives, structures apt to render the immediacy of an urgent voice" (142). Lindberg-Seyersted pays close attention to the nature of Dickinson's rhymes — especially where the rhyming is "so charged with meaning that they express in a sort of shorthand condensation the subject of the whole poem" (174) — and cites as an example Fr1654; J1633: "Still own thee — still thou art / What surgeons call alive — / Though slipping — slipping I perceive / To thy reportless Grave — . . ." Lindberg-Seyersted explains: "Anguished thoughts of the beloved, who is slipping away into the 'reportless' . . . join the unjoinable: alive-Grave; the speaker's 'I perceive' is inserted between the rhyme words as part of the pattern of consonant rhymes and as part of the meaning: the 'I' is a helpless witness to the death process" (174).

Whereas Lindberg-Seyersted regards the diction and syntax Dickinson uses to approximate the language of oral discourse as the defining characteristics of her style, Cristanne Miller constructs a more detailed "grammar" as a basis for determining the way "structure and syntax affect meaning in her poems" (20). She organizes her grammar into five categories: compression, disjunction, repetition, syntax strategies, and speech strategies. Each category consists of particular operations, as follows:

Compression (of syntax; of the poetic structure itself)
- ellipsis of function words
- dense use of metaphor
- highly associative and abstract vocabulary
- recoverable deletion (e.g., it is as [IF] a Vesuvian face / Had let its pleasure through" [Fr 764; J754])
- non-recoverable deletion (e.g., omission of words or phrases that supply logical links between statements, such as in Fr778; J742: "Four Trees — upon a solitary Acre — / Without design . . . / Maintain —" [maintain *what*?])

Disjunction
- unconventional or ambiguous punctuation and capitalization
- metrical irregularity

- unexpected shifts in tone
- unselected variant words and phrases
- unconventional grammar (changes in the grammatical function of words; e.g., verbs used as nouns, as in "The Daily Own — of Love" [Fr426; J580])

Repetition
- (e.g., of function words, indefinite pronouns, relative pronouns)

Syntax Strategies:
- *hypotaxis* (containing subordinate-clause connections)
- *parataxis* (disjunctive, coordinate in contrast to subordinate, linking)
- *negation and contrast* (clauses linked by the conjunctions "or," "but," "yet"; negative definitions, as in "It was not Death, for I stood up" [Fr355; J510])
- *syntactic doubling* (e.g. "He stirred his Velvet Head // Like one in danger, cautious, / I offered him a Crumb" [Fr359; J328], whereby "Like one in danger, cautious" modifies either the "He" of the preceding line or the "I" of the following line — or both!)

Speech elements:
- colloquialisms
- "feminine" diction and syntax

In her concluding chapter Miller places her analysis of Dickinson's grammar into a feminist language-use construct. We see in Dickinson a strategy of linguistic disruption — disruption being one of Dickinson's conscious strategies (160) that is best explained by feminist analysis (161). Perhaps the most dramatic examples of disruption can be seen in poems wherein the speaker, a deferential female or child supplicant, confronts an unjust deity with powerful, disruptive implications, as in Fr215; J193:

> I shall know why — when Time is over —
> And I have ceased to wonder why —
> Christ will explain each separate anguish
> In the fair schoolroom of the sky —
>
> He will tell me what "Peter" promised —
> And I — for wonder at his woe —
> I shall forget the drop of anguish
> That scalds me now — that scalds me now!

"The speaker here," Miller explains,

> apparently forgives Christ for failing to answer the ceaseless question of "why" ... He allows the "drop of Anguish" she presently suffers. Yet the repetition of "That scalds me now" and the concluding exclamation mark call more attention to her overtly minimized anguish — "drop" — than to her indirect apology for his inadequacy. Moreover, the very posture of apologizing for the divinity's failure to answer essential questions ... amounts to an extraordinary indictment of His justice. (168)

Here, then, is one scholar's way of synthesizing a formalist analysis of poetic artistry with a feminist one. Dickinson's unusual linguistic and stylistic manipulations of language, we might say, are in effect strategies for advancing a feminist cause.

Noticing that no other scholar after Cristanne Miller "gives more than a passing glance to the innovation that most obviously characterizes [Dickinson's] voice — her strangely deviant rhymes," Judy Jo Small in *Positive as Sound: Emily Dickinson's Rhyme* (1990: 5) conducts an unprecedented in-depth analysis of the poet's intricate rhyming strategies and their contributions to the thematic and structural integrity of a given poem.

Small's first order of business is to establish Dickinson's "musical aesthetic": "Dickinson exploits the songbird convention of contemporary female poetry" (36), her musical aesthetic also embraces both that of Poe, who in his preface to *Poems* (1831) asserted that the object of poetry was to produce "an *indefinite* instead of a *definite* pleasure," and of Thomas Carlyle, who, in *On Heroes, Hero Worship, and the Heroic in History* (1841), conceived of a musical thought as "one spoken by a mind that has penetrated into the inmost heart of the thing; detected the inmost mystery of the thing" (both qtd. Small 36). Dickinson saw in music "the unstable blend of invitation to ecstasy and painful elusiveness that she associated with awe" (60).

Next, Small examines Dickinson's use of rhyme, which "is not only a phonic repetition, a pleasant musical chime, [but] also an indicator of poetic structure, a marker of units and patterns of verse. Rhyme shapes a poem in a reader's ear" (71). One especially intriguing example of Dickinson's use of rhyme as a rhetorical device occurs in "Better — than Music!" (Fr378; J503), which begins with one kind of rhyme, full rhyme:

> Better — than Music!
> For I — who heard it —
> I was used — to the Birds — before —
> This — was different — 'Twas Translation —
> Of all tunes I knew — and more —

shifts in the third stanza to another, partial rhyme:

> Children — so — told how+ Brooks in Eden —   +assured that
> Bubbled a better — melody —
> Quaintly infer — Eve's great surrender —
> Urging the feet — that would — not — fly —

then returns to full rhyme for the sixth and final stanza:

> Let me not spill+ — its smallest cadence —   +lose * waste
> Humming — for promise — when alone —
> Humming — until my faint Rehearsal —
> Drop into tune — around the Throne —

The meditation on the parallels between music and poetry is beautifully echoed in the rhyming strategy. Small explains how the speaker, "rhapsodizing first about a wonderful 'strain' the speaker has heard," digresses "to a consideration of legends about Eden and its 'better — Melody,' and at last returns to the wonderful 'tune.' The digression is apparently triggered by an association between this 'Keyless Rhyme' and a lost paradisal music now only dimly perceived" (93). Most cleverly, continues Small, "Eve's surrender of paradise is portrayed in terms of 'feet — that would — not — fly,' a phrase that applies both literally to her unwilling feet and metaphorically to plodding, recalcitrant metrical feet, onomatopoeically suggested by a series of monosyllables interspersed with dashes" (93–94).

Small also examines the relationship between Dickinson's rhyming strategies and her strategies for poetic closure or non-closure. Cautioning scholars to heed the distinction between "unfinished" and "inconclusive poems," Small explains how Dickinson employed full and partial rhymes to manipulate "closural and anti-closural forces" (197). In some poems the only stanza employing full rhyme is the last, as in "The Months have ends — the Years — a knot —" (Fr416; J423), in which the speaker comments on the way mortals, like unruly children, resist the "ultimate repose" of death. In this poem, life "is pictured as a 'Skein of Misery,' best ended," Small explains; and the simple harmony of the final rhyme — because it sounds just "right" — supports the idea that in the proper course of things a "*Day*" is meant to close with putting things "*away*" (180–81). Small then contrasts these "full-closure" poems with those of inconclusive closure, like "She rose to His Requirement — dropt / The Playthings of Her Life / To Take the honorable Work / Of Woman, and of Wife — . . ." (Fr857; J732). "The shape of the poem," Small explains, "lies in the progression from the definite fact set forth at the opening . . . and from the conventional assurance that her action is 'honorable' and right, to this quiet incertitude about the 'unmentioned' depths of a wife's experience."

Small's in-depth analysis of what would first strike readers as a superficial poetic device demonstrates the power of close analysis and the insights into the relationship between sound and sense that it can yield. These insights need not be taken as definitive, of course. In her concluding chapter, Small acknowledges the countervailing argument that "ears are fashioned differently" because "reading has a subjective dimension"; nevertheless, the aural strangeness of Dickinson's poetry "is designed, and it has designs on us." Quoting from "This World is not Conclusion" (Fr373; J501), Small reminds us that "internal difference" of unusual combinations of sounds is "where the meanings are." Small uses, as an analogy, Beethoven's *Fifth Symphony,* in which the opening three G notes and an E-flat later combine with notes to generate "tremendous and complicated meanings, meanings that elude language" (216). Dickinson practices this sort of musical alchemy throughout her oeuvre.

Dickinson's Poetic Artistry: Reassessing Formalist Approaches

The New Critics have been faulted for their insistence — central to their view of criticism — that a poem (or any work worthy of the term "literature") is to be studied for its intrinsic, aesthetic properties. It is sometimes mistakenly assumed that the New Critics disregarded the historical or the biographical, but that is not the case. What they asserted, generally speaking, was that the historical and biographical, while obviously of importance to literary *history,* were not essential for literary *analysis.* Of course, this view of the New Criticism (but not necessarily of formalism in general[7]) has come under consistent fire during the past thirty years.

---

[7] Other types of formalism include Russian Formalism and its successors in the Prague Linguistic Circle (which, through its principal figure, Roman Jakobson, gave rise to Structuralism). The Chicago School of Criticism combined formalist with historical critical approaches. The term "New Criticism" was adopted after John Crowe Ransom published *The New Criticism* in 1941, although the term itself, according to Grant Webster in *The Republic of Letters* (1979), was first used by Joel Spingarn as the title of a lecture at Columbia in 1910. Spingarn was referring to the beliefs of Benedetto Croce; the lecture later became the title essay for an anthology of literary criticism edited by Edwin Berry Burgum in 1930 (Webster 63). Be that as it may, the methods of close textual analysis advanced by the New Criticism profoundly influenced the teaching of literature in the academy after the Second World War — especially with the publication of the foundational formalist-training texts *Understanding Poetry* (First Edition, 1938) and *Understanding Fic-*

"Contemporary criticism's very sense of identity," observes Mark Jancovich, "is defined through its opposition to the New Criticism" (137). Part of the reason has to do with the Southern-agrarian paternalism of some of its early adherents, but most of the opposition is centered on formalism's insistence on the ahistorical character of the individual art object. Poetry may be situated in history and culture and in the particular circumstances of the poet's life, but its artistry is governed by imagery, symbolism, word-play, and so on. Formalism also regards literature, embracing as it does the complexities, conflicts, and ironies of human experience, as a major contributor to the aesthetic education of its readers. Literature in this regard differs from science (or at least scientific positivism), which aims to resolve conflicting ideas, simplify and demystify the world (including human experience). Biographical or historical matters are sometimes raised in the context of a close formalist reading, but only if the text warrants it — as when Dickinson mentions Amherst in "If I could bribe them by a Rose" (Fr176; J179) and in "What is — 'Paradise' —" (Fr241; J215). The "I" of a poem is assumed to be a persona not identical to the author, even if the speaker alludes to events or individuals that are known to be part of the poet's life: the aesthetic directive of the work demands it. Emily Dickinson herself demanded it: she told T. W. Higginson that when she says "I" it is always "a supposed person" (L268). John Emerson Todd regards this key proclamation as a clear allusion to Dickinson's poetic technique, on which he bases his 1973 monograph, *Emily Dickinson's Use of the Persona,* a study of the way Dickinson's persona operates in her poetry. (Todd's book will be discussed further below.)

In actual practice, formalists quite commonly allude to aspects of the writer's life in order to make a connection, say, between a geographical or historical allusion in the work and its real-world referent. For example, Cleanth Brooks, in his well-known close reading of Herrick's carpe-diem poem, "Corinna's Going a-Maying" notes in his discussion of the conflict between Christian and Pagan elements in the poem that the poet was an Anglican parson.[8] Because they considered non-textual influences on liter-

---

tion (First Edition, 1943), both edited by Cleanth Brooks and Robert Penn Warren. For a history of the development and influence of the New Criticism in its various manifestations, see Mark Jancovich, *The Cultural Politics of the New Criticism* (Cambridge UP, 1993). For a contemporary reassessment of the New Criticism see Daniel Green, "Literature Itself: The New Criticism and Aesthetic Experience," *Philosophy and Literature* 27.1 (2003): 62–79.

[8] "We have still not attempted to resolve the conflict between the Christian and pagan attitudes in the poem, though the qualifications of each of them, as Herrick qualifies each in the poem, may make it easier to discover possible resolutions which would have appealed to Herrick the Anglican parson who lived so much of

ary production to be irrelevant to the integrity of the works in question, the New Critics were routinely attacked and ultimately discredited; but it is simply not true, as a quick glance at any volume of criticism by Allen Tate, Cleanth Brooks, I. A. Richards, John Crowe Ransom, Yvor Winters, or R. P. Blackmur will attest, that these critics purged extra-textual matters from their critical commentary. Indeed, when such references did appear, they often detracted — ironically — from the objective and meticulous analyses they championed and, indeed, performed so well. Winters, in his 1938 essay "Emily Dickinson and the Limits of Judgment," points to Dickinson's "countrified eccentricity" as a way of explaining what he thought to be the "defects" of the limited range of her metrical schemes (29). Austin Warren, after inserting a virtual sermon on the distractions of earlier critics' obsessions with Emily Dickinson's love life ("I heartily wish that conjecture about Emily's lovers might cease as unprofitable"; "Emily Dickinson" 109), lapses into idle biographical speculation himself a few paragraphs later: "There were, I think, many loves in Emily's life, loves of varying kinds and durations. There were infatuations with Sister Sue and Kate Anthon, perhaps with Helen Hunt Jackson — loves 'natural' enough and permitted by 19th century standards. There was a succession of males to whom she attached her devotion" (110) — and this from the co-author (with René Wellek) of that virtual manifesto of New Criticism, *Theory of Literature* (Third edition, 1956). But as Richard Foster notes in *The New Romantics: A Reappraisal of the New Criticism* (1962), "perhaps the largest share of the pieces by New Critics that have become classics of modern criticism have been 'essay' — semi-poetic revery and personal impressionism — rather than 'analysis'" (15). Holistically speaking, then, it still holds true that the New Critics generally practiced what they preached, but were willing to overlook their central tenet rather than become parochial or stilted.

The first book-length study of Emily Dickinson's poetry from a strictly artistic perspective is Charles Anderson's *Emily Dickinson's Poetry: Stairway of Surprise* (1960). George Whicher's *This Was a Poet: A Critical Biography of Emily Dickinson* (1938) and Richard Chase's *Emily Dickinson* (1951) also pay close attention to Dickinson's poetic craft, but within a biographical framework — one that several critics have continued to adopt more recently.[9] Rebecca Patterson's *Emily Dickinson's Imagery* (1979), William

---

his life in Devonshire and apparently took so much interest, not only in the pagan literature of Rome and Greece, but in the native English survivals of the old fertility cults." (*The Well-Wrought Urn*, 71).

[9] In one of his chapters, "A Poetry of Ideas" (a phrase used by Allen Tate to describe Dickinson's poetry) Richard Chase calls attention to Dickinson's deliberate generation of ambiguity between sexual and sacramental symbolism in poems like

H. Shurr's *The Marriage of Emily Dickinson: A Study of the Fascicles* (1983), Jerome Loving's *Emily Dickinson: The Poet on the Second Story* (1986), and Bettina L. Knapp's *Emily Dickinson* (1991) are notable examples.

Anderson not only conducts keen analytical readings of Dickinson's poems, he provides a coherent framework for her entire project. According to Anderson, Dickinson explores four major themes: art; experience of the outer world (perception, forms, process); experience of the inner world (ecstasy, despair); and death and immortality.

Anderson, with access to Dickinson's complete body of work via Johnson's 1955 variorum *Poems* and Johnson and Ward's 1958 edition of the *Letters,* was now able to provide a comprehensive study of the poet.

Except for occasional lapses into biographical or psychological speculation and a ten-page biographical sketch that appears as an appendix, Anderson's study is a model of the meticulous and learned close reading that formalists value so highly. When not drawing from a given poem's internal evidence, he may reinforce his textual interpretation with reference to analogous passages from the correspondence, from unambiguous allusions such as the Bible or Shakespeare, from other similar poems, or — thanks to Johnson's variorum edition — to variant readings within the same poem. In his commentary on "Bees are Black, with Gilt Surcingles — / Buccaneers of Buzz. / Ride abroad in ostentation / And subsist on Fuzz...." Fr1426A; J1405), note how closely — and with such copious detail — he analyzes the artistry of Dickinson's word choice:

> By calling the bees buccaneers she conjures up those free-booters, like Sir Francis Drake, who raided the Spanish Main in the sixteenth century. The term, from *doucan,* was originally applied to wild hunters in Haiti who lived on the country, independent of civilized markets. So her black knights are land-pirates, mounted on horses rather than ships and ranging "abroad" over the countryside. Her epithet combines the suggestions of looting and swaggering. "Buccaneers" also fits the alliterative pattern which helps to puncture their pretentiousness, for "Buzz" along with its rhyme word "Fuzz" cuts them down to size.... The plunder they proudly carry off is just pollen. Though they seem free and self-sufficient, like Emerson's "Humble-Bee," they are dependent on the lowly fuzz if they are to "subsist." For all their "ostentation" their panoply is "gilt" not gold. Are these anthropo-

---

"I'm ceded — I've stopped being Theirs — ...." (Fr353; J508), as well as prefiguring gender/feminist criticism of the poet: "[O]ne must not neglect the striking affirmation of consciousness and the new power of making choices which womanhood confers.... She has found her first 'rank' too small. 'Crowing on my father's breast' she had been but 'a half unconscious queen'" (157).

morphic bees? A sly comment on men as pretentious swaggerers who are in the end dependent on the very nature they loot?

The second half of the poem moves in another direction with the theological overtones of "ordained." "Surcingle" in stanza one . . . prepares for this since it can mean the girdle of a cassock as well as a saddle-girth. Has the bee-buccaneer become a priest, pollen and the nectar from his "Jugs" now transformed into the elements of a miniature Eucharist? At any rate the bee's sustenance . . . is declared to be "ordained." This term suggests the stable order of creation as distinguished from what is accidental, what is appointed and decreed rather than merely "contingent." (104–5)

To a greater degree than most formalist critics, Anderson demonstrates a masterful ability to capture the extraordinary richness and complexity of meaning and controlled artistry that can be found in even a few lines of a poem by a great poet.

Like Anderson, Clark Griffith in *The Long Shadow* conducts extended close readings of key poems that resonate throughout Dickinson's *oeuvre* — except that Griffith limits his scope to poems that together probe "a world that is fraught with perils and profoundly contemptuous of human needs," and that respond to such a world in two different ways: "One is an attitude involving submission to tragic realities"; the other "countenances . . . a strategic retreat from the circumstances of tragedy" (17). Griffith first considers the second approach. Dickinson, he says, uses such devices as a child's persona or dramatic irony in creating poems like "I started early — took my Dog —" (Fr620; J520). He undertakes a six-page close explication of the poem: His first point is that Dickinson sets up expectations only to defy them. Instead of presenting us with "a characteristically Romantic celebration of childhood" whereby the child is seen as experiencing harmony with nature, the sea, despite initial signs of welcome, reveals a menacing side to the little maid, and goes after her. Although we may find this surprising, the child does not. "If the sea rejects, still he seems to make partial amends by giving the child the lovely gift of pearl" (19–21). Griffith then asks the reader: "Can it [the child's adventure] . . . be dismissed quite so lightly?" Here we encounter explication de texte at its best, which shows why the New Criticism became so widely accepted as a foundation of literature teaching: After guiding us through a detailed yet still superficial reading of the poem, Griffith says in effect — wait: let's go back and look more carefully at what's going on here.

> Consider, for instance, the characterization of the sea. Almost invariably in Romantic poetry, we would expect the ocean to be personified (if at all) in a *feminine* form. Here, by contrast, the usual personification has been reversed. . . . Nor, having put the child in

the clutches of an adult male, does Emily Dickinson permit so enormously suggestive a relationship to drop. Instead, she immediately goes on to magnify its suggestiveness by presenting the attack itself in terms that are distinctively and even baldly licentious.... (21)

And so on. Griffith repeatedly demonstrates the richness of insight that an extended close textual analysis of a great poem can yield.

We encounter the second approach Dickinson's speakers take to a world fraught with peril in poems that engage the circumstances of death and dying. The speakers approach these circumstances not in any despairing way, but from the perspective of stoic acceptance. For example, in "The last Night that She lived" (Fr1100; J1100) mourners attend a woman's final moments on her deathbed:

> The last Night that She lived
> It was a Common Night
> Except the Dying — this to Us
> Made Nature different
>
> We noticed smallest things —
> Things overlooked before
> By this great light upon our minds
> Italicized — as 'twere.

The mourners are left, at the end of the poem, after the woman has died, groping for what to do next:

> And We — we placed the Hair —
> And drew the Head erect —
> And then an awful leisure was
> Belief to+ regulate —   +With nought to — * Our faith to —

Griffith first provides us with an overview of what is going on thematically in the poem: "At the end, it is the living who must continue to act; when the anonymous *She* has become a corpse, the mourners are still faced with the terrible task of looking for consolation or purpose in the scene before them" (115). Griffith next scrutinizes Dickinson's style as it operates in this poem, "thereby to gain a firmer conception of the thought, the care, and the ingenuity that consistently enter into her style in general." First, he examines "the barrenness of diction" — words like narrow, jostled, italicized — "terms that are not normally thought of as possessing much poetic value." This leads him to conclude that "a striking inconsistency" exists "between the emotionalism inherent in the situation being presented, and the dry, spare, prosy diction which permits very little in the way of an overt emotional display" (116). This also holds true for the rhymes — which are not only slant rhymes but "as steadfastly unmusical as rhymes ever become without lapsing into prose altogether" (117). Griffith's explication, aside from being classic New Criticism, quite thoroughly dismantles the impressionist critics' charge that Dickinson's poetics were the result of a faulty ear, or based on sheer ignorance of proper form.

Griffith's next order of business in this chapter is to show how the themes and household tropes of "The last Night that She lived" recur in poems such as "'Twas warm — at first — like Us " (Fr614; J519), "There's been a death in the opposite House" (Fr547; J389), and "I heard a Fly buzz when I died" (Fr591; J465). With regard to the latter poem, Griffith pays close attention to the three "layers of significance" (135) generated by the image of the fly in this deathbed drama. On the simplest layer or level, the fly represents vitality in the everyday world: "As the fly disappears, sense is ebbing with it. When the fly is gone, the speaker herself has been transported to an ineffable other-world" (135). On a second, more complex level, Griffith continues, the fly embodies an awful vision of the death to come — "a hint that stink and corruption are death's only legacies" (136). On the third level the fly is perceived "at its most demonic ... [T]he insect continues to represent life [but] it remains the only animate object in a room which moves steadily toward inanimation. ... It forces us to see that while death may carry one ineluctably to the fly, still it is no less true that only through death can the fly be escaped" (137). In one analysis after another, Griffith demonstrates the wealth of meaning that close attention to literary technique in a given work can generate.

In his first of two monographs on the poet, *The Art of Emily Dickinson's Early Poetry* (1966), David T. Porter, like Charles Anderson and Clark Griffith before him, avoids discussing Dickinson's poems from a biographical perspective, "not because that approach is wholly fruitless," as he explains in his preface, "but because it is excessively speculative." He then elaborates:

> We need not be troubled by wonder or frustration at the refusal of the life to explain the poetry. If anyone requires a demonstration that an artist can create situations he has not experienced, let him read *The Red Badge of Courage* in the knowledge that Crane had never gone to war. We need not commit the fallacy of believing Emily Dickinson felt sad when she wrote of sadness, nor need we succumb to the fetish of the single cause by trying to locate exact springs of creativity. (xii)

Despite this eloquent disclaimer, Porter nevertheless begins his study with "the formative years" (the title of his first chapter), focusing on Dickinson's letters to Higginson, pointing out how she masked her "confident self-regard" (8). In Porter's view, Dickinson's letters "are extremely mannered" and their "forced style . . . studiously avoids compromising her unique, often cryptic mode of expression." He then speculates, "One feels she was intent upon demonstrating to him the ways of an extraordinary woman" (8).

Porter's larger speculation, as the title of his monograph indicates, is that a close reading of the early poems will reveal more coherence and development than first meets the eye. Rather than the superficial topical approaches taken by many critics — which "err in being shortsighted (concerned too hastily with subjects, the metaphorical or analogical constructs)," Porter instead argues that a central theme, aspiration, is the cohering force behind her early poetry. In these poems "she savors the distance between desire and its goal" (157). The dramatic tension between "her questing condition and the recurrent recognition that mortality forever denies ideal fulfillment" generates the extreme emotional states controlled by her "consummate artistry" (157–58).

Instead of seeing Dickinson's body of poetry in terms of distinct categories, as does Charles Anderson with his aforementioned fourfold scheme, Robert Weisbuch, in *Emily Dickinson's Poetry* (1975), chooses instead to regard Dickinson's lyrics as one long poem, just as Whitman's lyrics constitute a *Leaves of Grass*. "It is a key tenet of romanticism . . . that a writer's work, in its totality, should constitute a biography of his consciousness." Weisbuch's method, then, is to identify characteristics uniting the poems (xiii). Making it clear to the reader that his book is a work of criticism and not a biography, he in effect subsumes the life to the poetry — such life-as-poetry comprising "two Emily Dickinsons, visionary celebrant and skeptical sufferer, who live together in the poems" (3). While he might seem to be making a wry comment on biographical criticism, Weisbuch is seriously reminding us that not only is "possibility . . . Emily Dickinson's synonym for poetry," it is also the realm in which she dwells. In her house of possibility, this poet has "discovered that the most ordinary word . . . could become a signifier of utmost mysteries, could grow like a vine into the upper air" (1). Weisbuch invokes "Sleep is supposed to be" (Fr35; J13) to call attention to Dickinson's "need to distinguish two antithetical modes of thought, to value the symbolic, possibility-building mind at the expense of mechanistic common sense" (6). In this poem the speaker impatiently makes clear "that even the advocates of father's 'real life' use figurative language — 'The shutting of the eye' is clearly synecdochic — and thus that their way of thinking is itself full of symbolic assumptions" (6–7).

What is the essence of Dickinson's poetic method? According to Weisbuch, it is *analogy*. "Dickinson's typical poem," he explains, "enacts a hypothesis about the world by patterning a parallel analogical world" (12); it is her way of being able to see the world afresh, stripped of the clichés of perception that characterize conventional world views. Using

"Who never lost, are unprepared" (Fr136B; J73) as a typical example, Weisbuch shows how Dickinson invigorates a stale theological truism, that "the soldier has 'lost' his life to find another, crowned life" (23):

> Who never lost, are unprepared
> A Coronet to find!
> Who never thirsted
> Flagons, and Cooling Tamarind!
>
> Who never climbed the weary league —
> Can such a foot explore
> The purple territories
> On Pizarro's shore?
>
> How many Legions overcome —
> The Emperor will say?
> How many *Colors* taken
> On Revolution Day?
>
> How many *Bullets* bearest?
> Hast Thou the Royal scar?
> Angels! Write "Promoted"
> On this Soldier's brow!

As Weisbuch notes, the analogy shifts from deserts to mountains and then to a battleground that soon becomes heaven. These scenes "finally find a home within a Christian tradition" (23). Dickinson has taken an example of abstract Biblical wisdom, and through the use of military analogies, has rooted the wisdom in traumatic human experience. In so doing she renders the human realm every bit as vital as the divine; in fact, the divine cannot not be truly comprehended, Dickinson seems to suggest, until it is recast experientially.

An intriguing contrasting (but not contradictory) reflection on the unifying aspects of Dickinson's poetic canon is offered by John Robinson in *Emily Dickinson: Looking to Canaan* (1986), in which he notes that Dickinson's thought did not progress in a systematic way; he sees her work "not as a development but as an amplification." Robinson concludes that "[s]he had no project for her work. She did not carry through a purpose" (16) — which echoes David T. Porter's claim in *Dickinson: The Modern Idiom* (1981). In regarding Dickinson as a poet of amplification rather than progression, Robinson is in effect placing her outside of western thought altogether:

> At her best she enlarges our sense of being alive, but her position is a radical one because it involves undermining the very habit of sequence

which is basic to many western thought processes: she challenges the idea of having objectives and seeking to reach them, of judging life by targets which are or are not attained. Such purposefulness ... makes someone vulnerable to circumstance, whereas her hope ... is that someone who manages in different terms may be liberated. (22)

Robinson cites "Superiority to Fate" as an illustration:

> Superiority to Fate
> Is difficult to gain
> 'Tis not conferred of any
> But possible to earn
>
> A pittance at a time
> Until to Her surprise
> The Soul with strict economy
> Subsist till Paradise.
> (Fr1043; J1081)

The speaker makes herself, in Robinson's words, "the celebrant of sky-high aspiration, of unrealized potential in herself and in the world. She believes potential will always be bigger than its worldly accomplishment" (22).

If one agrees with Robinson that Dickinson undermines sequentiality, how might that affect the way we approach the fascicles? Perhaps she arranges her poems for the very purpose of ironically playing out different sequencing possibilities — not to subvert traditional notions but to enlarge — or, to use Robinson's word, to *amplify* — the possibilities of sequence — not unlike the way her improvisations on hymnal meter play with the potentialities of hymn.[10]

What is often referred to as Dickinson's fragmented vision becomes, in Porter's reading, the basis for her brilliance. For example, to illustrate the way she captures the intense emotions generated by the contemplation of death, Porter quotes more than two dozen two-, three-, and four-line passages from poems composed in a three-year period, between 1858 and 1861. Porter discerns and provides examples for several different shadings of topic in these poems, including recognition of the inevitability of death —

> Good night, because we must,
> How intricate the dust!
> (Fr97A; J114)

— the experience of death without a guiding faith —

---

[10] For further discussion of sequence in Dickinson's fascicles, see chapter 4.

> Dying! Dying in the night!
> Won't somebody bring the light
> So I can see which way to go
> Into the everlasting snow?
> (Fr222; J158)

— and death's irreversible work, rendering the grief felt by mourners futile —

> Were useless as next morning's sun —
> Where midnight frosts — had lain!
> (Fr234; J205)

Porter's and Robinson's analyses of Dickinson's rhetoric of amplification (we might also think of it as a rhetoric of improvisation of variations on a theme, more commonly associated with musical progression rather than poetic progression) I consider to be a major insight into how Emily Dickinson should be read.

Dickinson's Rhetorical "I": The Matter of Personae

At first glance, Emily Dickinson's assertion to Higginson in 1862 that the speaker in her poems is "a supposed person" appears to invalidate any autobiographical interpretation of the poems. To be sure, as John Emerson Todd points out in the preface to his monograph, *Emily Dickinson's Use of the Persona* (1973), the "I" in many of the poems could not possibly be the poet, or else we would have to conclude that Emily Dickinson smoked cigars. — "Many cross the Rhine / In this cup of mine. / Sip old Frankfort air / From my brown Cigar" (Fr107; J123) — or, for that matter, experienced being buried alive — "I died for beauty — but was scarce / Adjusted in the Tomb" (Fr448; J449). However, the matter is not as easily resolved as Todd would lead us to believe. For one thing, a persona — that is, a mask, a disguise — may be "thin" in the sense that the poet could be alluding to events in her life obliquely — a facet of her riddling sensibility. Thus the cigar-smoking persona of the poem quoted above might be Dickinson's sly way of telling us that she fantasizes being male. We could follow through on this hypothesis quite easily with several other poems: the persona of "Wild nights!" (Fr269; J249) is male ("Might I but moor — tonight — in thee!"), which from a psychoanalytic perspective may imply a lesbian fantasy on the part of the poet.[11] In any event, Todd argues that Dickinson adopts various personae for purposes of staging dramatic

---

[11] See Rebecca Patterson, *Emily Dickinson's Imagery* (1979), especially chapter 1, "The Boy Emily."

scenarios that enact complex problems. While Todd clearly identifies these personae and illustrates the ways in which they are used, he neglects to demonstrate how the poems function as dramas.

Elizabeth Phillips, however, in her *Emily Dickinson: Personae and Performance* (1988) does succeed in building a convincing premise that Dickinson's personae function dramatically in the poems. In probing what she calls Dickinson's "histrionic imagination" (chapter 4), Phillips notes how the poems frequently take "a dramatic form":

> The speech is often colloquial but also personal, inviting the unwary reader to believe in what James Merrill has called "the illusion of True Confession" . . . There are so many performances in the poems that Dickinson may elude us. Adopting provisional attitudes and myriad voices, she changes point of view, role, situation, genre, language, and style with remarkable speed and adroitness. (78)

Phillips then provides a sense of the range and variety "of tones and perspectives," each of which is dramatic: a child enacting a scene with God ("Papa above!"; Fr151; J61); a young woman holding a mirror to herself and mocking her insignificance ("I'm saying every day / 'If I should be a Queen, tomorrow' —"; Fr575; J373); another young woman who declares herself to be both yielded up and emancipated ("I'm ceded — I've stopped being Their's —"; Fr353; J508).

Phillips's reading of Dickinson as a dramatic poet is important because it coincides with Dickinson's own view of perception as active engagement with the world, as experiment. "Experiment to me / Is every one I meet," she asserts in one of her poems from around 1865 (Fr1081C; J1073). Thus, we can read many of Dickinson's poems as demonstrations of the way an idea, perception, or emotion could be played out — another way, too, of dwelling in possibility.

To sum up, scholars have shown that an important dimension of Emily Dickinson's poetic artistry is revealed by her unconventional manipulation of words and meanings, figurative language (especially analogy), syntactic structures, and rhetorical strategies. The poetic text can also be regarded as a *discourse* — an audience-oriented communication that conveys an argument — that is, posits a claim and supports its validity with reasoning, illustration (literal, metaphorical, ironic, dramatic). Whereas old-style formalists are likely to see rhetorical modes on one hand and poetic or artistic modes on the other as separate or even opposed, "rhetorical" formalists see interplay — not only among author, text, and immediate audience, but also aesthetic interplay, involving the use of personae, dramatic scenarios, and other fictive devices.

Formalism lives on in Dickinson studies in that it has bequeathed to other critical approaches a way of reading a text closely for *any* reason, not necessarily for reasons that fall within the old paradigm of formalist criticism itself. In other words formalism continues to evolve. Consider, for example, Helen Vendler's use of close textual analysis in her *Poets Thinking: Pope, Whitman, Dickinson, Yeats* (2004), as a way of showing how acts of cognition result in producing thematically and structurally unified poems. The earlier formalists skirted around such a concern; to them it implied that poetry functioned as a mere conveyor of knowledge — a clear contradiction to their efforts to distance literature from other modes of knowledge. Although Vendler values the lessons learned from her formalist predecessors — from Allen Tate and John Crowe Ransom, who "argued for the psychological complexity that produces 'tension' and 'paradox' in both the substance and the texture of poetry"; from Cleanth Brooks and Robert Penn Warren, who "emphasized unity of structure and image and the autonomy of the work of art" (3) — Vendler nonetheless feels there is much more to a poem than its iconic "well-wrought urn" aspect; that poems possess "a fluid construction that could change its mind as it proceeded" (4). Rejecting the way a poem "is too often conscripted into illustrating a social idea not germane to its own inner workings," Vendler attempts "to illuminate . . . the way thinking goes on in the poet's mind during the process of creation, and how the evolution of that thinking can be deduced from the surface of the poem" (6). Her chapter on Emily Dickinson focuses on the poet's "invention of temporal structures that mimic the structure of life as she at any moment conceives it" (64). Consider, for example, "Oh give it motion," in which the speaker contemplates a corpse:

> Oh give it motion — deck it sweet
> With Artery and Vein —
> Upon its fastened Lips lay words —
> Affiance it again
> To that Pink stranger we call Dust —
> Acquainted more with that
> Than with this horizontal one
> That will not lift its Hat —
>   (Fr1550; J1527)

How is it possible, Dickinson seems to be thinking, to maintain temporal sequence even after death? Her solution: *reverse* the temporal sequence. We see in this poem "a macabre imitation of the chromatic steps of creation — resurrecting the dead body, giving it 'motion' backward into life" (77). Dickinson, Vendler concludes, "makes us conscious of the extent to which examining a poet's intellectual models of experience is indispensable to the understanding of art" (91).

2: Trends in Dickinson Biography and Biographical/Psychoanalytic Criticism

> *Biography first convinces us of the fleeing of the Biographied —*
> — E. D. to T. W. Higginson,
> February 1885 (L972)

> *Of all the scientific disciplines psychoanalysis has more in common with art. Both seek understanding of the human spirit.*
> — Louis Fraiberg, *Psychoanalysis & American Literary Criticism* (1960)

> *Her life, like the major vehicle of her poetry, was metaphoric.*
> — Richard B. Sewall, *The Life of Emily Dickinson* (1974)

HOW IS IT POSSIBLE in nineteenth-century Calvinist, patriarchal New England, students of Emily Dickinson inevitably wonder, that a young woman from a distinguished family rejects her family's and her culture's faith (or at least the protocols of that faith), chooses not to marry and raise a family, and — most astonishingly — "shuts the door" on society and throws away the key to pursue the vocation of poetry in her own utterly uncompromising manner? Formalists, of course, do not consider the question relevant to their critical agendas (although that does not preclude their being fascinated with the poet's life), but biographers and critics for whom the life informs the work consider the question essential. Was it emotional turmoil triggered by unrequited love? Was it agoraphobia or some other kind of phobia? Did her eye problems or other physiological afflictions stoke the engines of poetic production? Perhaps it had something to do with Dickinson's experience of what she mysteriously referred to in an 1862 letter to Higginson as her "terror — since September — I could tell to none,"[1] which led her, as she wrote in her second letter to

---

[1] Richard B. Sewall, in *The Lyman Letters* (1965), notes the similarity between "a terror since September" and the way Dickinson described, in a passage in a letter to Joseph Lyman, being compelled not to read while undergoing eye treatment in

Higginson, to "sing, as the Boy does by the Burying Ground — because I am afraid" (L261). Or perhaps the cause more closely parallels that of the cloistered nun who chooses to devote her entire life to Christ, for Dickinson chose to devote herself with equal commitment to poetry — even recognizing the religious character of her devotion when she alluded to herself in a poem as "the Wayward Nun beneath the Hill" (Fr745; J722), and in an 1853 letter to Susan Gilbert by saying "I find that I need more vail"[2] (L107). Maybe the white dress she always wore in her adult years served as her habit, the outward sign of self-election to the holy vocation of poetry.

Motives, underlying desires, subconscious impulses, connections between external actions and imaginative production — these are the concerns of literary critics and biographers who locate the roots of artistic production in the subconscious. "The language of desire is veiled," writes Elizabeth Wright in *Psychoanalytic Criticism: A Reappraisal* (2nd ed., 1998). "Psychoanalysis explores what happens when primordial impulse is directed into social goals" (1–2). Like literary criticism, psychoanalysis uses interpretation, "which calls into question the commonsense facts of consciousness" (2). Even by scanning the table of contents of Freud's *The Interpretation of Dreams* (1900), I might add, one notices the affinity between psychoanalysis and literary criticism. His chapter on "The Dream-Work," for example, breaks down the function of dreaming into what could easily pass as an analysis of the process of writing poetry: "condensation," "displacement," "means of representation," including "representation by symbols in dreams" and even immediate post-dreaming "secondary revision." And in an essay written some years later, "The Relation of the Poet to Daydreaming" (1908), Freud wonders how the poet is "able to carry us with him in such a way and to arouse emotions in us of which we thought ourselves perhaps not even capable?" (44). His attempt to answer the question takes him to ponder the nature of dreams — whether nocturnal dreams or daydreams — and to the possibility that both kinds represent "fulfillments of desires" (52).[3]

Boston: "Some years ago I had a woe, the only one that ever made me tremble" (74–76). See also James R. Guthrie's *Emily Dickinson's Vision: Illness and Identity in Her Poetry* (1998), 10.

[2] One of the meanings of *vail* (intransitive verb) in the Middle Ages and Renaissance, according to the OED, was "to have might or power; to prevail"; Dickinson's referent (literal or metaphoric) is that of a woman veiling her face. For a discussion of the way Dickinson puns with veil/vale, see Daneen Wardrop, *Emily Dickinson's Gothic: Goblin with a Gauge* (1996) 97–99.

[3] See also John S. Mann ("Dream in Emily Dickinson's Poetry," 1978), who reflects on the way Dickinson associates the elusiveness and evanescence of dreams with memory.

Dickinson Biographies: An Overview

Biographies of the poet either are internal ("intellectual" or "psychoanalytic") or external (emphasizing what is known of the poet's private life as well as her social and cultural milieu). Here, a bit of historical context may be useful. In 1930, the centennial of Emily Dickinson's birth, two full-scale "external" biographies (as distinct from intellectual biographies) of the poet appeared. First came Josephine Pollitt's *Emily Dickinson: The Human Background of Her Poetry*, which, despite the title, seldom mentions Dickinson's poetry at all — and even then, only in the context of social relationships, for example, how Helen Hunt Jackson's correspondence with her childhood friend Emily Dickinson led to the publication of "Success is counted sweetest" in Jackson's anthology, *A Masque of Poets* (1878). Pollitt's biography was followed a few months later by Genevieve Taggard's *The Life and Mind of Emily Dickinson* (1930), which attempts to link Dickinson's poetry to events and relationships in her life, especially Dickinson's putative romantic attraction to George Gould and Samuel Bowles. Pollitt and Taggard relied heavily on speculation and narrative coloration to weave their respective portraits of the poet, which are absorbing but overly subjective. Here is a sampling from Pollitt:

> Emily Dickinson came from the capital in a dreamy state of mind. She had formed a romantic and violent attachment for a man [Lieutenant Edward Hunt, Helen Hunt Jackson's first husband], under impossible conditions. It would seem that every thought of him should be spiked with the sense of Helen: Helen's hands, Helen's kiss, and confidences, and childhood's games at growing up.... Before she had time to shake herself thoroughly awake came the sermons and friendship of Dr. Wadsworth.... (127–28)

Taggard spends more time than Pollitt establishing plausible connections between the life and the poetry. For example, she argues that Dickinson absorbed many of her father's legal concepts and the vocabulary accompanying them, together with his strategies of argument, for poetic purposes, and lists nearly 300 legal terms found in her poems (see 278–81). However, she also slips into overly subjective coloration when, for example, she considers Dickinson's feelings about publishing: "Emily refused to have her poetry published even when she most pathetically desired the contact of readers ... [V]anity, turned into humility and shame, coursed in Emily's blood; she was prodigiously vain" (243). When reading such a passage, one can sympathize with the New Critics' eagerness to avoid falling prey to the biographical fallacy.

The first Dickinson biography to appear after the publication of Thomas H. Johnson's variorum edition of the *Poems* (1955) was Johnson's own *Emily Dickinson: An Interpretive Biography,* published that same year. As the subtitle suggests, Johnson devotes two thirds of the biography to the details of Dickinson's vocation of poet — most of this information, alas, having already been treated by other biographers. Following a three-chapter overview of the history and culture of the Connecticut River Valley (his premise being that Dickinson's life was inseparable from the valley's tradition), Johnson introduces us to her family, then to her "estate": her friends whom she valued with such emotional intensity that "she avoided direct contacts, or fled to escape them" (45). To put it another way, "the exuberance of living overwhelmed her" (46). This is as speculative as Johnson ever gets, part of his agenda being to *excise* the speculations of other biographers such as George Frisbie Whicher's *This Was a Poet* (1938). Well-crafted as Johnson's biography is, it seems bland when compared to other biographies before and since. It lacks the minutiae (however speculative) about the private person that readers have come to expect from a biography of the poet, even an "interpretive" one.

Emerson once said that the biography of a genius is internal rather than external. Albert Gelpi in *Emily Dickinson: The Mind of the Poet* (1965), moves in that direction, perceiving his individual chapters to be "a series of concentric circles of widening diameter" (vii) — the mind of a genius rippling outward to embrace the world. Like Johnson, Gelpi begins with the circumstances surrounding Dickinson's family life, the history and culture of the Connecticut River Valley, and leads up to the overarching theological and philosophical mysteries with which she grappled. He turns to Dickinson's correspondence as an important resource for tracing the growth of her thought. Whereas Johnson draws from the letters to reconstruct relationships with friends, Gelpi sees in the letters "the development of her imagination and her growing sense of poetic mission" (64). For example, in April 1850, the same year Dickinson received Emerson's *Poems* from her close friend Benjamin Newton, she sent a letter to another close friend, Jane Humphrey, conveying "a special sense of dedication" that indicates "the emergence of a poet" (65). Part of the letter reads as follows:

> I have dared to do strange things — bold things — and have asked no advice from any — I have heeded beautiful tempters, yet do not think I am wrong ... The winter was all one dream, and the spring has not yet waked me, I would always sleep, and dream, and it never should turn to morning, so long as night is so blessed. What do you weave from all these threads? (L35)

Gelpi next takes us to the following year, when she first conferred upon herself the title of poet: "We are the only poets, and everyone else is *prose*," she writes to her sister Sue (L56). A short while later, she writes a letter to her brother, filling it with rich autumnal imagery, and concludes it with a passage that Johnson had rendered as verse in his variorum edition (L58; J2[4]):

> "... there is *another* sky ever serene and fair, and there is *another* sunshine, tho' it be darkness there — never mind the faded forests, Austin, never mind the silent fields — here is a little forest whose leaf is ever green, here is a *brighter* garden, where not a frost has been, in its unfading flowers I hear the bright bee hum, prithee, my Brother, into *my* garden come!

Dickinson's famous "Brother Pegasus" letter to her brother two years later indicates that her sense of vocation was holding fast and firm: "Now Brother Pegasus, I'll tell you . . . I've been in the habit myself of writing some few things . . ." (L110).

Gelpi reminds us that one can be a biographical critic and still make good use of formalist analysis. His close reading of Dickinson's letters reveals, more than earlier biographies, how a poetic sensibility manifests itself over many years. Also, whereas Johnson regarded nature as one of Dickinson's "flood subjects" (the phrase Dickinson herself used in reference to immortality), Gelpi substitutes love: "In a body of poetry devoted to the main concerns of consciousness the principal themes are . . . love, death, and immortality: fulfillment, dissolution, and transcendence inextricably entwined" (109). In fact, love, for Dickinson "is the force which drives the cycle of life, death, and resurrection" (114) — as one of her mystical quatrains suggests: Love — is anterior to Life — / Posterior — to Death — / Initial of Creation, and / The Exponent of Earth — (Fr980; J917).

Using Dickinson's poems about the experience and the metaphysics of love, Gelpi effects a synthesis between the poet's life and the poet's mind: "As love moved between death and immortality, as consciousness moved between woe and bliss, the poetic imagination embodied the extremes of experience in contrapuntal themes: the bird . . . who yet can dominate the universe with melody; . . . the homely caterpillar whose 'dim capacity for Wings' becomes the butterfly bursting from the . . . cocoon" (115).

Another early post-Johnson biography that strives to effect a synthesis between external and internal elements is *The Capsule of the Mind: Chapters in the Life of Emily Dickinson* (1961), by Theodora Ward, the granddaughter of Dr. Josiah and Elizabeth Holland, both of whom were lifelong friends of the Dickinsons, and to whom Emily Dickinson wrote dozens of

---

[4] Franklin, in his variorum *Poems* (1998), removes the passage from Dickinson's poetic canon.

letters over the years.⁵ In the preface to her biography, Ward cautions that because Dickinson's images "are usually related to the conscious sensation or evaluation of the experience instead of being an outpouring from the depths of the psyche," it is necessary "to follow the experience as she became aware of it, rather than attempt an analysis of the images and symbols according to any preconceived idea of their significance" (viii). Essentially, then, Ward approaches many of the poems as biographical revelations, artistically transformed but transparent enough to point to a particular external experience. Even in an allegorical poem such as "Three times — we parted —Breath — and I —" Ward sees an external connection:

> Three times — we parted — Breath — and I —
> Three times — He would not go —
> But strove to stir the lifeless Fan+   +flickering fan
> The Waters — strove to stay.
>
> Three times — the Billows threw+ me up —   +tossed
> Then caught me — like a Ball —
> Then made Blue faces in my face —
> And pushed away a sail
>
> That crawled Leagues off — I like to see —
> For thinking — While I die —
> How pleasant to behold a Thing
> Where Human faces — be —
>
> The Waves grew sleepy —+ Breath — did not —   +The Ocean — tired
> The Winds — like Children — lulled —   *[The Ocean —] wearied —
> Then Sunrise kissed my Chrysalis —
> And I stood up — and lived —
>
>   (Fr514; J598)

Even though Ward admits that it isn't necessary to establish a one-to-one connection to an external circumstance, the temptation to do so remains too tempting for her. "The kiss of sunrise, that brought the butterfly out of its chrysalis," Ward asserts,

> is clearly something that has happened in the external world. Into the emptiness that had placed her in such danger has come the revivifying experience of falling in love. . . . Into the vacuum left by her struggle had come a man who carried the attributes of a God she could adore . . . It is not necessary to identify the man who stirred Emily so pro-

---

⁵ See Theodora Ward, *Emily Dickinson's Letters to Dr. and Mrs. Josiah Holland* (Cambridge, MA: Harvard UP, 1951).

foundly. It is not necessary to postulate the existence of any actual man as the object of her love, so closely was her emotion connected with her own inner involvement. Yet, drafts of letters exist in handwriting of this period to someone whom she called "Master." (48–49)

It is easy to sympathize with Ward's need to seek biographical clues in Dickinson's imagery; yet the impulse strikes me as naïve in that the speaker's "Breath" could just as easily be linked to a moment of spiritual or mystical transport as to a romantic one. Even if it were true that Dickinson had been thinking of "Master," whoever he or she might be, this poem loses its power if read through a biographical lens, as do many of Dickinson's other poems. The aesthetic experience of the poem is diminished if not altogether negated when the center of attention is shifted from the work of art to the life.

Emily Dickinson shunned conventional human interaction because she found the heart of life in aesthetic experience. As David Higgins reminds us in his *Portrait of Emily Dickinson* (1967), his correspondence-based biography of the poet, she "preferred to write to her friends rather than see them." In her letters as in her poems Dickinson condenses and distills her thoughts into metaphor. As Higgins insightfully points out, this was her way of living deliberately: she "preferred to present herself to the world only by deliberate art" (6), and her letters "were part of her art [and] the life she chose made them also her conversation and her autobiography" (24). Higgins fashions his biography around the correspondence because he believes that they reveal much about her poetry (24).

Higgins strikes a key chord in his epistolary biography when, in the context of discussing her earliest letters, he expresses his amazement at the vivacity of the eleven-year-old Emily in an 1842 letter to her brother Austin: "The reader finds himself caught up in the breathless detail of her daily life" (26). Here is a portion of that letter:

> Aunt Elisabeth is afraid to sleep alone and Vinnie has to sleep with her but I have the privilege of looking under the bed every night which I improve as you may suppose the Hens get along very nicely the chickens grow very fast I am afraid they will be so large that you cannot perceive them with the Naked Eye when you get home . . . (L1)

The stages of Dickinson's life are reflected in the letters, and inform Higgins's organization of his biography of the poet. He begins with "Home and Family," then proceeds to "Growth" — Emily's struggle with conversion as reflected in her letters to Abiah Root, for example, and her letters to Henry Vaughan Emmons, "which help to document a transitional period between her youth and maturity" (66). Higgins then brings us to the years in which Dickinson, who is starting to think of herself as a poet, begins seeking "preceptors" like Samuel Bowles and Charles

Wadsworth. The letters now acquire "the compact intensity of her poems" (92). As she pursued her vocation of poetry, says Higgins, "she valued all friendships more than before" (93). Higgins portrays the time of the "Master" letters as a "crisis" period in her life; the years of extraordinary poetic production her "royalty" and "Queen Recluse" periods. Finally the declining years arrive, climaxed by the sudden death of her eight-year-old nephew Gilbert ("Gib") — years that Higgins poignantly treats under the heading "The Weight of Grief." He notes that during the last three years of her life, Emily Dickinson wrote 248 letters despite her poor health — a great many more than during any other period.

Higgins's epistolary biography, in tracing the progress of Dickinson's life through the 1,049 extant letters[6] and 124 prose fragments that comprise the three-volume *Letters of Emily Dickinson* (1958), demonstrates how much insight we can gain into even a "veiled" life like Dickinson's through insightful readings of these primary texts.

One of the most controversial biographies of the poet is Rebecca Patterson's *The Riddle of Emily Dickinson* (1951), winner of Houghton Mifflin's prestigious Literary Fellowship Award, which still draws attention today. Patterson argues that Emily Dickinson and Kate Scott Anthon were lovers, and that even though Dickinson did cultivate "intellectual attachments to men, . . . from the days of her childhood women attracted her emotionally, and women alone had the power to wound her" (7). The poems, moreover, unveil a story, a literal story:

> "The mind of Emily Dickinson was literal. Her symbolism was only a word-play used to present familiar things in a new and startling light. She was a wit, not a mystic." (10)

---

[6] In addition to Joseph Lyman's recordings of portions of letters Dickinson had written to him, published by Richard Sewall as *The Lyman Letters* (1965), two new Dickinson letters have been discovered. In 1992 The Friends of the Amherst College Library published *Emily Dickinson: A Letter*. The letter, which is addressed to "Susie" (whether this is Susan Dickinson or Susan Phelps isn't clear), and dated 1858 by R. W. Franklin, begins: "You will forgive me, for I never visit." The second letter was first discovered among the papers of historian John Franklin Jameson (1859–1937) in 1990 by Morey Rothberg, published in *Dickinson Studies* 78 in 1991 (20–21), and authenticated ten years later by Morey Rothberg and Vivian Pollak in the article "An Emily Dickinson Manuscript (Re)Identified at the Library of Congress," *Emily Dickinson Studies* 10.1 (2001): 43–51. It reads as follows: "Excuse these / Brown Suggestions — / Wisdom is / seldom dressed / in Pink — E. Dickinson."

Patterson's biography captivated audiences, and it is easy to see why: the biography reads like a novel. For example, she describes Kate Scott's arrival at the Evergreens (Austin and Sue's house) this way:

> On a day of early March, 1859, a tall young woman, swathed in long furs, her dark hair crowned by a fashionable black hat, her dark eyes brilliant behind a widow's black veil, stepped down from Austin's sleigh to the snowy driveway of the Austin Dickinson house. Many bags and parcels were to be carried in, for this was to be a long visit of some three weeks. But Kate would not stop to oversee the moving of her luggage; she would hurry up the walk toward Sue. There would be exclamation and laughter and warm embraces for Sue; but at some point Kate would turn toward the small, auburn-haired young woman waiting eagerly to meet her. Emily had been hearing about Kate Scott for almost nine years. She was ready to like her, and if she was not already prepared to love her, then the love followed swiftly upon a sunny laugh, a musical voice, and the most excitable, moving personality that Emily was ever to know. (116)

Patterson draws her evidence for Emily's romantic relationship with Kate not only from the letters (see L203, for example), but from the poems as well; in fact she opens her biography with a poem that actually mentions "Katie" (Fr1429; J1410) — one of the few poems in Dickinson's oeuvre that mentions names of persons she knew:

> I shall not murmur if at last
> The ones I loved below
> Permission have to understand
> For what I shunned them so —
> Divulging it would rest my Heart
> But it would ravage their's —
> Why, Katie, Treason has a Voice —
> But mine — dispels — in Tears.[7]

Nearly thirty years after *Riddle,* and published posthumously, Rebecca Patterson's *Emily Dickinson's Imagery* (1979) appeared. In this study, Patterson attempts a psycho-biographical reading of the poems, approaching them as clusters of images — of colors, jewels, chemical elements, the

---

[7] Franklin, in a note to his variorum edition, comments that this 1877 poem was written "on a bifolium of notepaper," and signed ("Emily"). "Though prepared for a recipient, apparently Catherine Scott Anthon, who visited Amherst in 1877, it was not sent." Franklin also notes that Dickinson "used one of the folded surfaces to try to explain further why she would not see her visitor . . . "We shun because we prize her face" (Fr1430; J1429); (*Poems,* 1998).

cardinal points of the compass, that uncover a "geography of the unconscious," as she titles one of her chapters.

What I find most edifying in Patterson's analysis is her discussion of Dickinson's erotic sensibility as it becomes manifest in her imagery. Refuting a British reviewer who commented with apparent satisfaction that the "Love" section of an early collection of Dickinson's poetry "lacked eroticism," Patterson writes:

> There is, on the contrary, no more erotic poetry in the English language. This is the secret of its drive, of its febrile energy, of the inexplicable fascination it has for many baffled readers. Death is eroticized, pain is eroticized, religion is eroticized. She cannot write about a hummingbird without turning it into an erotic symbol; and her bees and flowers and butterflies are innocently, blatantly eroticized, almost but not quite to the point of comedy. Expressed in a slightly different way, she has but two subjects, which are in fact one subject — an eroticized death and what might be called a thanaticized eros. (30)

Patterson asserts that much of this erotic symbolism "came into consciousness"; that Dickinson "knew at least what or whom she was writing about and how far she was diverging into fantasy and wish fulfillment from real experience"; that Dickinson "did indeed create a drama of which she was by turns the happy or the tragic hero, but always with a basis in reality" (30). However, Patterson never actually elaborates on the consequences, biographical or literary, of Dickinson's erotic imagery becoming a part of her consciousness, or having its basis in reality. We might ask what difference it would make for the poet (for whom the imagination *was* reality) to make the shift from unconsciousness to consciousness, or from fantasy to reality.

Biographical Writing on Dickinson, 1974–2001

It wasn't until 1974, with the publication of Richard Sewall's National Book Award-winning *The Life of Emily Dickinson*, that "external" and "internal" biographical elements factors were most successfully integrated. The first hint we have of the extraordinary task Sewall has set out to achieve in his biography is his thirteen-page chronology, which begins not with Emily Dickinson's birth, but that of her paternal grandfather, Samuel Fowler (Oct. 9, 1775), and includes events that could be significant or not, depending on context and on future discoveries, such as the day on which a major religious revival in Amherst began (Aug. 25, 1846); the month in which Dickinson received Emerson's *Poems* from Ben Newton (January 1850); the day that Emily, Lavinia, and a group of friends climbed Mt. Holyoke (Oct. 9, 1849), or the day Edward Dickinson rang the church bells to herald the aurora borealis (Sept. 18, 1851).

In his opening chapter, "The Problem of the Biographer," Sewall stresses the degree to which Dickinson's life, "like the major vehicle of her poetry, was metaphoric" (4), thus making it difficult "to detach the real person from the stereotypes that have been imposed upon her" (11) — an insight many a biographical critic seems to have failed to grasp. Sewall then elaborates:

> To question the old clichés — the Broken Heart, the Tyrant Father, the Recluse — is not to say that her life reveals no shape at all. Keats said of Byron that he "cuts a figure — but he is not figurative." Emily Dickinson cut no figure at all, but in a deeper sense her life was figurative, metaphoric. (11)

Sewall divides his approach to the poet into two parts, each a separate volume. In volume 1 he examines the cultural milieu in the context of seven key individuals (each requiring his or her own chapter: the poet's paternal grandfather, Samuel Fowler Dickinson; the father, Edward; the brother, William Austin; the sister, Lavinia Norcross — and the then-startling revelation in his chapter on "Mabel Loomis Todd and Austin": the story of the adulterous affair between the poet's brother and the woman who would, in 1890, present Emily Dickinson's poetry to the world. The remaining chapters focus on Susan Gilbert Dickinson, and the circumstances leading to the posthumous publication of the poems. Emily Dickinson herself, as Sewall liked to quip, doesn't get born until volume 2. In the second volume Sewall follows a similar pattern of defining the subject's life by examining first its stages (childhood, schooling, early friendships); then the key players in it: Charles Wadsworth, Samuel Bowles, Thomas Wentworth Higginson, Helen Hunt Jackson, Josiah and Elizabeth Holland, the Norcross cousins Fanny and Louisa.

Sewall opens his commentary on Dickinson the poet by reflecting on her similarity to the metaphysical poets, agreeing with scholars like Judith Banzer, who in her 1961 article in *American Literature,* "Compound Manner: Emily Dickinson and the Metaphysical Poets," saw Dickinson as "poised between scepticism and faith, desire and renunciation, optimism and despair," her poetry manifesting "paradox, argument, and unifying conceits" (417; qtd. Sewall, 708). However, Sewall proceeds to show how unlike the metaphysicals she is:

> Her more precarious stance, her more self-conscious, detailed, and poignant exploration of the dark interior, her distant and often paradoxical God, set her apart from these poets and made for a different rhythm and language. . . . She lacked the sense of sin that plagued

Donne, and the prevailing serenity of Herbert. Her spiritual gait . . . is more spasmodic than theirs. (708)

Sewall also considers Dickinson's resemblance to the Romantic poets, especially Keats, and to the Victorians, especially Robert Browning — but once again, the differences overshadow the similarities. Regarding the latter poet, Sewall points out that although Dickinson might well "have found encouragement in Browning's distinctive form" — for example in "the conversational tone, the broken rhythms, the sudden shift ([e.g.] from Scripture to the stock market)" Dickinson's tone "was habitually more lyric, and she had very little of [Browning's] interest in creating characters" (716).

Beyond the similarities to the aforementioned great poets before her, Dickinson's poetic genius, for Sewall, lies in her innovative language. Even in her lesser poems, he argues, "the language is invigorated by an uncanny ear for sound, by unexpected juxtapositions, by single striking adjectives or verbs of action used as never before" (718).[8]

Perhaps the most audacious project in Dickinson biographical criticism is *The Marriage of Emily Dickinson* (1983), William H. Shurr's monograph in which he approaches all forty of Dickinson's fascicles as an elaborate narrative structure depicting the poet's betrothal and marriage to — and separation from — the Reverend Charles Wadsworth.[9] Jerome Loving in *Emily Dickinson: The Poet on the Second Story* (1986) also attempts to correlate aspects of Dickinson's life with her art by approaching the poems as a body of recollection: "The lives of the poet and the person," he writes, "had finally converged on the second story" (that is, in her sequestered space where her mind alone can function freely, apart from the demands of the "first floor" of corporeality). The second story is the abode of poetry, which Loving imaginatively characterizes as "a way of dying without death. It rejected in its celebration of the tensions of life any and all notions of catharsis or redemption through death" (5). A good many of those tensions, Loving tells us, were brought about from Emily's falling out with her once-intimate friend and current sister-in-law Sue, who once served as Emily's surrogate, who had been "Emily's way of remaining the experienced virgin, that individual who could retain the freedom of adolescence in adulthood — or sex in the subjunctive. But now, about the time of the birth of Sue and Austin's first child, Ned, which

---

[8] Sewall discusses writing Dickinson's biography in "In Search of Emily Dickinson" (1986).

[9] See chapter 4 for a discussion of Shurr's marriage-narrative hypothesis in the context of Dickinson's fascicle sequences.

resulted in "Sue's transformation into the soft, cherubic creature of motherhood, Emily felt the full weight of experience" (52–53).

Through recollection — through memory, which Loving equates with Dickinson's idea of circumference — the poet on the second story discovers that dying is a way of coming to life, to full consciousness of our existential dilemma. "God created us by killing off our bliss . . ." (73) and now, "We roam in Sovereign Woods" (Fr764; J754), "lured there by the Voice in the Garden that comes to us as a mere echo of our own voice": "And every time I speak for Him — / The Mountains straight reply —" God's voice is our own, Loving explains, "because God speaks through us, not to us" (73).

Loving, similar to Ward, Cody, and Shurr before him, prefers to privilege the life over the poetry — a reasonable enough preference if one is a biographer. But mining the poetry for insights into Dickinson's behavior leaves us with the notion that Dickinson turned to poetry as a reaction to negative circumstances in her life, rather than as a vocation, a notion that I find difficult to accept.

Like Richard Sewall, Cynthia Griffin Wolff begins her biography with an examination of Dickinson's family, past and present, her schooling and her growing sense of vocation. But there the similarity ends. Wolff devotes the remaining two thirds of the book to Dickinson's chosen vocation and the way that vocation took shape. It is fitting that Wolff begins with a consideration of Dickinson's poetic voice. In an age when women were conditioned to play out the social stereotypes of passivity, domesticity, and emotional sensitivity, Dickinson asserted herself intellectually through poetry, and in so doing defied the stereotype of poetess — contemptuously alluding to the flood of women's saccharine verse that filled the pages of periodicals such as the *Springfield Republican* as "dimity convictions." Dickinson understood that she lived in an age in which, as Wolff explains, "American poets could command considerable respect as thinkers because poetry . . . was held to serve a significant intellectual function" (174). One of her most important early accomplishments as a poet was to find a voice in which a female sensibility could be conveyed as seriously as a male's — and that was the voice of a child. "The child could serve as an Everyman because every adult had once been a child. Moreover, in childhood the prescribed roles for 'appropriate' male and female behavior were not yet fully enforced" (182). Eventually the child's voice modulates into the "wife's," symbolizing a new maturity and status — but not of the typical conjugal sort. The wife Dickinson becomes is the bride of poetry. This was a voice "of maturity and responsibility, wounded and sobered by pain" (202). This voice then morphs into what Wolff calls the proleptic voice: "essentially and deliberately literary. It speaks aloud, often indifferent to the listener. It does not trouble to aggrandize the self:

now one but death is competing for preeminence" (221). Wolff then presents the most renowned of the proleptic poems because of its ability to generate "a tension between the capacity of vision and the meaning of its extinguishment, between that which is willed and that which must be accepted passively" (225). The poem in question is among Dickinson's greatest: "I heard a Fly buzz — when I died —" (Fr591; J465). What commands our attention in this masterpiece, Wolff believes, "is the quiet of the Voice, the simple fortitude that will serve as guide through the suburbs of the Wilderness. ... In the moment of this poem, we are poised fastidiously between the order and coherence of life and the disintegration of death" (225).

It is an eloquently articulated insight, but Wolff's job as Dickinson's biographer becomes problematic in moments like this: how much time can the biographer devote to analysis of the subject's oeuvre without seeming to digress into purely literary scholarship? If we are to take the truism that Dickinson's life literally was her work seriously, then the answer must be, "A considerable amount of time indeed"; but then, can we still call the work a biography? The term "intellectual biography" strikes one as oxymoronic unless one is able plausibly to connect the poems with the life — an almost impossible task to achieve with conviction, in Dickinson's case! Moreover, "the life" in this context can mean many things, including the composing of letters echoing ideas in the poems. Wolff makes abundant use of such connections between the poems and the letters. In the case of "I heard a Fly buzz," for example, she calls attention to the way the speaker's "faculty of sight is slipping away," and that she cannot "maintain an ordered visual grasp of the world." Wolff relates this to a comment Dickinson made in a letter to Higginson: "The Ear is the last Face. We hear after we see" (226; L405).

In view of Sewall's amazingly well-documented biography of Dickinson, what could another full-scale biography possibly offer? Two things, Alfred Habegger tells us in the introduction to his *My Wars Are Laid Away in Books: The Life of Emily Dickinson* (2001): first, it can supplement the older materials with newly discovered ones, and second, it can correct a long-held but mistaken view of the poet, namely "that her art was static or airless and that we don't need to know about her stages, sequences, contexts in order to catch on" (xiii). The first of these aims Habegger fulfills convincingly; the second, only speciously, for the simple reason that he does not examine the poetry closely enough. He does make a valiant effort to link poems to particular situations, but such linkages are almost always purely speculative because Dickinson's poetry distanced itself metaphorically from particular life events (hence giving the impression of that "omitted center" Jay Leyda and other scholars have noticed). In trying to establish a clear connection between Dickinson's love poems and her private life, for example, Habegger admits to some uncertainty about the validity of his attempt:

> That the love poems were a response to an actual and painful relationship with a man seems the only plausible way to take them. Yet even as we scour them for news of the poet's life, we must keep in mind her predilection for fiction, fantasy, secrecy. She may or may not have had a special "Box — / In which his letters grew" ["I got so I could hear his name"; Fr292; J293[10]], but there probably was a correspondence. (412)

One of the most informative and satisfying parts of Habegger's biography pertains to Emily Dickinson's education — her seven years at Amherst Academy and her year at Mt. Holyoke Seminary for Women. We learn, through newly uncovered documents, for example, that Emily wrote marginalia in a Latin textbook she shared with her friend Abby Wood. The text, an edition of Virgil recently acquired by Amherst College from Abby's descendents, bears an inscription from *The Aeneid* in Emily's hand:

> *Forsan et haec olim meminisse juvabit* Aeneid 1–203.
> Afterwards you may rejoice at the remembrance of these
>   (our school days)
> When I am far away then think of me — E. Dickinson.
>
> (141)

Habegger's biography is filled with many little surprises like this, the result of casting the spotlight on often overlooked or slighted moments, which then take on unexpected significance. One of the most memorable involves the wife of Emily Dickinson's second cousin on her mother's side, Eudocia Converse Flynt from Monson, Massachusetts. She had come to Amherst College for commencement, attended the Dickinsons' reception, and

---

[10] Jane Donahue Eberwein, commenting on this poem in *Dickinson: Strategies of Limitation* (1985), understands that reading the love poems autobiographically is "often a misleading approach to Dickinson's work but always tempting"; nonetheless, this leads one to "discover an intense commitment to one man as the central figure of the poet's universe, a competitor with God for her devotion" (23–24). Be that as it may, Dickinson's poetic artistry becomes Eberwein's principal concern. Thus, in "I got so I could hear his name" Eberwein calls attention to the poem's "tight parallel organization which . . . breaks down in syntactic confusion" in the last stanza" (26). Of course, Eberwein is writing criticism, not biography; nonetheless, with Dickinson the alchemy of poetic craft — the sublimation of the poet in the persona (if not the erasure of the poet by the persona) — cannot be set aside even when the poems give the impression of being starkly autobiographical.

everyone apparently had a fine time. A short while later Eudocia received this "letterpoem" from Emily (manuscript lineation used):

> You and I, did'nt finish talking. Have you room for the
> sequel, in your Vase?
> All the letters I could
> Write,
> Were not fair as this —
> Syllables of velvet —
> Sentences of Plush —
> Depths of Ruby, undrained —
> Hid, Lip, for Thee,
> Play it were a
> Humming Bird
> And sipped just
> Me —
>
> Emily —
>
> (Fr380A; J334)

Habegger writes:

> As in the poem "My river runs to thee," sent the previous year to Mary Bowles and concluding, "Say — Sea — / Take Me!'" the writer almost seemed to be offering herself as an erotic treat to a woman who was several years older, not especially close, and married. The poems appear to invite an affectionate union, but in their original context they posed an enigmatic challenge to any conceivable response. They offered no recognizable social categories, only metaphors of union drawn from nature. (460)

Habegger gives the incident a cultural context by prefacing it with a reference to a book titled *Friendships of Women* (1868), by a Bostonian named William R. Alger, who "drew on European and American literature and history to characterize the patterns of women's closest relationships." One of Alger's chapters focused, according to Habegger, on "women's passionate but Platonic same-sex bonds. The topic was in the air" (459).

Another moment of intrigue occurs when Habegger comments on what he calls Austin Dickinson's "one surviving 'imaginative' composition," actually a fanciful letter he wrote to Emily likely dating from Emily's year at Mt. Holyoke.[11] This composition would not be of interest were it not for the fact that Austin appears to be quoting from a lost letter from

---

[11] Reproduced in 1955 in *Emily Dickinson's Home*, ed. Millicent Todd Bingham; 82–83.

Emily. In Austin's letter, Vinnie, Austin, and their mother are spending a quiet evening at home, when an unidentified man draws everyone's attention to a letter, which Austin begins to read. Suddenly he (Austin) breaks down in laughter, stomping his foot so hard that it causes such a concussion (and here Habegger quotes directly from Austin's letter) "that the whole firmiment [sic] was shaken, the whole planetary system was deranged ... and the clouds fell from the heavens." What caused this outburst? Habegger speculates that some of the sentences could well be taken from Emily's lost letter: "I [Emily] told her [Mary Lyon?] you [Edward Dickinson] were not afraid of her being too strict with me, and she replied, Tell him I am much obliged to him" (207–8). Habegger is apparently the first to notice the possibility that the quoted lines could well be Emily's. If so, as he points out, it would be only the second document we have of Dickinson writing to her father; the other being the startling "Dear Father — [large blank space] Emily" written on the back of the manuscript of Fr1333; J1325 ("Knock with tremor —") at the time of Edward's death.

Habegger has indeed produced a significant and highly readable biography; it is much closer to Sewall than to Wolff in his meticulously documented examination of Dickinson's social and cultural milieu, and even exceeds Sewall, I think, in recreating the social circumstances inferred from lost or overlooked documents that have never been alluded to in print. On the other hand, Emily Dickinson the poet of genius is slighted in Habegger, with the result that the two biographies balance each other.

Psychoanalysis as Biography

John Cody's controversial psychoanalysis of Dickinson, *After Great Pain: The Inner Life of Emily Dickinson* (1971) is a latecomer to psychoanalytic criticism, which enjoyed a flowering in the 1940s with works like Marie Bonaparte's *The Life and Works of Edgar Allan Poe: A Psychoanalytical Interpretation* (1949) and Ernest Jones's *Hamlet and Oedipus* (1949).[12] Psychoanalytic studies from the mid 1970s onward have shifted away from Freud and toward Jung, Lacan, and Cixous. Cody, a retired psychiatrist, anticipates challenges to a psychoanalytic reading of a great poet like Emily Dickinson: Cody asks that we assume, just for the sake of argument, that Dickinson's psychological problems can be diagnosed and their likely causes described. And suppose too that they "had a modulating effect on her creativity and that this influence can be demonstrated, and ... that

---

[12] For a discussion of these and similar psychoanalytic studies, see Scott Peeples, *The Afterlife of Edgar Allan Poe* (Rochester, NY: Camden House, 2004), 29–62.

the poems do contain allusions to psychic conflicts. The question is what has any of this got to do with literature? Can such investigations lead to a greater appreciation of the poems or help define Emily Dickinson's stature as a poet? ... The answer depends on one's conception of the nature of art" (4).

Cody then outlines those criteria that distinguish formalism from other critical methods. "It appears to be a matter of individual taste," he writes, "to what extent one inclines toward either side of these extreme positions [of a work of literature being an entirely closed system vs. its being an entirely open system]" (4). Acknowledging that it is important to read a poem carefully "before rejecting it as too narrowly personal," Cody nevertheless insists that a deep and careful reading of a poem includes "*all its psychological implications.* Only then is one in the proper position to render a judgment on the universality and esthetic quality of the poem" (4–5; emphasis Cody's).

However deep and careful a reading one may undertake of Dickinson's poems, one might counterargue, it still takes a great leap of faith to assume that the anguish or trauma depicted in them chronicles that experienced by the poet herself. Cody next turns to "After great pain" (Fr372; J341), the poem that provided him with the title to his book, and which he characterizes as "a threnody to a vanquished ego and to a paralyzed emotional life":

> After great pain, a formal feeling comes —
> The Nerves sit ceremonious, like Tombs —
> The stiff Heart questions "was it He, that bore,"
> And "Yesterday, or Centuries before"?
> ...

"How is it possible to believe," Cody exclaims melodramatically, "that the poet did not undergo the terrible prostration that she appears here to commemorate? By what creative magic could she, high on the safe shore of normality, plumb such depths of suffering? (23–24). "By what creative magic" indeed: do not all serious readers of Dickinson ask that question with every intake of breath triggered by eighteen hundred poems' worth of astonishing figures of speech and turns of phrase?

What I see in Cody's psychobiography is the working out of a hypothesis: *If* the poems do indeed reveal a case history of the poet's own psychopathology, then what does such a revelation contribute to the reader's *literary* interests in the poet — for we are, after all, engaged in the field of literary studies, not psychology.

Cody approaches Emily Dickinson as a patient — yes, a genius who has produced a body of great poetry, but a patient nonetheless, one whose symptomatology can be formally described:

> The failure of Emily Dickinson to achieve complete fulfillment socially and sexually and the anxiety and ambivalence which subverted her ambition to reach the reading public she merited are ultimately traceable to psychological determinants rooted in her transactions with her mother.... [e.g.] The lost "Dominions," "Kingdoms," and "Palaces" of the poem "A loss of something ever felt I" [Fr1072; J959] ... may be symbols unconsciously related in the poet's mind to her having been shut out at an early age from the heaven of maternal affection through some emotional unresponsiveness or incapacity on the part of her mother. In the poetry of the mature woman the child speaks, still grieving for a source of sustenance that had been lacking or withdrawn — the tenderness and shelter of a mothering woman. (42)

Cody then draws from family letters to reconstruct the personality of Dickinson's mother, Emily Norcross Dickinson: "One catches glimpse after glimpse of an habitually complaining woman, subject to depression and hypochondria. She appears emotionally shallow, self-centered, ineffectual, conventional, timid, submissive, and not very bright" (42).[13]

Whatever we can say literarily about the poetry, Cody implies, can only give a partial picture, not just of the poet, but of the poetry as well. And so, in Dickinson's "After great pain," Cody sees "both a summary of the major symptomatology and a general outline of the course of the entire acute phase of the poet's illness" (328). Here is his analysis of the first stanza:

> A precipitating stress ("great pain") has brought about the substitution of a compulsive, rule-bound, extrinsic mode of behavior for a spontaneous natural inner one ("a formal feeling comes"). The responsive sensory apparatus is suspended in a deathly stolidity ("like Tombs"). The emotional life is thus slowed and encumbered like rusted machinery, as if some great interval of time had clasped since it last tried to function (the "Heart" is "stiff"). There has also occurred such a complete loss of affective and meaningful contact with

---

[13] In *A Poet's Parents: The Courtship Letters of Emily Norcross and Edward Dickinson*, editor Vivian Pollak observes from these letters a very different sense of the personalities of Emily Dickinson's parents: "The Edward Dickinson who emerges in the courtship letters is more vulnerable and more of a feminist than tradition would have it; the Emily Norcross who emerges ... usually gets her way.... These letters help to delineate the poet's maternal legacy, modify our understanding of male dominance and female submission in the Dickinson household" (xxvii).

the human environment that time has lost its meaning. Even the events that engendered the catastrophic pain have lost their vividness and appear almost to have happened to somebody else or to have occurred in some infinitely remote past (the "Heart questions was it He, that bore, / And Yesterday, or Centuries before?"). (328–29)

There is no way, of course, to tie the pathological reactions delineated in this poem to a specific event in Dickinson's life without being wildly speculative. Cody is aware of this, and concentrates instead on the more general dynamics operating in her life, especially the maternal influence. So how do such dynamics, such psychic "disabilities" translate into artistic productiveness? Cody is convinced that "Mrs. Dickinson unwittingly provided her daughter with the conditions necessary for the development of her peculiar gifts. . . . It was Mrs. Dickinson's failure as a sufficiently loving and admirable developmental model that set in motion the series of psychological upheavals which were unmitigated misfortunes for Emily Dickinson *the woman*" (484; emphasis Cody's).

That last sentence is key to what Suzanne Juhasz, in her introduction to *Feminist Critics Read Emily Dickinson* (1983) regards as "especially damaging about Cody's book": not his efforts to show that the poet was insane or experienced some kind of psychotic breakdown, but rather

> his assumptions about "normal" female development, female (and male) gender identity, and the nature of creativity and achievement. Cody supposes that a woman acquires female identity through positive identification with her mother. If this does not come about . . . if she cannot find another woman to act as a role model, "she may at last be driven to pattern herself on a masculine model," and this will in the course of things lead to gender confusion . . . Cody associates creativity and achievement with the masculine. He asserts that it was Dickinson's abnormal identification with her father that "though blocking her completion as a woman, stimulated her to use her mind." (Juhasz, 3–4)

And what about Dickinson's "preoccupation with the theme of death" (267)? It seemed to have been a lifelong obsession, as Cody demonstrates. She herself was aware of it: "I think of the grave very often," she wrote to Jane Humphrey in 1852 (L86). In determining a cause, Cody rejects the theory that friends were dying all around her of consumption and other diseases; rather, "what afflicted her most profoundly was the fact of mortality itself and the precariousness of all life, including her own" (269). Moreover, Cody detects an element of perverse fascination with death: "In some obscure way death stimulated her" (270), and refers to the letter she wrote to her Norcross cousins regarding the death of Frazer Stearns, in which she expresses "her eagerness in gathering and conveying the precise circumstances of death" — for instance, "His big heart [was] shot away by a 'minie ball' . . ." (L255; qtd Cody 270). Cody also attributes Dickinson's death fixation to her Puritan culture as well as to Romanticism.[14]

In her introduction to Rebecca Patterson's posthumously published study, *Emily Dickinson's Imagery* (discussed above) Margaret H. Freeman regards Cody as "least convincing when he tells us that poets can imagine only events, not feelings," and that it is only necessary "to recall Aristotle's theory of catharsis, Keats's negative capability, or Coleridge's theory of the imagination to explode the naïve presumption of a direct correlation between experience and emotion." What we find so moving in Dickinson's poetry, Freeman goes on to explain, is that "it makes the feeling concrete at the same time as it delocalizes it, thereby removing it from its source" (vii–viii). All told, then, what Cody lacks in his study "is a theory of poetry" — which is precisely what Rebecca Patterson provides in her examination of Dickinson's imagery.

On several occasions in *After Great Pain*, Cody alludes to Emily Dickinson's agoraphobia, which *Random House Webster's College Dictionary* defines as "an abnormal fear of being in crowds, public places, or open areas" — but does not investigate this facet of her psychopathology other than to say that she had it (46; 91), to state that "she grew increasingly phobic about leaving the house (164), and to quote from a letter the poet had written to Sue [Susan Gilbert] in 1855 (when she was 24) about walking unaccompanied to church, in which Cody finds evidence of "psychological patterns . . . that are distinctly pathological" and "her beginning agoraphobia":

> I'm just from meeting, Susie, and as I sorely feared, my "life" was made a "victim." I walked — I ran — I turned precarious corners — One moment I was not — then soared aloft like Phoenix soon as the foe was by — and then anticipating an enemy again, my soiled and drooping plumage might have been seen emerging from just behind a fence, vainly endeavoring to fly once more from hence. (L177; qtd Cody 240)

As Cody points out in the foreword to Maryanne Garbowsky's study of Dickinson as agoraphobe, *The House without the Door* (1989), illness was a fact of Emily Dickinson's life and should be taken seriously "as an important reality of her existence" (13).

---

[14] See also Hastings Moore, "Emily Dickinson and Orthothanasia" (1979). The term, used by K. R. Eissler in *The Psychiatrist and the Dying Patient*, refers to words that attempt to pinpoint the specific meaning of dying. Dickinson, one could say, strove for language that could capture the precise experience of dying.

In a well-balanced inquiry, Garbowsky uses evidence from medical sources such as the *Diagnostic and Statistical Manual of Mental Disorders,* published by the American Psychiatric Association, to show how Dickinson's actions and descriptions of panic attacks and the like fit the symptoms of agoraphobia. But the most interesting part of Garbowsky's study is her insight into how the fascicle poems and the way they are sequenced shed light on the way Dickinson experienced her illness:

> As we look through the fascicle poems, we recognize the pattern of an agoraphobic life-style: the flight from fears, the need for protection within her father's house, the atmosphere of family conflict, and the desire for release from tormenting inner pressures. Without an understanding of agoraphobia, Dickinson's life appears erratic and eccentric without any direction or design. (79)

One of the poems that Garbowsky singles out as indicative of agoraphobic symptomatology is "Some keep the Sabbath going to Church / I keep it, staying at home" (Fr236; J324). Garbowsky asserts that "its pantheistic suggestions fade to reveal Dickinson's fear of crowds and public gatherings" (80) — tying the poem to her dread of being noticed by churchgoers. But Garbowsky's insistence on Dickinson's agoraphobia as the main reason for her not attending church does not seem warranted in light of Dickinson's lifelong rebellion against the tenets of established religion.

Fascicles 15 and 16, according to Garbowsky, "are especially significant because of their proximity to . . . the 'terror since September,' and . . . because they identify the emotional and mental anguish of that period" (90). One of these poems is "The first Day's Night had come — / And grateful that a thing / So terrible — had been endured — / I told my Soul to sing — (Fr423; J410):

> In this poem, Dickinson records her reaction to a complete, full-blown panic attack, something that left "her Strings snapt" and "Her Bow — to Atoms blown." . . . What she is describing here are two major effects of panic attack: the first is the fear of recurrence and the second is the fear of personality disintegration. Her question at the end of the poem "Could it be Madness — this?" shows Us her confusion and her fear, a fear she was probably reluctant to admit: "Something's odd — within — / That person that I was — / And this One — do not feel the same —"

In her concluding chapter Garbowsky states that Emily Dickinson "wielded the written word as a potent wedge against her fears, words bringing her a measure of control over a life she must have felt powerless to change" (147). Indeed, Dickinson triumphs as an artist in this way: it was the source of her power (in Gary Lee Stonum's sense of the word —

see chapter 7). Garbowsky too applies the word to Dickinson, but in a different sense: "For Dickinson words had power; they held the magic she needed to release herself spiritually and mentally from the emotional torments she felt." She quotes "On a Columnar Self — / How ample to rely / In Tumult — or Extremity —" (Fr740; J789) as a record of her "self-endurance" (148). Of course, one can argue that all writing fulfills some sort of psychological need for the writer, and that, hence, all writing can be viewed as therapeutic, but Garbowsky goes a step farther in demonstrating how Dickinson transformed a debilitating illness into an enabling one.

Dickinson's Compound Vision

The same could be said of the way Dickinson dealt with her physical ailments. Psychiatric disorders may be difficult if not impossible to diagnose accurately in an individual who lived before psychoanalysis was invented. Physiological disorders, however, may be deduced from medical records, and sometimes, as in the case of eye disorders, from photographic evidence. Regarding the latter, James R. Guthrie, in his *Emily Dickinson's Vision: Illness and Identity in Her Poetry* (1998) refers to an essay that Richard Sewall wrote in collaboration with the ophthalmologist Martin Wand, "'Eyes Be Blind, Heart Be Still': A New Perspective on Emily Dickinson's Eye Problem" (1979), which focuses attention on the 1847 daguerreotype of Dickinson. They conclude that the cornea of the poet's right eye is "deviated as much as fifteen degrees from true" (Wand and Sewall, 403; qtd. Guthrie 11). The disease is known as exotropia, and "prevents the sufferer from achieving perfectly binocular vision" (11). Could this eye affliction lie behind the following poem?

> Before I got my eye put out
> I liked as well to see —
> As other Creatures, that have Eyes
> And know no other way —
>
> But were it told to me — Today —
> That I might have the sky
> For mine — I tell you that my Heart
> Would split, for size of me —
>
> The Meadows — mine —
> The Mountains — mine —
> All Forests — Stintless Stars —
> As much of Noon as I could take
> Between my finite eyes —

> The Motions of The Dripping Birds —
> The Morning's Amber Road —[15]
> For mine — to look at when I liked —
> The News would strike me dead —
>
> So safer Guess —
> With just my soul upon the Window pane —
> Where other Creatures put their eyes —
> Incautious — of the Sun —
> (Fr336A; J327)

Guthrie, aware of other ways of reading the poem, leans toward that possibility, noting that the poem, if given a literal interpretation,

> narrates the consequences of Dickinson's failure to obey her doctor's command to shun direct sunlight. Another reading . . . is opened up, however, by her phrase "I got my eye put out," which shifts the blame to an external agent. Although it is initially unclear who has injured the poet or why, the text provides a few clues. Her description of scenes she would look upon, were she to regain full use of her eyes, is so rapturous that we may infer her transgression had been to admire the visible world excessively. (15)

Dickinson biography cannot fail to serve students of the poet, no matter how "formalist" their lines of inquiry. Besides, with this poet, as with Shakespeare, life and work seem virtually inseparable. Dickinson's life was lived through her creative intellect, so that whatever "happened" to her in terms of external events she would sublimate into her art.

Psychoanalytic study of the poet's work likewise serves scholars of all stripes, and such inquiry continues to this day. For example, in his article "Emily Dickinson and Schizotypy" (2004), Steven Winhusen, a physician and independent scholar, argues that a diagnostic category approved by the American Psychological Association in 1979 — schizotypal personality disorder — can be fruitfully applied to Emily Dickinson, thereby redressing Cody's failure "to explain adequately [Dickinson's] ability to write such coherent and reasoned work" during the periods in which she suffered her psychotic episodes. Among the APA's list of eight characteristics of the disorder, topping the list, Winhusen reports, was "odd communication," followed by "inadequate rapport in face-to-face interaction" (78).

---

[15] For the fascicle copy of the poem, Dickinson changed this line to read "The Lightning's jointed Road —" The version reproduced above was enclosed in Dickinson's fifth letter to Higginson, about August 1862. (See Franklin, 1998.)

Whether the insights of modern psychiatry or medicine can enhance our perception of Dickinson's poetry continues to be tirelessly debated. Although these matters may neither augment nor diminish her artistry, they are endlessly fascinating.

3: The Feminist Revolution in Dickinson Studies

> *My little force explodes*
> — Emily Dickinson to T. W. Higginson (1862)
>
> *From a feminist perspective, Dickinson's life was neither a flight, nor a cop-out, nor a sacrifice, nor a substitution, but a strategy, a creation, for enabling her to become the person she was.*
> — Susan Juhasz, introduction to *Feminist Critics Read Emily Dickinson*
>
> *The more we come to recognize the unwritten and written laws and taboos underpinning patriarchy, the less problematical, surely, will seem the methods she chose.*
> — Adrienne Rich, "Vesuvius at Home: The Power of Emily Dickinson"

FEMINIST LITERARY CRITICISM does not appear until the mid-1970s, nearly a quarter century after the rise of modern feminist writings such as Simone de Beauvoir's *The Second Sex* (originally published in France as *Le Deuxieme Sexe* in 1949; in the United States in 1953). Of course, feminist writing has a long and varied history that can be traced back centuries. Two treatises in English, Mary Wollstonecraft's *A Vindication of the Rights of Women* (1797) and Margaret Fuller's *Woman in the Nineteenth Century* (1845) are foundational.

Feminist Criticism of Emily Dickinson: Its Birth and Flowering

Despite the widespread influence of Beauvoir's book, augmented in the following decade by Betty Friedan's *The Feminine Mystique* (1963) and Andrew Sinclair's *The Emancipation of the American Woman* (Original title, *The Better Half,* 1965), it wasn't until the 1970s that modern feminist literary criticism took root.[1] James L. Machor, in "Emily Dickinson and

---

[1] In the 1970s and early 1980s, several important works were published: Kate Millett's *Sexual Politics* (1970); Susan Juhasz's *Naked and Fiery Forms: Modern*

Feminine Rhetoric" (1980) conducted a rhetorical analysis of Dickinson's poetry from a feminist perspective. Machor highlights feminist motifs in poems such as "I never lost as much but twice —" (Fr39; J49). Here, Machor notes how Dickinson

> commands the full force of her ironic and rebellious temperament. She establishes in the first stanza a self-effacing humility which is . . . suddenly undercut by the last stanza's final lines. There is no resignation here nor passive acceptance. Rather, the series of epithets culminating in the sardonic implication of "Father" denotes a frustration with . . . conventional attributes of feminine resignation. (139)

The groundbreaking studies by Machor, Homans, Showalter, Gilbert and Gubar, and others provided the foundation on which the burgeoning of feminist scholarship on Emily Dickinson in the 1980s built. Now in its fourth decade and continuing to flourish, feminist criticism has revolutionized the way the poet is studied. It seems surprising, in light of the fact that Dickinson herself alludes to the power of the female psyche, that feminist criticism had not taken root sooner. As Vivian R. Pollak states in the introduction to her *Dickinson: The Anxiety of Gender* (1984), "Gender was Dickinson's generative obsession" (18). And even if we agree that Dickinson always used a persona in her poetry, it does not change the fact that Dickinson *chose* to adopt a persona for whom gender was paramount in her artistic production.

Formalist critics (male and female alike) such as Charles Anderson, Clark Griffith, David Porter, Inder Nath Kher, and E. Miller Budick who pay no attention to Dickinson's gender in relation to her poetic artistry are following formalism's prime directive of keeping biography separate from criticism; but their principal reason for excluding biography seems not to be to reject the possibilities of biography (or history, or psychology or gender) as a means of illuminating art, but to give full attention to the complexities of meaning generated exclusively by the poetic language itself. Kher speaks for all formalists when he states in his introduction to *The Landscape of Absence: Emily Dickinson's Poetry* (1974):

American Poetry by Women, A New Tradition (1976); Elaine Showalter's *A Literature of Their Own: British Women Novelists from Brontë to Lessing* (1977); Sandra M. Gilbert and Susan Gubar's *The Madwoman in the Attic: The Woman Writer and the Nineteenth-Century Literary Imagination* (1979); Gilbert and Gubar's anthology, *Shakespeare's Sisters: Feminist Essays on Women Poets* (1979); Margaret Homans's *Women Writers and Poetic Identity* (1980); Cheryl Walker's *The Nightingale's Burden: Women Poets and American Culture before 1900* (1982); and James L. Machor's "Emily Dickinson and Feminine Rhetoric" (1980).

In order to achieve a proper appreciation of Dickinson's poetry, we should guard against the tendency to psychologize and to draw inferences of a purely psycho-biographical nature. We should keep our eyes steady on the text because our responsibility is to interpret poetry and not the person. . . . The creative I is the personality which the poet realizes as she creates it and realizes it persistently. This personality is not the ordinary individual; rather, it is a type which represents one's creative existence. (3)

Feminist critics, of course, operate according to a contrary directive. In Suzanne Juhasz's words, "[t]he central assumption of feminist criticism is that gender informs the nature of art, the nature of biography, and the relation between them. Dickinson is a woman poet, and this fact is integral to her identity" (1). The fault of formalist critics, Juhasz argues, is twofold: first they split Dickinson's identity in two: "woman" and "poet"; second, they sever any connection between her poetry and the *woman* poet who wrote it (1).[2] It then becomes the task of feminist critics to reassemble into a whole what has been unnaturally fragmented. Pollak sees such reassembly operating in Dickinson's own project — that Dickinson is "centrally concerned with the origins and consequences of her social isolation" (30) — a concern that ultimately (and perhaps paradoxically) results, through her art, in the integration of her psyche. In the "marriage" poems, for example, Pollak sees Dickinson "conveying the urgency of her quest for psychic integration" (169). Loss, isolation, conflict (including "irresolvable sexual conflict" [30]) become the raw ingredients out of which is crafted the "vivid Ore / [that] Has vanquished Flame's conditions" (Fr401; J365). Wendy Barker, in *Lunacy of Light: Emily Dickinson and the Experience of Metaphor* (1987) shares a similar insight into the feminist effort to undo gender-based systems of opposition that have acquired archetypal status over the ages. The female poet, she writes "subverts the old, impossible polarities of light and dark by metaphorically creating her own 'Blaze' within the dark" (102).

Gilbert and Gubar's groundbreaking study was surely the major catalyst to the feminist critical reception of Emily Dickinson, with its perceptive analyses of major fiction and poetry by nineteenth-century British and

---

[2] Two exceptions, I think, are Richard Chase and Clark Griffith. Chase recognizes that Dickinson, like the Brontës, wished "to invest the domestic lot of women . . . with a structure of imaginative meaning" (*Emily Dickinson* [1951], 150); Griffith, in the epilogue to *The Long Shadow: Emily Dickinson's Tragic Poetry* (1964), realizes (although rather fleetingly) that the givers of existence's great riddles of temporality and mortality — God (the divine father) and the human father — are both masculine. "It would appear, then, that maleness is to be identified with special privileges" (281).

American women — analyses that include examination of the motifs of enclosure, limitation, and captivity. In the chapter devoted to Dickinson, titled "A Woman — White: Emily Dickinson's Yarn of Pearl," Gilbert and Gubar argue that even though Dickinson "never wrote an extended narrative poem" as did Elizabeth Browning with her novel-in-verse *Aurora Leigh,* or Christina Rossetti with her "Goblin Market," Dickinson's life itself "became a kind of novel or narrative poem in which [she] ... enacted and eventually resolved both her anxieties about her art and her anger at female subordination" (581, 582). The key word is *enacted:* by creating in effect a great many small lyric dramas, adopting a wide variety of voices, or personae, Dickinson transcends what Juhasz refers to as "the double bind" of the woman poet: on the one hand, the impossibility of self-assertion for a woman, on the other hand, the necessity of self-assertion for a poet (584).

In *Women Writers and Poetic Identity* (1980), Margaret Homans presents a clear rationale for the role that a feminist perspective can play on the study of poetry by women. "Though poetry is ideally unconditioned by gender," she writes, there are nonetheless "implicit male biases." Moreover, when "the poetic self represented in a text identifies itself as masculine or feminine, the reader must ask why it does so, and to what effect" (3). One particularly intriguing example of gender subtly calling attention to itself that Homans detects in Emily Dickinson's poetry is Dickinson's habit "of characterizing many external things as masculine — truth and falsehood, the world and its renunciation — [which] illustrates a mind defining its own interior operations as feminine. . . . Her freedom from literal meaning originates in her sense of femininity" (176). Dickinson, then, in Homans's view, poetically re-genders internal and external reality.

The first book-length work to provide a comprehensive range of explicitly feminist readings of Dickinson's oeuvre is Suzanne Juhasz's *Feminist Critics Read Emily Dickinson* (1983), a collection of nine essays that demonstrate the different ways in which Dickinson asserts creative control of her art and her life, drawing from her particular situation as a woman in a restrictive Puritan and patriarchal culture. If we can speak of a common denominator among the essays, it would be that they all explore the nature or origin of Dickinson's astonishing artistic power. As Juhasz writes in her introduction, "[d]efinitions of power are clarified and enlarged as feminist critics explore the literary and biographical implications of gender." The essayists demonstrate the several ways in which Dickinson is "responding to the repressions that surround and threaten to control her. . . . Her power — of appropriation, of role-playing, of disrupting and reversing — is not an evasion but an active and radical engagement with those forces" (17). Margaret Homans amplifies the idea of Dickinson's "radical engagement" in her essay "'Oh, Vision of Language': Dickinson's

Poems of Love and Death," by noting how many of our basic perceptions of dualism and of subject-object relationships originate in gender difference (114). Homans shows how Dickinson subverts traditional hierarchic relationships — God-and-mortals, Master-and-(female) servant, and so on. In the poem "The Daisy follows soft the Sun —" (Fr161; J106) the conventional hierarchical relationship between passive-female Daisy and imperious-male Sun "is exposed as illusion" (118):

> The Daisy follows soft the Sun —
> And when his golden walk is done —
> Sits shily at his feet —
> He — waking — finds the flower there —
> Wherefore — Marauder — art thou here?
> Because, Sir, love is sweet!
>
> We are the Flower — Thou the Sun!
> Forgive us, if as days decline —
> We nearer steal to Thee!
> Enamored of the parting West —
> The peace — the flight — the amethyst —
> Night's possibility!

Homans notes that "[t]he daisy's name makes her like the sun: a flower called a day's eye is being defined not as itself but in comparison to the sun" (118). But then, "[t]hrough a strategy of mock humility the daisy gently dismantles the sun's pretensions to absolute power, but she can increase her power only by deceasing his" (119). With nightfall the romantic but oppositional relationship collapses, opening exciting new possibilities for the daisy, no longer defined by an Other. Dickinson conveys a similar theme, I might add, in "Sunset at Night — is natural — / But Sunset on the Dawn / Reverses Nature — Master — / So Midnight's — due — at Noon" (Fr427; J415). Ostensibly about a solar eclipse, as the second stanza makes explicit ("Eclipses be — predicted — / And Science bows them in —"), a second, ironic meaning of "reversing nature" surfaces: reversing nature, as in the darkness produced by an eclipse, is also natural even if highly unusual — just as a woman's ability to assume traditional male roles should be considered natural; indeed it, like the scientifically predicted eclipse, is "*due* — at Noon."

Barbara Antonina Clarke Mossberg also provides one startling illustration of Dickinson's "radical engagement" in her essay, "Emily Dickinson's Nursery Rhymes." She sees the poet's little girl persona as "a brilliant . . . metaphor for her experience as a woman poet in her culture, reflecting and resolving her 'small size'" (47). Littleness, in Dickinson, Mossberg argues, "does not reflect her physical or psychological reality, so much as her conscious choice to be "little," to play along with society's view of her insignificance and turn it to her own advantage" (55). The poem that demonstrates this most remarkably is "They shut me up in Prose —":

> They put me in the Closet —
> Because they liked me "still" —
>
> Still! Could themself have peeped —
> And seen my Brain — go round —
> They might as wise have lodged a Bird
> For Treason — in the Pound —
> (Fr445; J613)

Of course, there are plenty of instances in which Dickinson appears to be speaking in her own voice and asserting her womanly rights and authority.[3]

Juhasz also mentions that early biographical studies of the poet distinguish sharply between the life and the art. Most notable in this regard is Whicher's 1938 biography, which Juhasz points out is actually divided into biographical and literary units, without any ideological relation to each other (3). The closest Whicher ever comes to linking Dickinson's gender with her poetic sensibility comes when he asserts that when she wrote "At least — to pray — is left — is left / Oh Jesus — in the Air — / I know not which thy chamber is — / I'm knocking — everywhere —" (Fr377; J502), "[s]he was all woman" (Whicher 272). Whicher regards this poem as a cry of despair, a record of a mind overcome by an emotion it cannot expunge, of the way a heartbroken child has no room for anything but its own grief (272). Clearly, Whicher associates womanhood with the uncontrolled emotions more appropriate for a child than for a mature adult. In fairness to Whicher, such was the paradigm with which not only male but female critics regarded women.

One of the most provocative essays in Juhasz's anthology is Joanne A. Dobson's "'Oh Susie, it is dangerous': Emily Dickinson and the Archetype of the Masculine." Dobson's essay provides additional insight into the power dimension of Dickinson's poetry by calling attention to the poet's construction of a masculine archetype, one that is "simultaneously omnipotent, fascinating, and deadly. . . . In poem after poem we see the poet's persona presented as . . . overwhelmed by the near presence of an

---

[3] Sandra Runzo, for example, in her article, "Dickinson's Transgressive Body" (1999), calls attention to "Mine — by the Right of the White Election!" (Fr411; J528) in which Dickinson "rehearses a language of legal and social authority." Noting that the poet composed this poem about fourteen years after the Seneca Falls convention, Runzo sees Dickinson here writing "her own 'declaration' of rights — she is elected, crowned, vindicated" (63–64).

arbitrary and rapacious masculine power" (8). Dobson's reading of Emily's relationship with Sue anticipates that branch of feminist writing concerned with issues of gender and sexual (lesbian) issues.[4] In her 1989 monograph, *Dickinson and the Strategies of Reticence,* Dobson elaborates on social pressures placed on women authors to perpetuate, in fiction and poetry, the paradigm of women as grown little girls, so to speak: "[t]he use of a little girl protagonist screened out the mature woman with her disconcerting potential sexuality and guaranteed the woman writer a comfortable, and thus approving, audience" (62).

Representations of the poetic self, of course, need not be explicitly gender based in order to reveal gender-related concerns at work. Consider, for example, *Emily Dickinson and the Image of Home* (1975), Jean McClure Mudge's study of Dickinson that antedates Gilbert and Gubar's *The Madwoman in the Attic* by four years. As the title suggests, Mudge argues that "home" in Dickinson's poetry and letters transcends its conventional domestic referent to embody consciousness itself. She quotes the fifth stanza of "I am alive — I guess —" (Fr605; J470):

> I am alive — because
> I do not own a House —
> Entitled to myself — precise —
> And fitting no one else —

This, I would argue, constitutes an ironic — and feminist — reading of houses in Mudge's sense of the word: the speaker does not own a house, not just because of her gender, but because, as an external acquisition, it is unnecessary. As Mudge sees it, "Dickinson's *body* was her most private house" (22; emphasis added). Instead of seeing this in a strictly feminist context, however — that is, that Dickinson in effect secedes from her literal home with its patriarchal rule and confinement, to the liberated female space of artistic consciousness — Mudge follows a more psychoanalytic track earlier laid down by John Cody in *After Great Pain* (1971). Aware of the "too often reductionistic" applications of psychoanalysis to literary works — a danger Freud himself recognized — Mudge cautiously attempts to "align Dickinson's attitudes with certain concepts of Freud and [Erik] Erikson, since they all touch basic realities, the givens of biology and the experience of neurotic feeling or behavior"; but at the same time, Mudge continues, "her poetry . . . and her symbols are extraordinarily personal, probing beyond biology, psychology, or anyone's 'explanation,' not excepting my own" (22). In this sense, the distinction between a

---

[4] See especially Ellen Louise Hart and Martha Nell Smith's edition of the Emily/Sue correspondence, *Open Me Carefully,* discussed below.

"psychoanalytic" reading and a "feminist" one (or any other mode of critical reading, for that matter) ultimately becomes blurred when we think of Dickinson's efforts to carve out her own psychological space: "If Emily cherished security and liberty from convention inside her father's house," Mudge argues, "still she almost perpetually waged a personal battle for psychological freedom and religious affirmation" (197).

In *The Undiscovered Continent: Emily Dickinson and the Space of the Mind* (1983) Suzanne Juhasz also regards Dickinson's liberated artistic consciousness — the house of one's own — not only as artistic space sealed off from patriarchal rule (an image, one could argue, of reactiveness, even of victimization), but as a re-appropriation of power. "Traditional ideas about power are reversed here," Juhasz asserts, alluding to "The Soul selects her own society" (Fr409A; J303). "Not control over vast populations but the ability to construct a world for oneself comprises the greatest power, a god-like achievement" (15). Dickinson conveys this with lines such as "The Brain has Corridors — surpassing / Material Place —" (Fr407; J670); and in a later stanza: "Ourself behind ourself, concealed — / Should startle most." (See also "They shut me up in Prose" [Fr445; J613], discussed below.)

Mary Loeffelholz goes another step further. She argues in *Dickinson and the Boundaries of Feminist Theory* (1991) that within her self-imposed interior home space (a space re-commandeered, as it were, from her father), Dickinson revises male-defined Romanticism — a Romanticism of the outdoors — by interiorizing it, placing it in a feminine space. She does this by bringing outdoor nature music indoors:

> Domesticating male Romanticism's outdoor music, Dickinson despecularizes the structure of its quest romance. In Dickinson's indoor Romantic music, the characteristic Wordsworthian struggle between hearing and sight is often transposed either into the single register of sound (looking is not so privileged for her indoors), or into a synaesthesia of sound and touch rather than of sound and sight. (121)

Similar to Mudge and Juhasz in their synthesis of psychoanalytic and feminist insights, Barbara Antonina Clarke Mossberg, in her *Emily Dickinson: When a Writer is a Daughter* (1982), concentrates on the dynamics of the relationship between the poet and her parents — a dynamics that first required rejecting her mother's religion "as a way of warding off her mother's anatomically defined and confined destiny.... Saying 'yes' to Christ is saying 'yes' to the oppressive maternal matrix — the same kind of submission to a patriarchal order that has effaced her mother" (52). Dickinson's rejection of the father was equally radical. Mossberg calls attention to the way her letters "make erosions upon her father's public dignified image; they show a Halloween villain whose threat is not to be taken seriously (68). Even though she agrees with John Cody that Edward's ambivalent attitude toward his family resulted in three emotionally disturbed children (69), Mossberg takes a major feminist step away from such a reductively psychoanalytic criticism by arguing that Emily Dickinson resolved her own ambivalence toward her father, and in several ways — for example, by conforming to the dutiful daughter's role and concealing her rebellious, "masculine" identity as a poet by writing late at night (72). She also avidly read the books her father had ironically purchased for her but begged her not to read (as the poet explains in her second letter to Higginson [L261]). Clearly we see, even if on a small scale, a rather startling role reversal: underneath the dutiful daughter exterior we see a dutiful *father* conceding to the demands of his intellectually imperious daughter. While it is certainly true, as Mossberg says, that Dickinson ultimately abandoned any attempt to convince her father of her worth, and, instead went in search of other father figures through her letters — men who took a more positive view of women poets (72), we can also argue that, far from giving up on her father, she eventually helped him to understand her needs.

Consider, too, the "Master" letters from a feminist perspective. Traditionally regarded as evidence of Dickinson's loss of emotional control after being spurned by a male lover or would-be lover, these letters, when read from a feminist perspective, can reveal a contrary situation, as Helen Shoobridge demonstrates in her article, "'Reverence for each Other Being the Sweet Aim': Dickinson Face to Face with the Masculine" (2000). Shoobridge argues that Dickinson's strategy in these letters is to call attention to the woman's position, and alludes to Luce Irigaray's point, in her *Speculum of the Other Woman* (1985), about the advantages a woman can have "in deploying hyperbolic femininity to inhabit and engage with the discourses that produce her" (Shoobridge 88).

Mention should also be made of Rebecca Patterson's already-discussed *Emily Dickinson's Imagery*, edited by Margaret H. Freeman and published posthumously in 1979. Calling attention to the fact that Martha Dickinson Bianchi, in her *Life and Letters of Emily Dickinson*, "had called her aunt Emily 'an instinctive feminist' indignant from her youth 'at being counted as *non compos* in a man's world of reality'" (7), Patterson examines, in a chapter titled "The Boy Emily," the poet's imagery more from a gender-transgressing perspective than a feminist one. Thus she examines images associated with Dickinson's male speakers, as in "We don't cry, Tim and I" (Fr231; J196); "So I pull my stockings off" (Fr1271; J1201); "The Savior must have been / A docile gentleman" — which contains the line, "Since he and I were boys" (Fr1538; J1487), and so on. In her earlier work, *The Riddle of Emily Dickinson* (1951) Patterson had fashioned a lesbian biography of Dickinson, Susan Gilbert, and Catherine Scott Anthon — a biography marred by unwarranted speculations and readings of the poems forced onto the Procrustean bed of her thesis. Cheryl Walker, in her 1982 book *The Nightingale's Burden*, offers a more judicious account of the young Emily Dickinson's relationship with Susan Gilbert: yes, Emily was in love with Sue, but in the sense that Sue became a sanctuary for her. Walker quotes from L85: "And I do love to run fast — and hide away from them all; here in dear Susie's bosom, I know is love and rest." While agreeing with many feminist scholars that "passionate letters between women were not unusual in the nineteenth century," Walker goes on to suggest that Dickinson's feelings were unusual even among nineteenth-century women. But Walker, rather than concluding that the poet experienced a lesbian attraction for Sue, concludes instead that for Emily Sue embodied female power (105). Evidence for this appears in several letters, as Walker shows (106–7) — although they date from the last fifteen years of the poet's life. For example: "To see you, Sue, is power" (L364; Sept. 1871); "Cherish Power — dear — Remember that stands in the Bible between the Kingdom and the Glory, because it is wilder than either of them" (L583; ca. 1878). Walker's insights nicely synthesize formalist and feminist approaches by showing how Dickinson's gender figures in her production of poetic meaning.

Re-Gendering Hierarchical Symbols of Light and Darkness

Throughout history the sun, along with daylight, generally has symbolized the generative force of power, activity, and masculinity, whereas the absence of sunlight has represented inactivity, passivity, and femininity — a dualism that has long dominated Western culture. But Dickinson in effect re-symbolizes sunlight, characterizing it as "seductive but abandoning," as Wendy Barker argues in her 1987 *Lunacy of Light* (59). Barker offers as evidence the following poem:

> Of this is Day composed
> A morning and a noon
> A Revelry unspeakable
> And then a gay unknown
> Whose Pomps allure and spurn
> And dower and deprive
> And penury for Glory
> Remedilessly leave
>
> (Fr1692; J1675)

Here we see daylight as a dowry that has been revoked, leaving the poet as if she were an abandoned bride, in "penury" rather than "Glory" (59). Conversely, Dickinson embraces darkness — and by so doing, as Barker explains, "[r]esists the environmental forces that dominate her world in much the same way that . . . American writers like Cooper, Melville, and James resist these forces. . . . [S]he manages to create through metaphors of darkness a place where her own consciousness can be free" (75). Indeed, midnight becomes her new morning: "Good Morning — Midnight — / I'm coming Home —" (Fr382; J425).

Dickinson thus sweeps away the old hierarchical associations of light and darkness (light = masculine energy; darkness = female passivity) into new archetypal associations (if not a reverse hierarchy) whereby light takes on the characteristics of an oppressor and darkness a wellspring of untapped female power. In "She sweeps with many-colored Brooms" (Fr318A; J219), for example, the defining tool of female domesticity, a broom, is transformed into a cosmic force that sweeps away the dust of male-dominant convention before being mythically transformed into stars, a usurpation of the once male-defined heavens:

> She sweeps with many-colored Brooms —
> And leaves the shreds behind —
> Oh Housewife in the Evening West —
> Come back — and — dust the Pond!
>   . . .
> And still, she plies her spotted Brooms —
> And still the Aprons fly,
> Till Brooms fade softly into stars —
> And then I come away —

Barker notes: "These 'spotted Brooms' . . . like Dickinson's own 'freckled human nature,' are in their very irregularity capable of creating a spectacular horizon. And with the sun's eye safely over the hill . . . this housewife's brooms are transformed from ordinary implements of housekeeping into triumphant images of art" (107). Barker's study, then, is valuable for its convincing demonstration of Dickinson's ability to transform traditional connotations of light and darkness from masculine to feminine; and the conventional imagery from associations of domesticity and feminine servitude to associations of celestial and mythic power.

One obstacle to understanding the importance of Dickinson's gender in relation to her art surfaces in modern times, in psychoanalytic criticism, the most influential example of which is Cody's *After Great Pain*. According to Cody, women establish their female identity by identifying with the mother; but if Dickinson could not do so for whatever reason (for example, her mother did not "care for thought," as she told Higginson [L261]), then she would be likely to develop an "abnormal" identification with her father. The result is Dickinson's consequent identification with her father, who evidently did care for thought. In Cody's estimation, then, any woman who thinks — a male activity — is behaving abnormally.

A refreshing antidote to Cody's linking of what he sees as Dickinson's abnormal masculinized thought processes to her alleged psychosis is Helen Vendler's 2004 *Poets Thinking: Pope, Whitman, Dickinson, Yeats*, an examination of the way Dickinson thinks by way of her poetic structures. According to Vendler, Dickinson adopts a chromatic form of thinking whereby serial progression, like every possible musical note, is sounded with connectors such as "and then."[5] But then, Vendler explains, this chromatic progression "encounters unavoidable fissure, fracture, rupture, or abyss, and we get poems such as 'I felt a Cleaving in my Mind / As if my Brain had split — / I tried to match it — Seam by Seam — / But could not make them fit'" (Fr867B; J937). What Vendler sees Dickinson overtly interrogating, then, is not an unjust social order that marginalizes women as thinkers (although one could argue that this is conveyed indirectly), but rather her own earlier poetic formulations. And although Vendler sees "a falling off ... in the latter years of her life, a regression ... to earlier and easier formulations," Dickinson nevertheless continues to craft her poems with an aphoristic mixture of tenses within a single formulation centered around a catastrophic incident (83) — as in "Were it to be the last / How infinite would be / What we did not suspect was marked / Our final interview" (Fr1165; J1164).[6] "Dickinson's epigram of cognitive impossibility," Vendler explains, "indulges ironically in a tense-play and mood-play on the verb to be, the verb of existence no sooner invoked than extinguished" (83). Dickinson thinking is Dickinson *enacting* — her artistry and her artistic authority, giving us a new sense of "how human experience can be adequately represented" (84).

Dickinson's Textual Ecstasies

Many scholars, feminist or not, have found ways of repudiating what is considered to be a too-reductive way of accounting for the wellsprings of Dickinson's artistic authority. Aside from the formalist position that psychoanalytic criticism is simply irrelevant, an offshoot of the biographical

---

[5] Cristanne Miller discusses this strategy in terms of parataxis in her *Emily Dickinson: A Poet's Grammar* (1987).

[6] This poem formed part of a letter Dickinson wrote to her aunt Catherine Sweetser after learning of the death of her son (L469). The letter begins, "There are no Dead, dear Katie, The Grave is but our moan for them."

fallacy and incapable of shedding light on the aesthetic or textual complexities of the work in question, feminist critics such as Sylvia Henneberg, in "Neither Lesbian Nor Straight: Multiple Eroticisms in Emily Dickinson's Love Poetry" (1995), tend to regard seemingly biographical elements in Dickinson's love poetry as a textual issue, not a psychoanalytic one. With regard to the poem "All the letters I could write" (Fr380; J334), for example, Henneberg argues that Dickinson's speaker "does not experience an ecstatic moment with a man nor with a woman but with a text" (8) — a point that calls to mind the fact that Dickinson would sometimes send the same passionate poem to more than one person, as Helen McNeil notes (1986: 87). A case in point: "Title divine — is mine!" (Fr194A; J1072) was first sent to Samuel Bowles; then, a few years later, to her sister-in-law Susan Dickinson. "Everything — including Emily Dickinson's sexual orientation — is suddenly less clear," McNeil writes, asking, in regard to the line "The Wife — without the Sign!," "Just how literal is 'Wife' meant to be?" (24). Referring also to the two versions of "Going to Him! Happy Letter" (Fr278; J494) — one version alluding to a male recipient, the other to a female — McNeil speculates that "[v]ery likely Emily Dickinson was in love with both Bowles and Sue. Very likely too that she generalized from her experiences, distorting, condensing, and displacing them as she restructured them. The biography is raw material" (24). In other words, Dickinson the artist reworks the raw material of her life to suit the rhetorical situations of a particular poem — a theory that gains persuasiveness when we compare this poem, as John Evangelist Walsh has done in his *The Hidden Life of Emily Dickinson* (1971), to a passage in Elizabeth Barrett Browning's *Aurora Leigh* in which Romney muses on the meaning of life: "Is there any common phrase / Significant, with the adverb heard alone, the verb being absent, and the pronoun out?" (667–69). "For Dickinson," McNeil asserts, "writing was a form of love; to write is a love-act, expressed throughout her poetry by language of power and ecstatic pleasure" (92).

Dickinson's Anxiety of Influence

A strictly feminist reading of Dickinson's response to Emersonian Romanticism factors in gender. Joanne Feit Diehl, in *Emily Dickinson and the Romantic Imagination* (1981), the first feminist monograph on Dickinson, penetrates the idealistic veneer of Emersonian Romanticism, exposes the gendered underpinnings and the concomitant anxieties of influence that Dickinson, as a woman poet, inevitably experienced in relation to a male-generated vision of nature and man's place in it. In the case of the young male poet, Diehl explains, appropriating Harold Bloom's anxiety of influence theory for a feminist context, "[t]he relationship between the male poet and his muse is a private courtship upon which the presence of the father impinges but in which the younger poet, depending on his strength, may win his muse from the father . . ." But for Emily Dickinson, the situation is fundamentally different. "Her dilemma of influence is at once complicated and radically simplified by her perception that the Composite Precursor and her muse are the same. The muse gains stature and his or her power increases through this identification. When Dickinson envisions her muse as male, she fears his priapic power and wards him off with intense anxiety as she simultaneously seeks to woo him" (18–19). Diehl cites "We shun it ere it comes" as an example of this conflicting urge:

> We shun it ere it comes,
> Afraid of Joy,
> Then sue it to delay
> And lest it fly,
> Beguile it more and more,
> May not this be
> Old Suitor Heaven,
> Like our dismay at thee?
> (Fr1595; J1580)[7]

A poem that seems more suitable for Diehl's thesis, then — one that is able to capture "the sense of struggle when confronting the combined power of muse and male precursor" (Diehl, 24) — is "A little East of Jordan" (Fr145B; J59). Here, the metaphor, quoted from Genesis 32:26, of Jacob's wrestling with the Angel, and the Angel's warning "I will not let thee go / Except thou bless me" serves as a fitting analogy to the female poet's efforts to assert her voice and her art in a male-controlled domain.

Vivian R. Pollak, in *Dickinson: The Anxiety of Gender* (1984), in effect narrows the scope of Diehl's thesis to the circumstances of her home life. Pollak sees Dickinson as "a woman whose quest for sexual identity has been terminally thwarted," adding that "she is nature's victim" (29). Although

---

[7] Brief mention should be made of the original context for this poem: Dickinson had incorporated it into a note to Joseph A. Chickering, who, according to R. W. Franklin in his variorum note, "had been helpful after the death of ED's mother on 14 November 1882. . . . When Professor Chickering asked if he might call, ED was unable to see him after a postponement" (Franklin, 1998). Franklin then quotes from the beginning of the note: "I had hoped to see you, but have no grace to talk, and my own Words so chill and burn me, that the temperature of other Minds is too new an Awe." This context suggests that even if the helpful caller had been female, Dickinson's reaction would have been the same. Being one who typically felt extremely uncomfortable around other people, she would have been especially so during this period of grief.

Dickinson manages through her poetry to separate herself from a world intent "on shutting her up in prose" she is unable fully to liberate herself "from the suspicion that she was engaged in an anxious rationalization of a uniquely neurotic plight" (30). Beth Maclay Doriani, likewise, in *Emily Dickinson: Daughter of Prophecy* (1996), argues that Dickinson's poetic voice parallels the prophetic voices in Biblical, classical, and Romantic traditions (ix) — and in doing so, adopts the "very rhetorical resources she sought to undermine." Thus, says Doriani, "Dickinson found a way to speak as an authoritative daughter of prophecy in the tradition of Joel 2:28: 'Your sons *and daughters* shall prophesy'" (1; emphasis added) — and to do so "despite [her] culture's patriarchal slant" (2). After all, the Muse, as Margaret Fuller had asserted in *Woman in the Nineteenth Century* (1845), was "the especial genius of woman" (qtd. Doriani 9).

Camille Paglia, in her 1990 book *Sexual Personae*, also acknowledges Dickinson's revolt against Transcendentalist idealism; but unlike feminist scholars such as Diehl, Paglia centers Dickinson's power not in her "womanhood" in the socio-historically constructed sense of the word, but rather in her "womanhood" in the chthonic, earth-mother sense. From this perspective Emerson the poet fails to achieve the ideals of Emerson the visionary Romantic essayist: "The joyful, spontaneous poet is what he longs to be but is not" (598). Part of Emerson's problem is that his Transcendental ideal of self- reliance excludes the female principle. This, for Paglia, prevents Emerson "from activating the other crucial component of Romantic consciousness, the sexual archetypal, without which no Romantic poem can be written." A far stronger Late Romantic poetic voice is Emily Dickinson, "Amherst's Madame de Sade," as Paglia titles her chapter on the poet. "Academic views of [Dickinson]," she insists, "are too genteel" — and she goes on to catalogue many of the sadomasochistic images that inhabit poems like "One Anguish — in a Crowd —" (Fr527; J565):

> A Small Leech — on the Vitals —
> The sliver, in the Lung —
> The Bung out — of an Artery —
> Are scarce accounted — Harms —

"The leech," Paglia explains, ". . . is Dickinson's Sadean shorthand for a nagging anxiety, an invisible hemorrhaging wound, like a stress ulcer. Its ancestor is Prometheus' perforated liver" (626). Paglia, like Wendy Barker (albeit more audaciously), effectively demonstrates Dickinson's ability to use imagery in a powerful, transformative manner.

Dickinson's Rejection of Patriarchal Authority

One of the most provocative voices in feminist criticism of Dickinson is that of Paula Bennett, who, in *Emily Dickinson: Woman Poet* (1990), argues that Dickinson's anomic (or illegal) poetics reflects the poet's rejection of past masculinist truth. The world that Dickinson constructs in her poetry is one that lacks certainties, "and in which, therefore, the ideals of order and perfection (the foundation stories of Western phallocentrism) give way to process and incompletion." It is this fact, Bennett wishes to emphasize, that helps to legitimize the variant readings of Dickinson's poems as *"part of the very substance of the text"* (19; emphasis Bennett's).

In her chapter "Genre, Gender, and Sex," Bennett carries her feminist "incompleteness theorem" into the realm of eroticism. Here we see, through Bennett's eyes, Dickinson overturning two millennia of masculinist literary tradition, in which, "[f]rom Homer and Milton to Whitman and Mailer, the concepts of creative power and sexual power have been intertwined" (153). Bennett's argument in this chapter is that the "patterns of genital imagery in Dickinson's work . . . suggest that she experienced female sexuality (and female creativity) as a separate and autonomous power equal to, but different from, men's own: a 'little' but 'explosive' force" (154) — the reference being to the poet's disclosure, in her fifth letter to Higginson, "when I try to organize, my little Force explodes — and leaves me bare and charred —" (L271).

Bennett amplifies her idea of Dickinson's breaking free of masculine eroticism by calling attention to what she regards as "a network of specifically female genital images, including both the vagina and the clitoris (represented . . . by persistent references to crumbs, berries, peas, pearls and other small, round objects)," found throughout her work (154), but first appearing in her early letters to Susan Gilbert. "Only think of it, Susie," she writes in 1852, "I had'nt any appetite, nor any Lover, either, so I made the best of fate, and gathered antique stones, and your little flowers of moss opened their lips and spoke to me, so I was not alone" (L202; qtd. Bennett 155–56). In this and other similar passages, Bennett explains, "[w]omen are flowers. As flowers, they (or their sexual parts) are to be held, savored, lingered over and physically enjoyed" (156). Because Dickinson was "[p]rofoundly attracted to the female body" (166) it is no surprise that her most erotic poetry is homoerotic. Even poems that appear to be heterosexually oriented on the surface (male lover bee; female flower, both of which appear in "Come slowly — Eden"; Fr205; J211), the poem "is written in a homoerotic mode" (165–66):

> Come slowly — Eden!
> Lips unused to Thee —
> Bashful — sip thy Jessamines —
> As the fainting Bee —
>
> Reaching late his flower,
> Round her chamber hums —
> Counts his nectars —
> Enters — and is lost in Balms.

Bennett notes that this poem and "Did the Harebell loose her girdle / To the lover Bee" (Fr134; J213), "are . . . written from an ambiguous point of view. They are about the joys of entering but who is doing the entering? . . . With whom does [the speaker] identify?" What is clear to Bennett is that the poems "are imbricated with layer upon layer of female sexual imagery — Eden, lips, bashful, sip, Jessamine, faint, flower, round, chamber, nectar, balm . . . The speaker's awareness of the sheer physical enjoyment of female sexuality, symbolized by the idea of losing oneself in balms, is almost overwhelming" (167).

If Paula Bennett's feminist stance is strongest in its effort to identify in Dickinson an effort to secede from a masculinist poetics, Susan Howe's, in her *My Emily Dickinson* (1984), is strongest in its effort to show how Dickinson's innovative poetic language revolutionized the way we apply language to experience. Like Gertrude Stein half a century later, Howe says, Emily Dickinson "conducted a skillful and ironic investigation of patriarchal authority over literary history. Who polices questions of grammar, parts of speech, connection, and connotation? Whose order is shut inside the structure of a sentence?" (10).

The most striking feature of *My Emily Dickinson*, though, is its expressionistic mode of scholarship. Like D. H. Lawrence's *Studies in Classic American Literature* or William Carlos Williams's *In the American Grain* (from which Howe extracts the epigraph for her book), Howe foregrounds her personal voice (as the title implies) in a manner that entertains as it edifies: "[Dickinson's] first labor . . . was to sweep away the pernicious idea of poetry as embroidery for women" (17). And note the way Howe approaches Dickinsonian hesitation to implicate a culture that has excluded women from mainstream intellectual life:

> Emily Dickinson . . . built a new poetic form from her fractured sense of being eternally on intellectual borders, where confident masculine voices buzzed an alluring and inaccessible discourse . . . Pulling pieces of geometry, geology, alchemy, philosophy, politics, biography, biology, mythology, and philology from alien territory, a "sheltered" woman audaciously invented a new grammar grounded in humility in hesitation. HESITATE from the Latin, meaning to

stick. Stammer. To hold back in doubt, have difficulty speaking. "*He* may pause but *he* must not hesitate" — Ruskin. Hesitation circled back and surrounded everyone in that confident age of aggressive industrial expansion and brutal Empire building. Hesitation and Separation. The Civil War had split American [*sic*] in two. *He* might pause, *She* hesitated. Sexual, racial, and geographical separation are at the heart of Definition. (21; emphasis Howe's)

Moreover, by intertwining the quotation from Ruskin (a favorite of Dickinson) and a dictionary definition of hesitation ("for years my Lexicon was my only companion"), Howe cleverly emulates Dickinson's own subtle manner of diminishing the perceived universality of male visionaries. Dickinson had applied similar surgical procedures to Emerson and Higginson, and even to God. "Dickinson takes sovereignty away from God and bestows it on the Woods" (80).

Recent Trends in Feminist Scholarship on Dickinson

Recent feminist scholarship on Dickinson extends the range and versatility of this mode of critical inquiry. Especially important for its ability to link issues of authority to gender, as well as for convincingly reversing the image of Dickinson as an oppressively somber poet, is *Comic Power in Emily Dickinson* (1993) by Suzanne Juhasz, Cristanne Miller, and Martha Nell Smith. These feminist scholars not only call attention to the pervasively comedic nature of so much of Dickinson's poetry, they link it to the "subversive and disruptive modes that offer alternative perspectives on culture"; more specifically they show how, "through formal elements of voice, image, and narrative, Dickinson teases, mocks, even outrages her audience in ways that are akin both to the gestures of traditional comedy and to specifically feminist humor" (1). For example, Juhasz, Miller, and Smith point out how, in "I taste a liquor never brewed" (Fr207; J214), "the little Tippler / Leaning against — the Sun —" "smirks at the mythic and the sacred, deflating pretentious characterizations of poets' endeavors. Yet she does this not in a scoffing or belittling way, but with charming, delightful description" (19). The authors demonstrate, in their three separate chapters, how Dickinson appropriates three of the "central modes" of comedy — "tease, cartooning, and excess or grotesquerie" — in her poetry (22). "Dickinson's humor," the authors conclude, "reshapes the components of the world that she knows so that the poem becomes a site for a transforming vision" (137). What is so refreshing about this study is that it helps us to realize how Dickinson uses humor to generate the same kind of profound insights as her "somber" or "darker" poems.

For feminist critics of Dickinson or any female poet, the poems must be placed into a larger socio-cultural contest before they can reveal their full meanings. Using as a starting point Bakhtin's insights into the relationship between a writer and the social group he or she is addressing, Lynn Shakinovsky argues in her 1994 essay "No Frame of Reference: The Absence of Context in Emily Dickinson's Poetry" that "the complexities surrounding the notion of context for a woman writer shed light on some of the more puzzling aspects of [Dickinson's] poetry" (21). One of these "puzzling aspects" is the shifting or changing frameworks of her texts. "Her poems resist closure. Our attention is inevitably drawn to the frame of the poem, and we are invited to play with limits and boundaries, with the contexts within which we read the poems" (23). This makes wonderful sense when we think of how Dickinson used a wealth of stylistic devices, including compression, parataxis, syntactic doubling to produce manifold rather than singular truth. Unfortunately, Shakinovsky all but contradicts this fine insight in the next paragraph when she states that Dickinson "deliberately denies her readers the frames of reference inside which they may read her poems" (24). Dickinson, I would argue, does indeed deny a *singular* frame of reference, perhaps (appropriate as that paradigm might be to a patriarchal worldview); but generates multiple potential frames of reference, any one of which would serve to validate a corresponding interpretation.

The importance of Dickinson's gender in relation to her poetic sensibilities can also be realized when we consider her letter-writing. In *A Vice for Voices: Reading Emily Dickinson's Correspondence* (2001), Marietta Messmer argues that an examination of Dickinson's letters illuminate many aspects of her innovative poetics. More specifically, Messmer considers Dickinson's letter-writing "as a performative act in which she effectively appropriates a multiplicity of discursively constructed voices that engage in an intergeneric dialogic exchange in order to critique prevailing gender constructions . . . rewrite existing power relations, and challenge traditional forms of author(iz)ed and authoritative patriarchal discourse." Messmer extends Helen McNeil's project of demonstrating Dickinson's manipulation of rhetorical strategies to produce artistic effects — in this case, in epistolary production, a radical departure from nineteenth-century expectations for female letter-writing: that letters written by females would be "confessional" in nature. Dickinson's letters, Messmer explains, "become spaces for rhetorical performances, for entertaining an audience, and, ultimately, for controlled acts of self-representation deliberately tailored toward a specific recipient. The letter-writing act itself is consequently redefined as a creative, literary task dependent on imagination and inspiration" (77; emphasis Messmer's).

The central question posed by the feminist critics I have called attention to in this chapter is the one articulated most explicitly by Margaret Homans in 1980: "How does the consciousness of being a woman affect the workings of the poetic imagination?" (3). Dickinson regarded herself "not just as a poet but as a woman poet" (162); but more than that, she characterized much of the world as masculine, which, for Homans, "illustrates a mind defining its own interior operations as feminine" (176). Like their formalist counterparts, feminist critics pay close attention to poetic and rhetorical elements, but within the context of Dickinson's female sensibility and her awareness of herself as a woman writing — wielding language in a way that dismantles the paradigm that holds the Word (divine or otherwise) to be masculine.

Feminist criticism, then, has deepened our understanding of Emily Dickinson's artistry mainly by calling close attention to the poet's own feminist agenda in her poetic project. Feminist critics have taught us to appreciate the inseparability of gender from poetics; indeed, to read Dickinson from a feminist perspective is to re-read Dickinson from a formalist perspective and to discover that the latter is enriched rather than contradicted or superseded by the former.

4: The Manuscripts of a Non-Print Poet

> *Publication — is the Auction*
> *of the Mind of Man —*
> (Fr788; J709)
>
> *One cannot look long at the little volumes — any*
> *of the forty — without seeing Dickinson's self-*
> *determination as an organizing poet, a crafter of*
> *books as well as of stunning and complex lyrics.*
> — Eleanor Elson Heginbotham, *Reading*
> *the Fascicles of Emily Dickinson:*
> *Dwelling in Possibilities* (2003)
>
> *Any editorial work is a construction upon the poems.*
> — R. W. Franklin, *The Editing of*
> *Emily Dickinson* (1967)

VENTING HER ANGER IN A LETTER to Thomas Wentworth Higginson over the way one of her poems, "A narrow Fellow in the Grass" (Fr1096B; J986) was misprinted in the *Springfield Weekly Republican* (the details of which I will get to shortly), Emily Dickinson asserted that she "did not print." She had chosen her words carefully. "Print," unlike "publish," conjures up conventions of typography, not just conventions of literary taste, and she concluded that those conventions would not and could not accommodate her conception of how a poem should appear before readers' eyes. If she had been undecided before writing to Higginson, then he clinched it for her. Being a Unitarian minister, abolitionist, supporter of women's rights, essayist, and literary talent scout, he must have been the likeliest person to determine accurately not only whether her poems breathed, but whether they could breathe in print. He judged that they could not. Her poems would remain "poetry of the portfolio."

Dickinson's Chirography and the Limitations of Print

Whether Higginson's judgment is valid or not, editors today continue to wrestle with the best way to represent Emily Dickinson's poems, including whether they should even be represented in print. Some scholars believe that Dickinson neither composed her poems nor assembled them into fascicles with print publication in mind. Instead, they argue, creating fascicles was simply her way of keeping track of everything, as R. W. Franklin suspects (*Manuscript Books,* ix), or as end products for *private* publication, oxymoronic as that may sound. Martha Nell Smith, elaborating in 1992 on a point made by Franklin in *The Editing of Emily Dickinson* (see the epigraph at the beginning of this chapter), reminds us that "any translation of a text into mass reproducibility is a product shaped by editorial opinion" (126), a fact that Dickinson seemed painfully aware of. In "Emily Dickinson's Visible Language" (1993; reprinted in Farr 1996), Jerome McGann suggests that sometime around the winter of 1861, beginning with her stretching the metrical unit normally comprising one line in a given metrical scheme over two scriptural lines of a poem, Dickinson decided to use her "textpage [as] a scene for dramatic interplays between a poetics of the eye and a poetics of the ear" (41). Smith, writing in 1998, concurs with McGann by noting that "in the first eight fascicles, Dickinson was obviously writing bibliographically, or with the book and the printed page in mind — her poetic forms in these are regularized variations on the tercet and quatrain, predictably lineated" ("Dickinson's Manuscripts," 115; cf. McGann 42). This would be consistent with the theory that Dickinson had publication in mind when she first contacted T. W. Higginson in 1862 to ask him whether he thought her verse was alive. There are two problems with Smith's qualification, however: first, it seems conceivable that Dickinson could have adhered to traditional poetic lineation and stanza patterning in the early fascicles without having print publication in mind; and second, Smith's qualification does not account for other non-print "irregularities" that are present in these early fascicles — most notably her liberal use of the dash. Edith Wylder, in her 1971 study of Dickinson's punctuation, *The Last Face: Emily Dickinson's Manuscripts,* considers them to be elocutionary marks (see discussion below). If this is true, would not casting even early-fascicle poems in conventional type distort Dickinson's intentions? My own answer is yes, but that would not be a sufficient reason for denying them conventional publication. In any case, the debate over the manuscript originals versus their print transmutation is far from being resolved. Domhnall Mitchell, for example, in *Measures of Possibility: Emily Dickinson's Manuscripts* (2005), insists that the poet's punctuation is "idiosyncratic," not artistically determined, noting that their appearance in early correspondence, "strongly suggests that the continued vagaries of their direction, extent, and placement in the *later* work represents a sustained habit of the handwriting" (2005: 59; emphasis Mitchell's).[1]

---

[1] See also Ellen Louise Hart's review of Mitchell's *Measures of Possibility* in the

Other topics of interest in regard to Dickinson's manuscripts include the following:

- Manuscript variants and the notion of a "final" or "finished" text
- Text as artifact: cross-textual play; collage
- The rationale underlying the order of the fascicles
- Bound fascicles versus unbound "sets"
- Genre-blurring: poems in the context of letters they accompany or into which they are integrated.

Sometime before of during 1887, the year Mabel Loomis Todd began editing Emily Dickinson's poems, the fascicles were disassembled to permit ease of copying, editing, and screening for an eventual book-length collection (eventually submitted to Thomas Niles at Roberts Brothers and published as *Poems* in 1890), no record of the original sequences was retained. Despite the meticulous efforts of Thomas H. Johnson to reconstruct the fascicle sequences for his variorum *Poems of Emily Dickinson* in 1955, there were many problems, which Franklin recounts in *The Editing of Emily Dickinson* (1967). For example, Franklin writes,

> Mr. Johnson assumes that there was a unity in Emily Dickinson's intent, that she was trying to establish *a* reading [emphasis Franklin's]. Multiplicity, however, did not bother this poet, and she would without qualms change a reading in order to make it appropriate for different people and different occasions. Each of these fair copies is "final" for its person or occasion, but that cannot be equated with final intention for publication. Sending a poem to a friend is a type of publishing, but it fixes the poem only for that person on that occasion; sending a poem to a publisher . . . fixes the form of the poem for all people and all time. (132)

Franklin's point about multiple variants of a given poem not "bothering" Dickinson, as we shall see, becomes an important issue in current textual scholarship. Who is to say what Dickinson would have considered to be a final version for publication, since Dickinson (as current scholars make clear) rejected the convention of publication as mechanical reproduction — publication, as "the Auction / of the Mind of Man" (Fr788; J709)? In any case, scholars now may examine the poems exactly as Dickinson wrote

---

EDIS Journal, Nov.–Dec. 2006: 11–14. Hart calls attention to Mitchell's objection to making manuscript study central to Dickinson scholarship because it takes attention away from the poetry.

them, and in their original sequences, thanks to Franklin's *Manuscript Books*.²

The major concern among Dickinson scholars now is whether the manuscripts bring us any closer to an understanding of how Dickinson intended to perpetuate her poetry in the world, assuming she had such intention. Morris Eaves, in his 1994 article "'Why Don't They Leave It Alone?' Speculations on the Authority of the Audience in Editorial Theory," poses two questions all Dickinson textual scholars must sooner or later ask. First, can a conservative editorial policy for conventional publication honor Dickinson's intentions or does it violate them by prying even further into a secret life expressed in those unconventional minutiae? Second, if Dickinson had overseen the publication of her poems, would she have translated her personal codes of poetic discourse into the more public codes of conventional published print? (97) From the perspective of editorial theory — at least from Eaves's perspective as an editorial theorist — the notion that editing corrupts a text "is the dominant myth of modern editing" (86). But Eaves also points out that there is a countermyth: that editing improves a text. A mature editorial theory, according to Eaves, "would run between these two alternative myths, one producing respect for the unique original, the other producing the consensus necessary to give the reprint its dignity" (87). Applied to Dickinson, Eaves notes, alluding in particular to "Publication — is the Auction," that "[t]he decision to drag this agoraphobic poetry into the light . . . to 'reduce' this 'Human Spirit / To Disgrace of Price,' is ours, and only ours, to make. Respecting her intentions, we might have burned her poems, acting in the spirit in which some physicians assist suicides" (96). Instead, we have chosen "to betray her intentions with several rationales" — among them being that the poems have become "a public resource" (97).

It seems to me that the "public resource" rationale is a valid one. True, Dickinson intended her poetry to be shared intimately, just like her letters — that is, shared with specific recipients in mind; and the recipient must be made to feel that the poem-letter is for him or her alone, and not for a general readership; but this holds true *only so long as the poet is alive*. Once she is dead, it becomes the responsibility of editors to determine how best to represent her for the ages. "Disgrace of price" (to use Dickinson's phrase from Fr788; J709) it seems to me, applies only to the poet herself, not to her surviving kin or to future editors. What should today inform the appearance of a Dickinson poem in print are whatever clues Dickinson herself left behind — and she has left us with at least two very important ones.

---

² Franklin meticulously examined pinholes, stains, and watermarks to re-establish Dickinson's original page sequences within a given fascicle.

Martha Nell Smith recounts the story, which I mentioned in the beginning of this chapter, of Dickinson's voicing her displeasure to Thomas Wentworth Higginson at the way the printed version of her "A narrow Fellow in the Grass" (Fr1096B; J986) in the *Springfield Weekly Republican* had been "robbed of me — defeated too of the third line by the punctuation" (L316; Smith 11). The editors had inserted a question mark where one *conventionally* belonged, but Dickinson had deliberately left it out.

- Dickinson's manuscript version:

    You may have met Him — did you not
    His notice instant is

- The *Springfield Weekly Republican* version:

    You may have met him — did you not?
    His notice instant is,

As Smith explains,

> The question mark separates "not" from "notice," spoiling the anaphoric pun. "Not," followed so quickly by "notice," with no pause underscored between, brings to mind 'Did you note?' On the other hand, the divisive punctuation discourages the punning and ambiguity made possible in its absence. By emphasizing the break between lines, the punctuation mark practically insists on a particular reading, whereas its omission makes the relationship between the two lines more indeterminate, hence encouraging more interaction by the reader and more possibilities to create meaning. (12)

Editorial overriding of unconventional punctuation, then, is one clear reason behind Dickinson's rejection of print publication. Besides omitting punctuation where punctuation is conventionally required, she often employed orthographic marks that were not used for printing poems. Dashes were used, but not her style of rising or falling dashes that would indicate inflection. Such elocutionary marks were certainly available in typeface; Ebenezer Porter uses them in his *Rhetorical Reader* (1832; see discussion below), but they were not part of the convention of poetry reproduction.

A second important reason why Dickinson rejected print publication has to do with the inflexible layout conventions associated with poetry. Her line divisions that break up established metrical lines, for example, are largely ignored even today, simply because it is assumed that Dickinson intended lines of conventional tetrameter or trimeter lengths, but frequently ran out of room at the edge of the page. The first scholar to reproduce the lines as they appear in the manuscripts is Paula Bennett in *Emily Dickinson: Woman Poet* (1990). Even Dickinson's variorum editors

Thomas H. Johnson and R. W. Franklin reprinted the poems with conventional lineation, as if assuming that Dickinson had simply run out of room before completing the line.[3]

The most comprehensive study of Dickinson's manuscripts thus far is the most recent: Domhnall Mitchell's aforementioned *Measures of Possibility: Emily Dickinson's Manuscripts* (2005). Mitchell begins his study by calling attention to the "increasing acceptance" among Dickinson scholars "that the layout of a Dickinson autograph is deliberate or motivated: at the very least it is hers, not that of her editors" (21); he cautions against leaping to the conclusion that her autograph "peculiarities" constitute proof that printing Dickinson's poetry was tantamount to translating it into another language, hence fundamentally distorting it.[4] By paying close attention to often overlooked features of Dickinson manuscripts, such as line spacing, enjambment practices, even the way the poet shaped her words and individual letters, Mitchell provides new insight into Dickinson's sense of her own textual authority.

Mitchell first presented his views on the fundamental authority of Dickinson's manuscripts in his earlier study, *Emily Dickinson: Monarch of Perception* (2000). Mitchell considers it reasonable to assume that Dickinson scorned print publication (for reasons discussed above); but he also considers it just as plausible "that she might not have wanted to publish for reasons that have as much to do with class as with a concern for artistic control" (155) — reasons shared by her closest friend and sister-in-law Susan Gilbert Dickinson. Mitchell elaborates as follows:

> Emily's and Susan's objections to print may . . . be seen as part of an internalized middle-class ideology of the feminine that insists on domestic privacy for women as an important aspect of a family's identity and respectability. . . . Publication brings publicity, which threatens personal and familiar integrity. (156)

Mitchell also places this class-based rationale in the context of intellectual and artistic discourse — that is, he sees Dickinson's refusal to publish conventionally as her attempt

> to exclude wider social discourses and realities in favor of an individualized idiom of emotions, abstractions, and essences. . . . "Subjects hinder talk," Dickinson once wrote in a letter to Susan, and the

---

[3] Franklin, however, notes the manuscript line breaks (which he refers to as "divisions") for each poem.

[4] See also Lena Christensen, *Editing Emily Dickinson: The Production of an Author* (2008): "The emphasis on the aura of the original [manuscripts] must be questioned, for it represents a desire for an immediacy that is not attainable" (116).

phrase has a typical resonance and indeterminacy. It can be read as a kind of dismissive, imperious pronouncement: actual topics or issues . . . impede important significant expression. (156–57)

Mitchell's point is well-taken, especially in light of Dickinson's attitude toward publication as an auction whereby the poet compromises her integrity for advantages that seem more mercenary than artistic. On the other hand, she undoubtedly sought wider recognition in 1862, or she would not have bothered with soliciting Higginson's opinion, which she knew would be conventional. My sense, then, is that Dickinson did indeed consider "printing," but quickly came to realize that the conventions of mechanical print reproduction would inevitably rob her poems of one of their most important attributes, its tone — its *breathing*.

As has been mentioned above, Edith Wylder, writing in 1971, was the first to identify and describe the function of Dickinson's "odd" marks of punctuation, including what Wylder considered to be elocutionary marks. She also established an important link between the poetic and the rhetorical elements in Dickinson's work. According to Wylder, Dickinson became keenly aware of the potential of literary works to be declamatory by way of Ebenezer Porter's widely-used *Rhetorical Reader,* one of her textbooks at Amherst Academy. Porter locates the essence of expressiveness in the voice, and considers silence to be the highest expression of passion. When words nonetheless try to capture this passion, Porter asserts, the voice "speaks only in abrupt fragments of sentences" (Porter, 1832; qtd. Wylder 14). But while Porter adheres to conventional punctuation, placing his inflectional marks over the stressed vowels, Dickinson, Wylder argues, replaces the conventional punctuation with rhetorical marks (22). These include angular slants, reversed slants, horizontal marks, and curved marks, all of which the poet employs to modulate the voice in specific expressive ways (9).

The question arises whether even the members of Dickinson's select society would have been able to distinguish, in the poet's chirography, between an angular slant and a conventional comma, or between a horizontal mark and a conventional dash. Wylder, as if anticipating this concern, has taken precise measurements of the marks in question. For example, she observes that the "'irregular' notations measured approximately one-sixteenth of an inch, their length varying slightly with the proportionate size of the handwriting or with its normal irregularities" (9). Of course, one could argue that, assuming Dickinson was indeed "rhetorically marking" her poems, she was doing so for her own benefit, perhaps to test their expressive power orally, or even with a mind to reading the poems aloud to family members. Martha Ackmann relates in a 1996 article a wonderful story from a Norcross descendent — Anna Jones

Norcross Sweet, the daughter of Emily Dickinson's mother's younger brother. "As a frequent visitor to the Dickinson Homestead," Ackmann writes, "Anna had many interactions" with Emily, including witnessing Emily "declaim her poetry" (120–26). This parallels another extant eyewitness report that Ackmann describes, this one by Dickinson's cousin Louise ("Loo") Norcross, who, writing in *The Woman's Journal* in 1904, describes the times she sat on a footstool behind the pantry door listening to Emily reading her poems aloud to her (Ackmann 123). Norcross's testimony helps shed light on why so many of Dickinson's poems begin with the word "I." As Archibald MacLeish observed, few other poets have used "the live locutions of dramatic speech . . . written as though spoken" as did Emily Dickinson (105).

Helen McNeil, writing in 1986, corroborates Wylder's and MacLeish's views. In calling attention to the rhetorical dimensions of Dickinson's poetry, she notes that "In mid and late nineteenth century New England, social discourse played a role whose importance is difficult to assess today, so greatly have our modes of communication changed. Emily Dickinson lived in an age of speech, an age of great public orators. . . . Literature was meant to be read rhetorically" (75, 76).[5]

In his monograph *Inflections of the Pen: Dash and Voice in Emily Dickinson* (1997), Paul Crumbley extends Wylder's investigation by focusing on Dickinson's "heteroglossia," which her early editors attempted to remove: "Instead of finding one single poetic voice," Crumbley explains, "stylistic countercurrents — provoked primarily by punctuation, capitalization, and diction — invariably suggested a divided self. . . ." (2). Dickinson's dashes especially "seemed to belie the orderliness of her poetry's common measure and ballad and hymn meters, transforming a poem such as 'This is my letter to the World' (Fr519; J441) from a paean to universal harmony to an angry assertion of the poet's outsider status in the cosmos" (2).[6] Drawing from Bakhtin's ideas of dialogics, Kristeva's ideas on the way the self is constituted, and even from Noah Webster's definition of the dash in the 1828 edition of his *An American Dictionary*,[7]

---

[5] See chapter 1 for a more detailed discussion of McNeill's views on Dickinson as a rhetorical poet.

[6] See Kamilla Denman, "Emily Dickinson's Volcanic Punctuation" (1993). Denman argues that Dickinson used her distinctive punctuation "to disrupt conventional grammatical patterns and create new relationships between words; to resist stasis in linguistic expression; to create musical and rhythmical effects; and to assert the silent and the nonverbal" (24).

[7] Part of the definition, quoted by Crumbley, reads: "A mark or line in writing or printing, noting a break or stop in the sentence; as in Virgil, quos ego — [what I am; that which I am]." Virgil's words, Crumbley suggests, "are an assertion of

Crumbley demonstrates the way Dickinson employed her dashes to generate polyvocality. Once they are aware that "no voice exists in isolation," readers can then "appreciate the way disjunctions remind [them] to join speakers in the negotiation of specific linguistic environments" (27). Crumbley sees Dickinson proposing "an alternative to the 'culturally monitored feminine community of expression' that [Joanne] Dobson states was designed 'to screen out personal expression'" (Dobson, 1989, xii; qtd. Crumbley 30). Crumbley considers the poem "Estranged from Beauty" (Fr1515; J1474), in which he says Dickinson suggests that "to be alive . . . is to know that identity is a temporary state, something we 'lease' as a departure from the reality it attempted to exclude" (30), as a case in point:

> Estranged from Beauty — none can be —
> For Beauty is Infinity —
> And power to be finite ceased
> +Before Identity was creased — +   +When Fate incorporated us
>   +leased

Crumbley first calls attention to the clever play between variant words — "That 'lease' is a variant for 'crease' points to the tension between a transient leasing and the permanence of a crease in one's face, the page of a book, or even an article of clothing that would have to be ironed again." As for the dashes, they "rupture the second and third lines [which] emphasize the way that the phrase 'none can be' immediately resists the finite, hierarchic state described in the phrase 'Estranged from Beauty.'" The subsequent line then implies "that identity, the 'power to be finite,' is an illusion" (30–31). Thus, Crumbley concludes, "this poem challenges romanticist assumptions that being alive means being alienated from infinity" (31). Even more fundamentally, Crumbley convinces us that because of the polyvocality generated by dashes or other ambiguous marks of punctuation (or lack thereof), along with word and phrase variants, print publication of the poems need to be as faithful to their manuscript versions as possible.

---

identity, but a markedly inconclusive one: Virgil asserts that he is something, but does not further define what that something is. The appearance of Virgil's assertion within a definition describing the disjunctive function of the dash associates identity with syntactic structure. The dash, then, becomes a form of punctuation that both challenges the linear progression of sentences and emphasizes the uncertainty of identity" (15).

Dickinson's Worksheet Drafts: Progression or Regression?

But should this also hold true for Dickinson's so-called "worksheet drafts"? Jeanne Holland, in "Stamps, Scraps, and Cutouts: Emily Dickinson's Domestic Technologies of Publication" (1994), argues that the poet's move from bound fascicles to unbound sets to writing penciled drafts on "scraps" represented not a regression but a progression to what Holland calls "domestic technologies of publication" (141). Focusing on "Alone and in a Circumstance" (Fr1174; J1167), a collage manuscript from 1870, Holland believes that Dickinson chose not to create a fair copy of this poem (during a time in which she had resumed making fair copies) because it "visually and textually dramatizes Dickinson's joyful play with writing's construction of the body. Dickinson affixed a postage stamp bearing the image of a locomotive, together with two printed words "*GEORGE SAND*" and *Mauprat* (the title of Sand's 1837 novel), clipped from a review in the May, 1870 issue of *Harper's,* to the page. The collage stages that interrogation by letting child's play subvert the law. Moreover, "the exchange between image and text exposes the inextricability of 'private' epistolarity from the 'public' literary culture of print, rehearsing Dickinson's class interests and her response to marketplace ideology" (141). In determining the connections between the holographic image of the manuscript and the poem itself, Holland begins with the iconography of the particular postage stamp, regarding it as "synecdoche for the poet's father; a locomotive was named in his honor in 1862. Bringing the railroad to Amherst was one of the consuming passions of Edward Dickinson's life." Holland thus suspects that Dickinson's choice of this particular stamp "resonates with patriarchal significance," and proceeds to describe an experiment she conducted with the manuscript:

> To view the locomotive correctly, we have to turn the paper sideways. Yet that perspective makes the poem look skewed. Seen sideways, "Mauprat," the male protagonist's name, is easily legible, as is the carefully crossed-out word "bandits" [included in the clipping] underneath. . . . When we rotate the paper, privileging the father's perspective, the daughter's texts — poetry and "GEORGE SAND" — are thrown out of kilter, and vice versa. This visual pun recalls Dickinson's letter to her brother that "we do not have much poetry, father having made up his mind that its pretty much all real life" (L65). . . . But the oppositions between locomotive/poetry, father/daughter, male/female are put into question by the cutout figure. Dickinson makes the locomotive the center of the image she constructs with cutouts. This suggests that she intuits the presence of the Father, a patriarchal power, at the heart of her work. (146–47)

Holland convinces us that the distinction between "scrap" or "draft" and "fair copy" breaks down with these worksheet drafts. Just as Dickinson had earlier blurred the boundary between poem and letter, she is now blurring the boundary between poem as text and poem as visual artifact. Perhaps, if we take her chirography and formatting of individual poems into consideration, we may conclude that she envisioned poems as visual artifacts from the very beginning.

Some scholars regard Dickinson's manipulation of textual materials as a means of commenting satirically, rebelliously, on social conventions. Martha Nell Smith, in her 1993 chapter "The Poet as Cartoonist: Pictures Sewed to Words," describes how Dickinson actually mutilated pages from sacrosanct texts such as her Bible, her *New England Primer*, and the family's collection of Charles Dickens in order to create cartoon-like collages with the manuscripts of some of her poems and letters. "By manipulating the material embodiments of texts," Smith explains, "Dickinson clowns and toys with convention, and thereby overturns the dicta of her day." Smith identifies five forms of cultural authority that Dickinson "critically exposes": poetic tradition, patriotism, romantic thralldom, the patriarchal family, and the rigidities of printing (72).

Another reason to give renewed attention to the worksheet drafts is that they may convey what Sally Bushell terms, in "Meaning in Dickinson's Manuscripts: Intending the Unintentional" (2005), "enactment of unintentional meaning" (52). For example, in "That sacred Closet when you sweep" (Fr1385; J1273), which reflects upon the care one must take when sweeping out memories, Bushell notes that Dickinson has chosen "to run words up the margin and invert the last two lines along the top of the page, thus partially enclosing the 'sacred Closet' of the poem itself." Bushell also observes that the poem is written "on the final back page of a four-sided bifolium sheet" and that "[t]he final words written along the bottom, up the side and finally upside down upon the page read: 'You cannot super — / sede itself / But it can / silence you." This Bushell sees as a kind of "silencing" or "sealing in, of a certain kind of activity within the manuscripts" (54). It is not her intention, Bushell explains, to use these manuscript observations as a rationale for favoring the manuscripts over Johnson's and Franklin's print versions, but to show that in Dickinson's case, responding to every facet of the manuscript page permits a critical analysis (58).

The Fascicles: Questions of Coherence

Another facet of non-print publishing includes fashioning one's own books or booklets out of manuscript pages — a project Dickinson undertook in earnest in 1858, but with which she had experimented years earlier. It seems likely that Dickinson learned the art of fascicle gathering, or private book-making, at Amherst Academy. As R. W. Franklin explains in the introduction to his variorum *Poems of Emily Dickinson* (1998): "[S]tudent writing [at Amherst Academy] was put out in a manuscript called 'Forest Leaves,' a form of juvenile journalism often hand-copied on single sheets of folded paper to form a volume" (9). Franklin goes on to explain how Dickinson would send "little volumes" to friends such as Henry Vaughan Emmons, together with published books she wanted her friends to read. In all likelihood, according to Franklin, these little homemade volumes "may have been gatherings of her poems, arranged on individual unbound sheets of stationery" (9).

This kind of "private publishing" was not uncommon among poets, was sometimes referred to as "poetry of the portfolio" — a phrase apparently introduced by Emerson in *The Dial*, and applied to Dickinson's poetry by Higginson in his essay "An Open Portfolio,"[8] intended to introduce Dickinson's poetry to the world (and undoubtedly to help promote the publication of *Poems* two months later). "Such poetry," Higginson explains, "when accumulated for years, will have at least the merit of perfect freedom, accompanied, of course, by whatever drawback follows from the habitual absence of criticism" (Buckingham 3–4). This is a rather disingenuous assertion when applied to Dickinson, considering the criticism he had given her (which we can infer from her second letter to him, in which she thanks him for the "surgery"; and to which he refers in his November 1891 essay in *The Atlantic*, "Emily Dickinson." Much of what Higginson considered a "drawback" to Dickinson's poetry — as evidenced by the "creative editing" he and Mabel Loomis Todd performed on the poems — would eventually be regarded as hallmarks of her genius.

Scholars have long wondered about Dickinson's literary objectives in actively arranging her poems into fascicles for six years (the better part of twenty years if we count the unbound, irregularly maintained "sets"). What ordering principle did Dickinson follow when gathering the "fair copies" of her poems into fascicles? Was it based on chronology, theme, motif, image, or symbol relationship? Is it possible that she followed no ordering rationale at all? Perhaps, as Franklin suggests, one of her motives "was to reduce disorder in her manuscripts. . . . As she copied poem after poem onto uniform sheets of stationery, she destroyed earlier versions . . . Each bound unit replaced multiplicity and confusion" (1981: ix–x).

The first three studies to consider an underlying design to the fascicle arrangements are Ruth Miller's *The Poetry of Emily Dickinson* (1968), M. L.

---

[8] First published in the *Christian Union* in September 1890 and reprinted in Willis Buckingham's *Emily Dickinson's Reception in the 1890s* (1989).

Rosenthal and Sally M. Gall's *The Modern Poetic Sequence: The Genius of Modern Poetry* (1983) and William H. Shurr's *The Marriage of Emily Dickinson: A Study of the Fascicles* (1983). Miller sees the fascicles being organized around very general themes such as "quest, suffering and resolution" (Miller 249).[9] Rosenthal and Gall, considering sequence to be one of the defining features of modern poetry (beginning with Whitman's *Leaves of Grass* and extending into the twentieth century with Pound's *Cantos*, Eliot's *The Waste Land*, Yeats's sequences dealing with the Irish Civil War, Williams's *Paterson*, and the meditative sequences of Stevens and Auden), assert that Dickinson's Fascicles 15 and 16 emerge from "violent psychological and artistic upheaval" (48), and perceive that such poems in sequence as "The First Day's Night had come" (Fr423; J410), "The Color of the Grave is Green" (Fr424; J411), 'Twas like a Maelstrom, with a notch" (Fr425; J414), "I gave myself to Him" (Fr426; J580), and so on, closing with "I had been hungry all the Years" (Fr439; J579), generate "a process of tensions and counter-tensions in motion, self-contained and yet not rigid" (48–49). "We have been carried from terrified whirling to a quietened desolation," Rosenthal and Gall suggest (54). The problem with this approach, as Robert Weisbuch points out in his 1983 assessment of scholarship on Whitman and Dickinson in *American Literary Scholarship: An Annual* (1983), is that one can find the same degree of coherence anywhere among Dickinson's poems, whether arranged by fascicle or not.[10]

William H. Shurr's thesis in *The Marriage of Emily Dickinson* (1983) is considerably more daring than Rosenthal and Gall's. Shurr sets out to demonstrate that all forty fascicles and fifteen sets represent a coherent "private communication to a specific lover" (10). Shurr then outlines the narrative that the poem-epistles unfold. He identifies five phases:

- Phase 1 (Fascicles 1–8): Here the nature of the relationship is established; the recipient is not yet the sender's lover; the language is liturgical, as if the recipient were a clergyman (52); the sender refers to herself as "Daisy" (as in the Master letters) or Anemone, identifying herself with the flowers she is sending him, as in Fr7; J31: "Pray gather me — / Anemone — / Thy flower — forevermore!" (53).
- Phase 2 (Fascicles 9–13): Here Shurr points out that the speaker announces "I'm Wife" (Fr225; J199) — in the poem that opens with that phrase, a poem that "memorializes a major change in the way Dickinson identifies herself in the fascicles" (60). Shurr also notes

---

[9] Tamaaki Yamakawa, in "Emily Dickinson's Mystic Well — an Aspect of Fascicle 14" (1988), takes a similar approach.

[10] See Heginbotham's commentary on Weisbuch's assessment of Rosenthal and Gall (*Reading the Fascicles of Emily Dickinson*, 2003: 10).

that a dozen poems in these second-phase fascicles describe meetings between the lovers, with the speaker comparing their temperaments, as in Fr221; J190, "He was weak, and I was strong — then —"

- Phase 3 (Fascicles 13–19): In this phase, according to Shurr, the speaker expresses "a crippling sense of her aloneness, the result of the separation that took place immediately after their private marriage ceremony" (73). Shurr cites evidence for this from "There came a Day at Summer's full" (Fr325D; J322): "So faces on two Decks, look back, / Bound to opposing lands"; from "You see I cannot see — your lifetime — / I must guess — / How many times it ache for me — today" (Fr313; J253); and other similar poems.
- Phase 4 (Fascicles 20–35): Here, says Shurr, the speaker becomes keenly aware of her professional identity as poet "to match the professional status of her beloved" (85). Paradoxically, it is the lover's absence — or rather his presence-through-absence, as Shurr phrases it, together with their shared experiences, "which furnish the best subject matter and motivation for her as a professional poet" (85). Both of these themes, observes Shurr, converge in "The Soul's Superior instants / Occur to Her — alone — / When friend — and Earth's occasion / Have infinite withdrawn — . . ." (Fr630B; J306).
- Phase 5 (Fascicles 36–40): Here the end of the affair is, says Shurr, "expressed most succinctly" in "It dropped so low — in my Regard — / I heard it hit the Ground — / And go to pieces on the Stones / At bottom of my Mind — . . ." (Fr785; J747). As Shurr sees it, Dickinson, in the five fascicles of this final phase, "works hard to write herself out of a situation which has come to a dead end" (113).

The most troubling aspect of Shurr's formulation is that he uncritically equates the speaker of the poems with Dickinson herself and asserts that the marriage was a literal if utterly private one. Shurr answers the question, "Was Dickinson actually married?" elusively: "If we restrict this question to the world of her fascicles, there is no doubt in the mind of the speaker that she was." Shurr seems unable to recognize the gulf existing between Dickinson's personal life and the fictive universe unfolding in the fascicles, nor does he seem to be open to other possible connections between the poems in different fascicles. Weisbuch (1985) dismisses Shurr's thesis as "sexist and sophomoric" (88).

Sharon Cameron undertakes an important new line of inquiry into the poet's arrangement of the fascicles in her 1992 book *Choosing Not Choosing: Dickinson's Fascicles* (1992). Cameron considers what she calls "amplified contexts" whereby fascicle gatherings undermine rather than enhance conventional intertextuality among the poems. In other words, instead of regarding single poems as entities, they might best be perceived as variants of one another, just as within a single poem, variant word choices might best be perceived as part of the internal integrity of the poem instead of external revisions for possible substitution. We are ultimately left with the question, says Cameron, "What *is* the poem?" (5). Poems read in isolation take on new meaning when read in the context of their respective fascicles. As an example, Cameron cites "It's like the Light —" (Fr302; J297) from Fascicle 12. By itself, the poem has no specified subject; but in its fascicle context, "it is explicitly defined within that context as the middle of three poems [the others being Fr301; J296 — "One Year ago — jots what?" and Fr303; J298 — "Alone I cannot be"] . . . on the same subject": the pain of parting from a lover. No single poem of Dickinson's can stand in isolation without loss of significant meaning. "Dickinson's poetry," Cameron concludes, "dramatizes the impossibility of wholeness understood as boundedness" (182). In her 1998 *Emily Dickinson Handbook* article, "Emily Dickinson's Fascicles," Cameron also refers to Dickinson's awareness of the impossibility of certainty, using Fascicle 15 as a case in point. According to Cameron this fascicle includes poems that are governed by antithetical claims, one of them being that madness is unstoppable, as in "The First Day's Night had come —" (Fr423; J410), and that madness can be stopped, as in "We grow accustomed to the Dark —" (Fr428; J419) (151).

Most textual scholars limit their theories of fascicle coherence to just a few of the fascicles. Dorothy Huff Oberhaus's *Emily Dickinson's Fascicles: Method and Meaning* (1995) focuses on the coherence of a single fascicle, Fascicle 40. Oberhaus argues that the unity of this fascicle rests upon "the poems' allusions to the Bible, their allusions to one another and to preceding fascicles, and their echoes of the Christian meditative tradition" (3). It is tempting to voice skepticism here: couldn't one find similar unity in the entire corpus of Dickinson's poetry? Interestingly, Oberhaus goes on to say exactly that:

> The intertextuality forms a network of signals leading the reader to discover that the fortieth fascicle is a carefully constructed poetic sequence and the triumphant conclusion of a long single work, the account of a spiritual and poetic pilgrimage that begins with the first fascicle's first poem. (3)

Fascicle 40, according to Oberhaus, exemplifies the Christian meditative tradition by serving as a conversion narrative, in which the narrator renounces the world, "suffers the pain of self-denial necessitated by her chosen way of life," and ultimately experiences "union with Christ" — although this does not last, and she continues to experience "the pain of realizing that while she has renounced everything to attain her poetic and spiritual goals, she has no assurance she will attain either." Oberhaus then concludes, "Reading the forty fascicles sequentially shows that F-40's conversion narrative is a reprise of events that occurred in the earlier fascicles" (80).

In the second half of her study Oberhaus takes us through the poems of Fascicle 40 to illustrate their respective thematic coherence. Her groupings are as follows:

- Poems 5–16: Living the life of "circumference" (sub-groupings: poems 5–8, The "house"–"home" cluster; poems 9–11: the "flowers" poems and the problem of "need"; poems 12–16: the "circumference[s]" of time and eternity).
- Poems 17–21: The poems of faith: "He who in Himself believes" (Fr835; J969)

In her concluding remarks, Oberhaus, aware that her reading may seem to force the religiously rebellious Dickinson into a Christian mold, notes that "even within their fascicle context, Emily Dickinson's poems do not immediately reveal the Christian nature of her mind and art, because she, who believed riddles to be 'healthful' (L362), tells 'all the Truth' but tells it 'slant' so that the truth she tells dazzles 'gradually.'" Dickinson, that is to say, is no less Christian for her intense scrutinizing (187).

Similar in scope to Oberhaus's study, Eleanor Elson Heginbotham's *Reading the Fascicles of Emily Dickinson: Dwelling in Possibilities* (2003), concentrates mainly on Fascicle 21. Heginbotham is concerned mainly with textual interplay, however. Careful not to slip into the intentional fallacy, she argues that it is useful "to see what proximate poems can tell us about each other and what the selections — for they are that . . . rather than repositories — suggest about the concerns of their author at the moment she bound them together" (xi).

What intrigues Heginbotham most about Fascicle 21 is the apparently deliberate positioning of the two centrally important poems not only in the literal center of the fascicle gathering but of all the fascicles: "[M]idway through a fascicle that is midway through her entire self-publishing project Emily Dickinson declared her aesthetic principles" (5). The poems in question — "They shut me up in Prose" (Fr445; J613) and "This was a Poet —" (Fr446; J448) — traditionally have been regarded as "disparate entities," Heginbotham explains; but "when explored together . . . they become new artifacts by virtue of their proximity. On the left . . . is the image of the speaker who resists being 'shut . . . up in Prose'; on the right . . . is a triumphant response to that resistance in the exploration of why 'This was a Poet —' On these pages 'Prose,' visually, almost viscerally, confronts 'Poetry'" (5).

Another approach to fascicle coherence is presented by Daneen Wardrop in her 2002 essay "Emily Dickinson and the Gothic in Fascicle 16."

Wardrop calls attention to "a skillful interplay of Gothicism and the problems inherent in identity formation" (142). Drawing from Julia Kristeva's insights (in *Revolution in Poetic Language*, 1984), into the way modernist texts fragment reality and thereby "threaten the unity of the individual," Wardrop shows how Dickinson uses Gothic motifs to call attention to the fragmented subject, which is powerfully introduced by the poem that opens the fascicle, "Before I got my eye put out" (Fr336A; J327). The "Gothic heart" of the fascicle — both figuratively and literally (it is positioned precisely in the middle, with five poems before and five after), is "'Tis so appalling — it exhilarates — / So over Horror, it half Captivates" (Fr341; J281), in which extreme opposites are played against each other, reminding us of "the psychological fact that what can scare the most remains what is closest" (144). Other poems in the fascicle that play out Gothic themes include "I felt a Funeral, in my Brain (Fr340; J280), and this poem, which, as Wardrop points out, "continues with the meditation of the divested self":

> Of nearness to her sundered Things
> The Soul has special times —
> When Dimness — looks the Oddity —
> Distinctness — easy — seems —
>
> The Shapes we buried, dwell about,
> Familiar, in the Rooms —
> Untarnished by the Sepulchre,
> The+ Mouldering Playmate comes —   +Our
>
> In just the Jacket that he wore —
> Long buttoned in the Mold
> Since we — old mornings, Children — played —
> Divided — by a world —
>
> . . .
>   (Fr337; J607)

Wardrop describes Dickinson's perspective in this poem as that of a speaker "who is dead and has returned home, to the things of her material existence that no longer belong to her now that she is incorporeal" (154), terming it "a phasing of consciousness" which Dickinson uses "to elicit chilling effects [and] a Gothicized way to elicit the problems of self-identity." Self and other have suddenly become disjunctive in a truly Gothic disorientation (154). In Dickinson's interior universe the self is often threatened with disintegration; it is a threat we sense in many of her poems

In three consecutive essays that form part of her collection *Emily Dickinson's Poems: Bulletins from Immortality* (1999), Tomoko Sato examines what she perceives to be the three-part structure of Emily Dickinson's first fascicle, assembled in 1858. In the first part Dickinson creates the setting for the speaker's meditation, opening with "The Gentian weaves her fringes —" (Fr21; J18), "a pantheistic blessing" (160)[11] set in late summer when "subtle changes [in] the natural world" take place (162). The second part of the first fascicle Sato characterizes as "contemplation of loss and gain," signaled by "We lose — because we win — / Gamblers — recollecting which / Toss their dice again!" (Fr28; J21). The third part of Fascicle 1 consists of "dialogues with a Master" in which (Here Sato refers to "Summer for thee, grant I may be" [Fr7; J31] and "When Roses cease to bloom, Sir" [Fr8; J32]) "Dickinson collapses the distinction between flowers and poems, and thus poems and the poet. Both poems signify her earnest entreaty that the intended reader collect her work" (182). Sato's conclusion is that Fascicle 1 is the beginning of a spiritual and poetic pilgrimage that culminates with Fascicle 40, in which "she succeeds in reaching the ultimate goal, where through faith she sees the New Horizon of eternity" (194).

Each of the preceding five non-biographical approaches to fascicle interpretation offers a fascinating (if not entirely convincing) alternative to viewing the poems as isolated entities. Cameron's "amplified contexts"; Oberhaus's "intertextuality" in the context of Biblical themes; Heginbotham's textual interplay based on the way poems are positioned within a fascicle; Wardrop's focus on how recurring motifs such as those associated with gothicism call attention to problems of identity formation; Sato's perception of the entire fascicle sequence as a spiritual pilgrimage — if nothing else, these theories greatly enrich our experience of Dickinson's canon.

Teaching the Fascicles

How might one go about introducing Dickinson's fascicles to undergraduates? In "Certain Slants of Light: Exploring the Art of Dickinson's Fascicle 13" (1989), Douglas Novich Leonard shares his classroom experience in getting students to think about fascicle sequence and coherence. Before giving his students the assignment of determining a sequential scheme for a particular fascicle (he likes to work with Fascicle 13), Leonard discusses lyrical sequences by other poets — Whitman's "Song of Myself" and Blake's *Songs of Innocence* and *Songs of Experience,* for example. The class then reaches consensus regarding sequence criteria: intro-

---

[11] Franklin (1998) regards "The Gentian weaves her fringes" as three separate poems (Fr21, 22, 23) instead of Johnson's single poem of three stanzas (J18). Sato is commenting on stanza 3 of the Johnson version: "In the name of the Bee — / And of the Butterfly — / And of the Breeze — Amen!"

ductions and conclusions, transitions between adjacent poems, tonal dynamics, clusters, repetitions of thematic or technical features, literary or biblical allusions; movements from the general to the particular and vice versa, climactic positioning of major poems, and repeated metrical patterns (125).

Leonard's students noticed that five of the poems, positioned in the middle of the fascicle, are about sunsets — for Dickinson, symbols of dying: "She sweeps with many-colored Brooms" (Fr318; J219; #8 in the fascicle), "Blazing in Gold" (Fr321; J228; #11); "Good Night! Which put the Candle out?" (Fr322; J259; #9); "The lonesome for they know not What" (Fr326; J262; #16); and "How the old Mountains drip with Sunset" (Fr327; J291; #17).[12] The students also noted that sixteen of the nineteen poems in the fascicle include light imagery of some kind. The consensus: "The poems are slants of light on death and grief. In elegiac fashion, the fascicle presents a different perspective on the loss of a loved person" (128); moreover, "[t]he careful student will discover that the light motif . . . can be grouped into five periods, each suggestive of a spiritual or psychological state" (129). Leonard discovered that in order to give his students "the fullest possible experience with poetry on their own," he ought to have allocated more time than he had (two weeks) to pursue such intensive creative analysis, and to allow it to go forward with less, not more, guidance.

Poems in the Context of Letters

In "Editing Dickinson's Correspondence," the second chapter of her 2001 study of Dickinson's letters, *A Vice for Voices,* Marietta Messmer calls attention to the "transgressive play with generic boundaries" that resulted in the production of what she calls "letterpoems" instead of letters and poems, or poems integrated into letters or accompanying them. Thomas H. Johnson's "sharp division between the formalities of verse and prose," Messmer points out, resulted in his violating Dickinson's original lineation by printing "the metrical prose margin to margin and the spatially disordered verse in 'correct' metrical lines" (55). Messmer adduces the argument that Ellen Louise Hart, another scholar of Dickinson's letters, had made in her 1995 article "The Elizabeth Whitney Putnam Manuscripts and New Strategies for Editing Emily Dickinson's Letters," that "Dickinson did not visually separate prose and poetry in her letters. Her prose lines and the lines of a poem are similar in length, she did not consistently divide poetry from prose through spacing, and she did not vary margins" (49; qtd. Messmer 55).

---

[12] Compare this observation with Heginbotham's, in her discussion of Fascicle 21 (discussed above).

Hart and Martha Nell Smith, in *Open Me Carefully* (1998) their edition of Emily Dickinson's intimate letters to Susan Huntington Dickinson, reflect more fully on the "letterpoem" hypothesis, which they consider to be "a distinct and important Dickinson genre" (xxv). Whereas Thomas H. Johnson "arranged lines in letters to separate poems and make them look the way we might expect poems to look, Hart and Smith choose instead "to follow Dickinson's commingling techniques, mindful that conventional notions of genre can limit our understanding of Dickinson's writing practices" (xxv–xxvi); and just as Elizabeth Barrett Browning fused poetry with fiction in her verse novel, *Aurora Leigh* ("one of Dickinson's favorite works"), so do Hart and Smith "see Dickinson's blending of poetry with prose, making poems of letters and letters of poems, as a deliberate artistic strategy" (xxvi).

The commingling "letterpoem" technique also has its parallel in the worksheet drafts, where we see poems "commingling" with the material surfaces on which they are inscribed. In so doing, as Sally Bushell suggests in her 2005 article "Meaning in Dickinson's Manuscripts: Intending the Unintentional," Dickinson calls attention to the "fragile and ephemeral state" in which she wants her drafts to exist, thereby either "giving them new life as text" or conferring on them the status of "material [that] can easily be thrown away if it is no good" (44).

Dickinson's Late Manuscript Drafts and Fragments

Marta Werner's *Emily Dickinson's Open Folios: Scenes of Reading, Surfaces of Writing* (1995) in effect "un-edits" Dickinson's late manuscripts and fragments. That is, she returns us to their manuscript originals (reproduced in high resolution in this volume). For Werner, Dickinson's greatest gift is her ability "to affirm extreme inwardness while refusing its legislation, to withdraw into the several isolations of the writing closet while ceaselessly soliciting the other" (36). Dickinson's late manuscripts — the worksheets of poems and letters which may or may not have been mailed to Judge Otis Lord — "attest to continuing *desire for writing* even after there is no longer any chance of finishing what has been begun" (41; emphasis Werner's). By reproducing each individual manuscript "without regard for traditional generic categories" Werner knowingly counters all earlier editorial renderings of these documents (55). By avoiding editorial intrusion as much as possible (she does not use editorial symbols of any kind other than recording catalogue numbers and using the word *verso* to indicate the back of a page) Werner enables the reader to assume the role of witness to Dickinson's "scene of original inscription" (57), no longer muted by editorial restructuring.

"What is a Dickinson poem?" Suzanne Juhasz pointedly asks in her 1998 essay "Materiality and the Poet" (428). In light of the fact that Dickinson's writings "possess such fluidity that we cannot precisely say what is prose and what is poetry" (427), Juhasz explains, reading Dickinson must include awareness of the material aspects of her work: the way her poems take shape on the manuscript page, in the fascicles, in the context of letters, or *as* letters ("letterpoems"). If the poem exists in several versions, which one should be considered definitive — or should they all be? How do we read a poem in the context of a fascicle? Juhasz calls attention to Sharon Cameron's theory, put forth in her *Choosing Not Choosing*, that the poems in a given fascicle are variants of one another (429; Cameron 1992: 5). Do Dickinson's poems acquire new or different meaning when we read them as addressed to particular recipients? As Juhasz notes, the Dickinson Editing Collective "plans to edit the many 'books' Dickinson published to various correspondents" (428). Ellen Louise Hart and Martha Nell Smith, following this paradigm, have already published their edition of "letterpoems" to Susan Dickinson, *Open Me Carefully* (1998).

Now that the Emily Dickinson Electronic Archives is established (www.emilydickinson.org), Dickinson scholars all over the world are able to access images of the poet's manuscripts without having to visit the archives at Harvard University, Amherst College, or other sites. As invaluable as such a resource is for Dickinson scholars, I believe that print publication must continue — but with even greater fidelity to the manuscript versions. This means that Dickinson's line breaks should be reproduced without editorial second-guessing about whether she ran out of room at the edge of the page or separated the line for rhetorical purposes. Also, Dickinson's dash variants, which have been meticulously researched by Wylder, Crumbley, and others, who have pointed out their elocutionary as well as rhetorical effects, should be faithfully reproduced. Finally, the practice of providing variant words and phrases in the margins or in footnotes, already followed by some scholars, should become standard.

5: Dickinson in Cultural Context: Principal Critical Insights

The Queen, discerns like me —
Provincially —
(Fr256; J285)

To study the cross-influences and dynamics between the major and minor writers is to participate in the democratic spirit of the major authors themselves, all of whom in various ways expressed their profound debt to lesser writers.
— David S. Reynolds, *Beneath the American Renaissance* (1988)

Dickinson herself knew she was not entirely alone, not writing in a vacuum. She was both at home and at sea in her New England female context. The most accurate judgment we can make is that her work remembers others' poems even as it forgets them.
— Cheryl Walker, "Dickinson in Context: Nineteenth-Century American Women Poets" (2004)

JACK L. CAPPS NOTES in the opening line of the preface to his *Emily Dickinson's Reading* (1966) that the poet's "voluntary seclusion has often been mistakenly equated to intellectual isolation" (vii). Dickinson, as Capps's book demonstrates, was highly attuned to her society. She was an avid reader of current events, literary journalism, contemporary as well as classic literature, and, especially in her formative years, a devotee of innovative religious and scientific discourse. She was privy (despite the restrictions imposed on her gender) to her lawyer/civic activist father's and brother's professional activities. Her personal and family friends included journalists, theologians, educators, scientists, and publishers (or their spouses or children). The importance of this for her art, according to Capps, is that through her keen awareness of her surroundings and especially through her extensive reading, Dickinson acquired her vicarious experience and perspective and made her perceptive observations and penetrating analyses possible (145).

Dickinson's Cultural Connectedness

Dickinson scholars who are concerned with contextualizing the poet historically and socially wish to show how her poetry reflects many of the artistic, folkloric, domestic, and religious artifacts that saturated the society of her day. The fact that she was a recluse does not make her any less a product of her culture, as being reclusive does not mean being totally sealed off from the world. In Capps's words, "[t]o limit horizons to the house and garden of the Dickinson homestead is to underestimate grossly the capacity of her imagination" (vii).

A useful overview of Emily Dickinson's historical and cultural milieu is provided by *A Historical Guide to Emily Dickinson,* edited by Vivian R. Pollak (2004). Along with an introduction and a succinct fifty-page biography, it includes five essays that place Dickinson in the contexts of the Civil War, New England religious and political life, and other women poets. In "'Is Immortality True?' Salvaging Faith in an Age of Upheavals," Jane Donahue Eberwein discusses Dickinson's religious struggles in the context of her Puritan heritage and the evangelical revivals of her day. The Connecticut Valley had a tradition as a center of Congregational revivalism, and Dickinson experienced the greatest period of such religious zeal in Amherst (75). In her essay "Public and Private in Dickinson's War Poetry" Shira Wolosky examines the way Dickinson's poetry engages war motifs, noting that nineteenth-century poetry directly participated in discussions of the most urgent questions facing America, thereby giving women a special opportunity to engage in issues of public concern (109–10). As the daughter of a Congressman, Emily Dickinson was also deeply attuned to political issues, as we learn from Betsy Erkkila's "Dickinson and the Art of Politics": "Whig political culture inhabited her house," Erkkila asserts (139). While Dickinson very seldom makes any direct reference to specific political events, "her poetic landscapes — even her most interior ones — are full of 'public' attitude about the political, social, religious, sexual, racial, scientific, and economic contests that marked her time" (151). What about literary influences? Cheryl Walker argues in her "Dickinson in Context: Nineteenth-Century American Women Poets" that "by examining Dickinson's poems side by side with those of more published women poets of the nineteenth century . . . one can see more clearly what is valuable about these other poets, the ways that they confound stereotypes of the sentimental 'poetess'" (197). Cristanne Miller then invites us in her essay "The Sound of Shifting Paradigms, or Hearing Dickinson in the Twenty-First Century" to consider Dickinson's poems from an oral/aural perspective, concluding that Dickinson regarded her poems "as separable from any single manifestation of [their] material appearance" (223) — a conclusion validated by the fact that when

Dickinson copied her poems she "usually did not repeat nonmetrical or otherwise unconventional visual features, such as the arrangement of variant words on a page or a slant of handwriting on a particular kind of torn page" (223). Pollak caps her *Historical Guide* with an illustrated chronology and a bibliographic essay by Jonathan Morse.

There are two conspicuous oversights in Pollak's anthology. First, scarcely any attention is given to role of the visual arts in Dickinson's day (I'm thinking especially of the American Romantic painters such as Thomas Cole and Asher Durand, whose influence Judith Farr examines in depth in her 1992 *The Passion of Emily Dickinson;* see below). Second, there are only passing references to those American authors whose works permeated the consciousness of New England and whose writings Dickinson is known to have absorbed in her formative years — in particular, Emerson, Hawthorne, and Higginson. Pollak ought to have included more commentary along the lines of Cristanne Miller's comments on Longfellow — whose poetry, Miller says, "serves best to exemplify what Dickinson and her contemporaries admired" (209) — and his multiple, experimental, and irregular verse forms.

Dickinson's Puritan Teleology: A Ground to Dance On

Contradicting Inder Nath Kher's claim, in *The Landscape of Absence* (1974), that reading Dickinson's work within the context of American history and culture prevents one from acquiring a full sense of her poetic sensibility, Karl Keller in *The Only Kangaroo among the Beauty: Emily Dickinson and America* (1979) intends "to set her squarely in the center of American literary history" (4). Despite the fact that "she does not sit very well for a portrait" (5), Dickinson nevertheless gives us "America as a woman" (6) — a refreshingly feminist observation from a male critic writing in the 1970s — except that Keller in the same breath borders on flippancy in his portrayal of Dickinson's sensibility: "Where else but in America do we have a woman torturing herself with such puritanical flash? . . . Where else do we have someone who desperately wanted to be a poet and yet felt no obligation to be learned?" (6) Even so, Keller manages to convey the wisdom of his project. Emily Dickinson reminds him of Nabokov's description, in his novel *Transparent Things,* of someone "dancing in a variety of forms around one's own self" (qtd. Keller 7). In ten chapters that place Dickinson in the context of Bradstreet, Taylor, Edwards, Stowe, Hawthorne, Emerson, her own literary friends (for instance, her sister-in-law Sue, Col. Higginson, Samuel Bowles, Josiah Holland, Charles Wadsworth), the New England bluestockings (especially

Margaret Fuller),[1] Whitman, and Frost (and, in a coda, to the rest of the world), Keller attempts "once and for all . . . to demolish the stereotype of E.D. the Recluse, . . . the New England Nun" (6). Thus, in relating Dickinson to Bradstreet, Keller adds cultural significance to Dickinson's bold assertion that "Faith is *Doubt*" (10):

> For the Puritan woman of the early seventeenth century, the Puritan cosmic order was dignifying. She was called to salvation, not to keep house or have children — though that was, as it turned out, the socially preferred way. . . . [T]he duty of family governance and instruction gave her a common status at home with men; she was expected to assert her worth even as she joyfully submitted to men's will. . . . [H]er Puritan self-consciousness led her to discover in duty (and here is another of Puritanism's paradoxes) a kind of liberation. . . ." (10–11)

This in turn makes sense of Dickinson's seemingly self contradictory poem, "'Twas my one Glory" (qtd. Keller 11):

> 'Twas my one Glory
> Let it be
> Remembered
> I was owned of Thee —
>   (Fr1040; J1028)

In the chapter on Dickinson and Hawthorne, Keller finds common ground in their respective uses of ambiguity, beginning with her famous oxymoronic characterization of him to Higginson: "Hawthorne appalls, entices" (L622; qtd. Keller 126). Ambiguity, for both Hawthorne and Dickinson, was "a balanced contradiction opposed to resolution, a juxtaposition of contradictory terms of equal rank and emphasis, a compound of inclinations and responses. . . . All is shown, nothing wins. Something is many things" (129). As she proclaims in one poem, "'Tis Opposites — entice — / Deformed Men — ponder Grace — / Bright fires — The Blanketless — / The Lost — Day's face — . . . (Fr612; J355). For Keller, Hawthorne perceives early America "as an archetypal oxymoron," alluding to tales such as "The Great Carbuncle," in which readers confront "the ambiguity built into Christianity: to live for the prize is to live in vain; to lose it is to live more fully; loss is gain; hell is grace"; in *The Scarlet Letter* ("Hawthorne's most satisfying formulation of oxymoronic ambiguities") Hester Prynne "thrives on her humiliation, fails amid her epiphanal pride, experiences . . . depression and success simultaneously"

---

[1] "Bluestockings" is the word Keller uses, but, being largely a pejorative term for intellectual, activist women, it seems to me out of keeping with his championing of the feminist ethos in his book.

(139). Dickinson's poetry, says Keller, is replete with such "oxymoronic ambiguities":

> 'Tis this — invites — appalls — endows —
> Flits — glimmers — proves — dissolves —
> Returns — suggests — convicts — enchants —
> Then — flings in Paradise —
>
> (Fr285B; J673 [3rd stanza])

> Defeat whets Victory — they say —
> The Reefs in Old Gethsemane
> Endear the Shore beyond —
> 'Tis Beggars — Banquets best define —
> 'Tis Parching+ — Vitalizes Wine —   +Thirsting [Fr C]
>
> (Fr283B; J313 [4th stanza])

Yet in Keller's eyes, "as a pioneer of ambiguity . . . Emily Dickinson was a mess-maker" — by which he means that she lacks balance, that "her forms are elliptical and collapsed, her persona . . . unpredictable" — the very stylistic characteristics that feminist-rhetorical critics like Cristanne Miller regard as facets of her literary genius.

A Poet's Scrapbook

Barton Levi St. Armand, in his 1984 book *Emily Dickinson and Her Culture: The Soul's Society,* takes as his point of departure the claim that "the history of Dickinson scholarship has been bent on the establishment of a canon," resulting in her poetic production having been "so cut up, dismembered, picked over, anthologized, and selected that we are in danger of losing touch with the original sensibility that produced them" (15). He sets out to reconstruct that original sensibility, assuring us that Dickinson's "private reality can never be violated when it is seen in relation to the larger public reality of her culture" (17). Indeed, as he cleverly implies in the subtitle of his book, Dickinson's selecting "her own" society inevitably involved selecting a great deal of society at large, so that when the poet's soul "shuts the door" on that society, as she cavalierly proclaims in Fr409; J303, she had interiorized enough of the world to refashion it in her own image. Few formalists, I would argue, would disagree with such a characterization of the way an artist makes use of her cultural milieu; the danger lies — to return to St. Armand's disparagement of any hermetically sealed-off "essential Dickinson" — with those formalists who would reduce the poet to her decontextualized poetic masterpieces.

By placing Dickinson more in contact with the practices of American Victorian culture, St. Armand allows us to see how many of the poems draw from contemporary folklore and customs, using the portfolio system as a repository of keepsakes. Thus, in writing a poem like "The Spider as an Artist" (Fr1373; J1275) Dickinson joins the Victorian cultural arena alongside poets like Lydia Sigourney, whose spider poem, "The Insect Teacher," appears in the scrapbook of Dickinson's close friend Mary Warner. And while Dickinson's artist spider rejects Sigourney's dutiful-wife spider, both appropriate the spider as an allegorical figure established by the common culture:

The Insect Teacher

See! With what untiring skill, —
What an energy of will,
All unaided, — all forlorn,
Housewife's hate, and beauty's scorn, —
How the spider builds her bower
High in the halls of regal power,-
Is the mansion of thy care
Made by wealth and taste so fair,
By misfortune's fearful sway,
Laid in dust? — or reft away?
— Yield no thoughts to blank despair,
Firm in faith, and strong in prayer,
Rise! The ruin to repair.
For the Spider, homeless made,
    Hunted from each loved retreat,
Not dejected, not afraid,
Toiling thro' the gloomiest shade
    Gathereth vigor from defeat: —
Child of Reason! — deign to see
What an insect teacheth thee.

The Spider as an Artist

The Spider as an Artist
Has never been employed —
Though his surpassing Merit
Is freely certified

By every Broom and Bridget
Throughout a Christian Land —
Neglected Son of Genius
I take thee by the Hand —
              (Fr1373; J1275)

Unlike Sigourney's spider, which is "an object lesson in the virtue of perseverance," Dickinson's spider, St. Armand explains, "is a pagan artificer in an orthodox Christian world" (33) — a motif she plays out in "The Spider Holds a Silver Ball" (Fr513; J605). St. Armand then widens the cultural context for spiders in New England culture: Edward Taylor characterized the spider (in "Upon a Spider Catching a Fly") "as a noxious 'Venom Elfe' out to trap foolish souls" (34); Jonathan Edwards famously "characterized the spider as a 'noisome insect'" (34) in his sermon "Sinners in the Hands of an Angry God"; and Mary Howitt, the hymnist and children's author whose works, St. Armand tells us, Dickinson encountered in the pages of *Parley's Magazine,* wrote the famous nursery rhyme, "The Spider and the Fly: An Apologue," in which the demonic spider serves as a lesson to naïve children lulled by flattery (35).

In subsequent chapters, St. Armand explores the way Dickinson assimilates Victorian-American motifs (death, romance, Christian iconography, the natural world) into her poetry. For example, in his chapter "Lone Landscapes: Dickinson, Ruskin, and Victorian Aesthetics," St. Armand suggests that Thomas Wentworth Higginson's nature essays in the *Atlantic Monthly,* which embodied the ideals of such American landscape painters as Asher B. Durand and other members of the Hudson River School, had a stronger influence on Dickinson than Emerson's nature essays (219). And in his chapter titled "The Art of Peace: Dickinson, Sunsets, and the Sublime," St. Armand sees Dickinson as a nineteenth-century extension of William Blake's visionary poetics. Like Blake, who saw in a sunset "an Innumerable company of the Heavenly host crying, 'Holy, Holy, Holy is the Lord God Almighty'" (qtd. St. Armand 259), Dickinson saw sanctity in a sunrise or sunset, "a living representation of the deity" (261), as it was for Ruskin and for Mary Warner via her scrapbook. In poems such as "The Sun kept stooping — stooping — low!" (Fr182; J152), according to St. Armand, Dickinson emulates the American landscape painters in that "she devised an aesthetic strategy that captured the ghost or likeness of the sunset by an imaginative fidelity to the exact conditions of what she saw before her, in the open air, aided by a long attentiveness and obedience to the ways of natural phenomena and an informed understanding of their physical processes" (267). And because a sunrise or sunset was ephemeral, multifaceted in the way it changed from moment to moment, it embodied the mysterious nature of being:

> If this is "fading"
> Oh let me immediately "fade"!
> If this is "dying"
> Bury — me, in such a shroud of red!
> . . .
>
> (Fr119; J120)

After reading St. Armand's insightful analysis of the interplay of cultural artifacts in nineteenth-century New England culture, one is left with little doubt that for the extended Dickinson family, "art, life, and romance were indissolubly linked together" (315). St. Armand's study goes a long way toward grounding "the uncommon intensity of [Dickinson's] perception (221) in her time and place — yet, for me, it contributes little toward demystifying that perception. Dickinson's poetic genius remains inexplicable no matter how numerous the surface ties to cultural artifacts may be.

Dickinson's Iconography

Gilbert and Gubar, in their aforementioned 1979 study *The Madwoman in the Attic*, assert that Emily Dickinson's habit of wearing white was a form of role-playing or impersonating various types, which they list as little maid, virgin, nun, bride, madwoman, dead woman, and ghost (621), but Judith Farr in *The Passion of Emily Dickinson* (1992) rejects that assertion. Farr acknowledges that Dickinson indulged in such theatrical behavior as "sending notes, flowers, and glasses of sherry on salvers to . . . friends in the parlor (and keeping out of sight)," or of "introducing [herself] by handing someone two lilies" — acts that suggested a willingness to share in traditional modes of behavior. But Dickinson, according to Farr, was "genuinely shy, militant about telling the truth, opposed to anything she thought ostensible [and] wore white to affirm her true nature and her membership in a spiritual company . . . the company of those who suffered for the sake of truth and overcame the world" (40). Understanding Dickinson's need to manifest her true nature helps us to understand her need to associate "outer with inner landscapes, the developing soul with the maturing artist, her inspirational powers with Nature and Nature's God" (67).

Like St. Armand, Farr sees American landscape painting as having had a formative influence on Emily Dickinson's poetic sensibility. The most important of these artists, Farr argues, is Thomas Cole (1801–48) and his famous allegorical landscapes known as *The Voyage of Life,* painted in 1840 and reproduced in the form of steel engravings (Cole was commissioned to paint a second series a few years latter, also widely copied. It now hangs in the National Gallery of Art, Washington DC). Farr speculates that Dickinson had seen the engravings during her year at Mt. Holyoke Seminary in 1847–48. Like Cole, Dickinson saw divinity in nature: "I noticed, that the 'Supernatural' was only the Natural, disclosed —" she wrote to Higginson in 1863, quite likely an allusion to Cole's paintings (L280; qtd. Farr 74)., Farr argues that Dickinson drew from Cole's *Voyage of Life* in creating her own narrative of human progress (78). In her very first fascicle, for example, the poet copied two poems containing imagery suggestive of Cole's paintings: "Adrift! A little boat adrift!" (Fr6; J30) and "On this wondrous sea" (Fr3; J4). Moreover, what Farr calls Dickinson's archetypal narrative can be divided into two love narratives: The Narrative of Sue and the Narrative of Master. The former consists of poems that associate Sue with Eden ("Come slowly, Eden"; Fr205; J211), with Cleopatra ("Her breast was fit for pearls . . . / Her brow is fit for thrones —"; Fr121B; J84), and with heaven ("Distrustful of the Gentian"; Fr26; J20). The Master narrative, the poetic counterpart of the anguished "Master Letters," begin with "Title divine — is mine!" (Fr194A; J1072), which Dickinson sent to Bowles (to whom, according to Farr, the "Master Letters" were also addressed). "Dickinson's poem cycle for Master, like the concurrent cycle for Sue," Farr explains, "tells a specific story . . .: the speaker's humility before her beautiful and brilliant subject; her fear to displease the subject; her desire to serve and loathing at being parted; her grief at the realization that any permanent or physical union is forbidden on earth; and her determination . . . to 'love the Cause that slew Me'" (Fr841; J925; Farr 189). The Master lyrics, then, "compose a narrative that . . . moves boldly into a different and new design. With a profound concentration on the conceit of Master's face and a vision of him as the source of light and salvation, the Master lyrics are Dickinson's love poems for a man" (190).

There were other painters of the time, according to Farr, "whose evocations of the suffering mind or soul evoke Emily Dickinson's," particularly Albert Pinkham Ryder (1847–1917) and the poet-painter Elihu Vedder (1836–1923). Ryder, who "attempted to disclose 'the ideal world that lay behind the illusory screen of the physical real world,'" (88); produced a painting, *The Lost Mind,* that Farr sees as having much in common with Dickinson's "I felt a Funeral, in my Brain" (Fr340; J280). Both painting and poem explore the experience of madness and the extremities of consciousness — motifs that become increasingly prevalent in the painting and literature of the period. Ryder also chose many of his subjects from the Bible, such as his *Death on a Pale Horse,* depicting Death as a skeleton wielding a scythe, evoking Revelation 6:8: "And I looked, and behold a pale horse; and his name that sat on him was Death" (Farr 88–89).[2]

---

[2] For a more extensive comparison between Dickinson and Ryder see chapter 6 ("Dickinson and Ryder: Immortality, Eternity, and the Reclusive Self") of Barbara Novak's *Voyages of the Self: Pairs, Parallels, and Patterns in American Art and Literature* (2007). Novak notes, for example, how both poet and painter (Dickinson in her "Two swimmers wrestled on the spar —" [Fr227; J201] and Ryder with his *Jonah*) fluctuate between mystic serenity and metaphysical anxiety (124).

Farr's study brings Emily Dickinson's iconographic imagination to the forefront. This is a poet, remember, who would rather experience vicariously the "bright impossibility" of a painting capable of evoking intense emotions than paint such a picture, as she asserts in her well-known "I would not paint — a picture —" (Fr348; J505). In the universe of a work of art, Dickinson seems to remind us, I would add, even despair can be "sumptuous." Farr calls our attention to a letter Dickinson wrote to her Norcross cousins (Fanny and Louisa) following the death of her mother in 1882, in which she reveals "her desire to immortalize the beautiful, sublime, and picturesque in a fashion that was 'surprising,' as she liked to put it: a manner and a style that were unconventional enough to teach and convince" (255):

> I believe we shall in some manner be cherished by our Maker — that the one who gave us this remarkable earth has the power still further to surprise. . . . Mother was very beautiful when she had died. Seraphs are solemn artists. The illumination that comes but once paused upon her features, and it seemed like hiding a picture to lay her in the grave. (L785; qtd. Farr 255)

God, for Dickinson, as Farr aptly states, "is the sublime artist. . . . Dickinson's mother becomes an artistic image — a 'face' — to be hidden like her daughter's" (255).

What Farr makes strikingly clear is that Dickinson in her poetry parallels the great American landscape painters like Cole in the way the horizon — the meeting point of landscape and sky — serves as "a point of fusion of this world and the next" (302). One might argue, of course, that one need not invoke the landscape painters to appreciate Dickinson's poetic iconography, that the essence of her poetic project is to use words as pigments;[3] but Farr's study, with its reproductions of key paintings (several in full color), helps us to better appreciate the poetry-painting analogy.[4]

Farr's most recent study, written with Louise Carter, *The Gardens of Emily Dickinson* (2004), intended for a general audience, is also edifying

---

[3] Cf. her comment to Higginson, "I never consciously touch a *paint*, mixed by another person —" (L271; emphasis added).

[4] In "Emily Dickinson and the Visual Arts" (1998) Farr notes how Dickinson's poems were associated with the visual arts by the earliest reviewers of her *Poems* (1890): "[O]ne critic [in the May 1891 issue of *Art Amateur*] compared Dickinson's poetry to . . . the painting of the German Lucas Cranach (1472–1553) . . . and to 'impressionist pictures' — probably French impressionism . . . to which Mabel Loomis Todd would compare Emily Dickinson's verse" (64–65; see also Buckingham 1989: 135, 237).

for Dickinson specialists because of the thoroughness with which Farr and Carter examine the extent to which flowers and gardening comprise not only the poet's aesthetic vision but her very way of life. Flowers ("posies") and poetry ("poesie") were for Dickinson analogues of each other, much the way paintings and poetry were. Commenting on the essential role flowers played in Dickinson's life and art (and indirectly pointing out the value of such cultural-context criticism for illuminating the poet's

> So important were flowers to Emily Dickinson, so knowledgeable was she about botany, that the key to a successful reading of an individual Dickinson lyric can depend on one's knowledge of the background and identity of a plant or flower or of weather and climatic conditions to which the poet may familiarly allude. (9)

As Farr and Carter show, examples of Dickinson's rich botanical knowledge, rendered artistically, abound. Especially fascinating are those poems in which that specialized knowledge is used to illuminate larger themes, as in the following seldom-discussed poem (Fr843; J978):

It bloomed and dropt, a Single Noon —
The Flower — distinct and Red —
I, passing, thought another Noon
Another in its stead

Will equal glow, and thought no more
But came another Day
To find the Species disappeared —
The Same Locality —

The Sun in place — no other fraud
On Nature's perfect+ Sum —   +General
Had I but lingered Yesterday —
Was my retrieveless blame —

Much Flowers of this and further Zones
Have perished in my Hands
For seeking its Resemblance+ —   +similitude
But unapproached it stands —

The single Flower of the Earth
That I, in passing by
Unconscious was — Great Nature's Face +   +was ignorant that Nature closed
Passed infinite by Me —+   +My Opportunity
                                          *Went infinite by Me —

In this garden setting the speaker reports having seen a brilliant red flower that commands her attention — yet, Farr and Carter tell us, "negligently, she passed it by . . . enabled to do so, perhaps, by the fact that it died as soon as it had bloomed." Farr and Carter then explain that while no flower can do this precisely, "there was indeed one flower grown by the Dickinsons that blooms for only one day and then drops from the stem, often in noontide heat: the daylily or *Hemerocallis*.[5] . . . The event becomes the . . . source of the speaker's grief and shame in the last three stanzas. It teaches her her own 'retrieveless blame,' blame that can never be lifted because the flower she passed by turns out to be 'The single Flower of the Earth'" (135–36).

Wishing to "augment" St. Armand's and Farr's studies by "grounding Dickinson's poems in their native territory," Elizabeth A. Petrino in *Emily Dickinson and Her Contemporaries: Women's Verse in America, 1820–1885* (1998) is convinced that despite — or perhaps because of — their distinctiveness, they place "into bold relief a profound connection with the underlying topics of women's verse and allows us to see both her and her female contemporaries differently" (8). For cultural critics the individual poet cannot be separated from her cultural milieu without severe injustice to both.

Petrino's "augmentation" of St. Armand's and Farr's studies is most fully realized in her chapter on Dickinson in relation to Lydia Sigourney and the tradition of the child elegy. Unlike her contemporaries Sigourney, Hannah Gould, Helen Hunt Jackson, Emma Alice Browne, and others who call attention to "the pious and exemplary character of the dying child" in their respective poems, Dickinson "expresses her dissatisfaction with the contemporary consolatory myth that the child enjoys a blissful existence after death" (56). In Emma Browne's "Measuring the Baby" (1883), for example, parents measure their child regularly until the child dies:

> Ah, me! In a darkened chamber,
>   With the sunshine shut away,
> Thro' tears that fell like a bitter rain,
>   We measured the boy to-day!
> And the little bare feet, that were dimpled
>   And sweet as a budding rose,
> Lay side by side together,
>   In the hush of a long repose!
> . . .
>   (qtd. Petrino, 66–67)

---

[5] Dickinson also may have been thinking of the flower's ephemeral nature, and, analogously, that of her poems, which perhaps are most essentially themselves as fleeting moments of beauty — bolts of melody that ought not be "fossilized" in print. See Richard Howard, "A Consideration of the Writings of Emily Dickinson" (1973). According to Howard, Dickinson wished to give her poetry an ephemeral quality. The role that flowers played in Dickinson's life supports this (86).

Dickinson, by contrast, "invokes the invitation and envoi of gravestone inscriptions in order to undercut the Victorian myth that we can expect a blissful reunion with the dead in heaven" (69). In the following elegy, for example, Dickinson places us in the mind of a dead child actually recollecting her experiences as she is being carried to the grave:

> 'Twas just this time, last year, I died.
> I know I heard the Corn,
> When I was carried by the Farms —
> It had the Tassels on —
> . . .
> I wondered which would miss me, least,
> And when Thanksgiving, came,
> If Father'd multiply the plates —
> To make an even Sum —
>
> And would it blur the Christmas glee
> My stocking hang too high
> For any Santa Claus to reach
> The altitude of me —
> . . .
> (Fr344; J445)

Unlike Browne's poem, which retells the baby's death from the point of view of her family, Dickinson's poem, written from the viewpoint of the dead child, gives us, according to Petrino, an insider's vision of the grave, a vision that shifts from memories of home life to thoughts of being reunited after death with those who are still alive (69).

Emily Dickinson and Her Contemporaries makes an important contribution toward understanding the poet in her cultural context, for it enables us to appreciate just how determined Dickinson was not to accept the comforting platitudes of conventional piety. Petrino reminds us that for many American writers of the nineteenth century, heaven was an actual physical place (96); but for Dickinson, heaven was not only a place she could not reach (Fr310; J239); she wasn't sure it was even a place at all: "Contentment's quiet Suburb — / Affliction cannot stay / In Acres — Its Location / Is Illocality —" (Fr824; J963; qtd. Petrino 97).

On the other hand, Petrino's study reveals that even though Dickinson rejected the bowdlerizing of women's verse in print, she also was shaped by it (208). This is not as paradoxical as it first seems: an artist must first immerse herself in the prevailing conventions in order to break away from them in a meaningful way. Petrino cites the example of "We play at Paste" (Fr282A; J320) to show that Dickinson herself was quite aware of this.

> We play at Paste —
> Till qualified, for Pearl —
> Then, drop the Paste —
> And deem ourself a fool —
>
> The Shapes — though — were similar —
> And our new Hands
> Learned *Gem*-tactics —
> Practising *Sands* —

A tension always exists between artistic convention and originality — a tension experienced by artist and audience alike. What Dickinson makes clear in the above poem — and what Elizabeth Petrino emphasizes so well in her monograph, is that no matter how innovative a poet is, she is always indebted to the poets who have preceded her.[6]

Dickinson's Sublimated Civil War

It has sometimes been thought that Dickinson did not devote much attention to the Civil War despite the fact that the war years coincided with her greatest poetic output; but as Shira Wolosky makes abundantly clear in her 1984 study *Emily Dickinson: A Voice of War*, the opposite is the case. Indeed, the poet's very sensibility is warlike in that it projects an apocalyptic fury against conventional theology and language. Thus, instead of particular battles or wounded soldiers — of battle in essence, of woundedness in essence; of the bitter paradox of knowing victory only in defeat that she captures in "Success," one of her best loved poems:[7] "Success is counted sweetest / By those who ne'er succeed. / To comprehend a nectar / Requires sorest need. . . ." (Fr112C; J67). Such a definition of victory, says Wolosky, is "a definition of its lack" (85), and she quotes Richard Wilbur, who had earlier realized that the increase in awareness of this darker sort of victory is, for Dickinson, "the better bargain" (1963: 40–41; qtd. Wolosky 85).

For Dickinson, Wolosky asserts, "the war raised pressing questions, continuous with and framing her profoundest concerns" (41). Many religious

---

[6] Petrino also makes clear that Dickinson's indebtedness included not just the predominant male writers of her day (especially Emerson) as Harold Bloom argues in *A Map of Misreading* (1975) but women writers as well (most notably, in America, Lydia Sigourney).

[7] "Success" was one of the mere dozen poems by Dickinson that was published during her lifetime — and it was published twice: in the *Brooklyn Daily Union*, April 27, 1864, and in Helen Hunt Jackson's "No Name" anthology, *A Masque of Poets* (1878).

thinkers of Dickinson's day, according to Wolosky, considered the Civil War part of the "millennial pattern and even that pattern's ultimate moment." Yet, like Melville, who asserted in *White Jacket* that "war almost makes blasphemers of the best of men" (qtd. Wolosky 48), Dickinson rejected the notion of war as part of a divine plan, as we see in "My Triumph lasted till the Drums / Had left the Dead alone / And then I dropped my Victory / And chastened stole along / To where the finished Faces / Conclusion turned on me / And then I hated Glory . . ." (Fr1212; J1227). Unlike Julia Ward Howe's "Battle Hymn of the Republic," which presupposes a divine plan — "where a 'Fiery gospel' is 'read' in 'burnished rows of Steel'" — Dickinson, as Wolosky states, rejected war "as a moment in sacred history from which point of view it would be retroactively just. She denounced suffering and death, even after victory" (51).

Wolosky's study, in contrast to St. Armand's or even Farr's, demonstrates the way a cultural phenomenon like war, tragic as it is, inevitably becomes a rich metaphorical resource for advancing the poet's sensibilities, her ongoing exploration of the role of divinity in the world, and in the face of human suffering.

Dickinson as Critic of Her Own Culture

In a quest similar to that of St. Armand and Farr, Domhnall Mitchell, in *Emily Dickinson: Monarch of Perception* (2000), "aims to amend the tendency to privatize Dickinson's literary documents and to look instead at how and why her poetry relates to the social spaces and languages that surround it" (2). First, Mitchell examines "the ways in which Dickinson negotiated with the historical, even when the historical appears to be absent from the writing." Three of the cultural spheres with which Dickinson "negotiates," according to Mitchell, are the railroads (as the most important and revolutionary form of transportation in her day) as well as horticulture, and, finally, domestic life. Thus, with regard to the first institutions, Mitchell reads Dickinson's amusing poem about the locomotive as an example of "an almost direct attempt at understanding a contemporary phenomenon" (8):

> I like to see it lap the Miles —
> And lick the Valleys up —
> And stop to feed itself at Tanks —
> And then — prodigious step
>
> Around a Pile of Mountains —
> And supercilious peer
> In Shanties — by the sides of Roads —
> And then a Quarry pare

> To fit its sides +   +Ribs
> And crawl between
> Complaining all the while
> In horrid — hooting stanza —
> ...
>   (Fr383; J585)

Mitchell shows how Dickinson's poetry engages the commerce, horticulture and home life of her day. One particularly fascinating topic he investigates is how Dickinson was influenced by the history of financial transactions surrounding the sale and purchase of the Homestead (74). Dickinson writes in a letter to Maria Whitney that "Consciousness is the only home of which we *now* know. That sunny adverb had been enough were it not foreclosed" (L 591; qtd. Mitchell 2000: 75). Mitchell cites the definition of "foreclose" from the copy of Webster's *An American Dictionary of the English Language* that Dickinson owned: "To foreclose a mortgage, in law, is to cut him off from his equity of redemption, or the power of redeeming the mortgaged premises, by a judgment of the court" (qtd. Mitchell 75). As Mitchell explains, "death resembles dispossession (and the traditional literary and scriptural image of the body as a temporary home enabled that notion) because it was the greatest imaginable equivalent to the devastation of one's personal and social identity" (75). Like Jean McClure Mudge (1975), Mitchell explores the way in which Dickinson makes use of the concepts of "house" and "home" in her poetry. Here is an example:

> Paradise is that old mansion
> Many owned before —
> Occupied by each an instant
> Then reversed the Door —
> Bliss is frugal of her Leases
> Adam taught her Thrift
> Bankrupt once through his excesses —
>   (Fr1144; J1119)

Allusion to Eden, Mitchell suggests, "structures the idiom of bankruptcy and gives the situation described . . . a historical and theological depth" (76).

Another way to assess an artist's aesthetic interaction with her culture is to recognize discrete stages of her development. Aliki Barnstone, in *Changing Rapture: Emily Dickinson's Poetic Development* (2006), rejects the longstanding assumption that Dickinson's poetry did not develop over the years, asserting that recognizing such development is necessary in order "to understand a poet's artistic and intellectual achievement" (2). Barnstone does not support this premise convincingly in my opinion. For one thing, what she means by "development" and how it ties into "achievement" is never clearly explained. It appears that Barnstone is really reinforcing St. Armand's premise that Dickinson's (or anyone else's) artistic genius cannot be fully understood or appreciated unless placed into its cultural context and unless its lines of influence, whether adoptive or reactionary, are carefully traced — but is that not a different argument? Be that as it may, Barnstone sees Dickinson's oeuvre passing through four stages of development:

- Externalized arguments with Calvinism through satire (6): poems that critique assertions by others — for example, "A science — so the Savants say / 'Comparative Anatomy' —" (Fr147; J100)
- Poems of "self-conversion" (9) wherein the struggle with Calvinism is internalized — represented by such poems as "There's a certain Slant of light" (Fr320; J258) and "After Great Pain" (Fr372; J341)
- Poems that shift in focus "from Calvinism to Transcendentalism" — what Barnstone terms "the adventure of the self" (13), embracing "the subjectivity of perception and the possibility of relatedness that subjectivity creates" (21), typified by such poems as "There is a Zone whose even Years" (Fr1020; J1056)
- Letter-poems that erase the distinction between poetry and prose. Here Barnstone calls attention to the "editorial decision to excise portions of letters in order to create poems" — a failure to perceive the document in question as a letter-poem rather than as a letter with an embedded poem.

These stages do serve as a useful template for studying the spectrum of Dickinson's oeuvre, despite the fact that Barnstone does not provide us with a clear timeline for the alleged development. The problem of course is overlap. Dickinson may not have written "letter-poems" in the fashion of her later years, but one could nevertheless argue that all of Dickinson's letters blur the distinction between letter (understood to be prose) and poem.

Reconstructing the Culture of Reading in Dickinson's Day

A history of reading includes not only the places where reading materials were consumed (privately, publicly, within the home, in schools, and so on) but the way in which ideas from reading were disseminated and — in Emily Dickinson's case — assimilated into her poetry. In *Emily Dickinson's Shakespeare* (2006) Páraic Finnerty aims to go beyond the "cultural truisms" that take for granted Shakespeare's significance for Dickinson "to discover the central and constitutive role reading Shakespeare had in

Dickinson's life" — a daunting task, in that Finnerty is obliged to reconstruct "the social and cultural milieu in which Dickinson read Shakespeare in order to clarify her actual references to reading him and so as to speculate further on her attitude toward her preferred author" (3). And reconstruct it he does, by examining the way Dickinson draws from her culture's regard for Shakespeare to help convey her epistolary messages. For example, Finnerty cites an 1873 letter from Dickinson to Franklin Benjamin Sanborn (an editor at large and columnist with the *Springfield Republican,* which had published several of her poems by this time) in which she continued their ongoing conversation about books. Dickinson suddenly turns her attention to Sanborn's apparent request to see more of her poems, and in so doing invokes Shakespeare in a curious way:

> Thank you, Mr Sanborn. I am glad there are Books.
> They are better than Heaven for that is unavoidable while one may miss these.
> Had I a trait you would accept I should be most proud, though he has had his Future who has found Shakespeare —
>
> E — Dickinson
> (L402)

As Finnerty sees it, Dickinson here "contrasts her level of creativity with Shakespeare's overachieving accomplishments. Her reluctance to submit a poem is framed as a confirmation that Shakespeare supersedes all prospective authors, herself included" (78). She also seems to be setting herself apart from the prevailing views of her contemporary critics (Sanborn among them), "who sought a different future for American literature — as a literature distinct from its English counterpart" (78). That is to say, Dickinson regards Shakespeare as having pre-empted any future writer's opportunity to exceed him in brilliance and humanistic vision.

Finnerty wisely supplements his analysis of Shakespeare as cultural capital for Emily Dickinson and her times with commentary on Dickinson's strategies for appropriating passages from favorite plays such as *Othello* and *Anthony and Cleopatra* into her letters and poems to enhance her own literary effects. For example, Finnerty notes that in "We like a Hairbreadth 'scape / It tingles in the Mind / Far after Act or Accident / Like paragraphs of Wind" (Fr1247; J1175) Dickinson is evoking Othello's ability to enthrall Desdemona with stories of narrow escapes. Dickinson's speaker, like Othello, endures "hair-breadth 'scapes i' the imminent deadly breach; / Of being taken by the insolent foe / And sold to slavery, of my redemption thence" (I.iii.136–37). "The allusion," explains Finnerty, "compliments the gothic in her poem, evoking the exhilaration of narrow escape from the frightening" (132).

In *Beyond Criticism* (1953) the poet Karl Shapiro asserts, audaciously, that culture and art are enemies, "for Culture is what is done with Art . . .

the harnessing of Art for power and energy." The message for the poet is clear: "If the poet is to be rescued from the world of Culture and the world of History he must first be restored to himself as poet alone. Only then will he be able to view the world as he sees it, and not as he is told to see it" (2–3). How would a cultural critic respond to such a charge? Jane Donahue Eberwein, for one, notes in her 1998 article "Dickinson's Local, Global, and Cosmic Perspectives," how the poet "drew strength" from her female friends as well as from "the sentimental women's culture of her time" (38). Eberwein also quotes Joan Burbick, who argues in her 1980 article "'One Unbroken Company': Religion and Emily Dickinson" that Dickinson's spiritual pilgrimage "is more relational than individualistic" and Shira Wolosky, who argues in her 1984 *Emily Dickinson: A Voice of War* that Dickinson's poetry "can be seen as profoundly engaged in problems of the external world and aggressively so" (both qtd. Eberwein 39). The most important thing Dickinson drew from her culture, Eberwein concludes, "was a searching mind — and the resilience not to be overcome by mysteries that eluded religion, science, and the law"; moreover, that "searching mind" maintained its uncompromising integrity by demanding "experiential evidence in all areas" (42). Dickinson, we could say, through her vocation as poet, was demonstrating a new and higher standard of moral and ethical, not just artistic, integrity.

6: Probing Dickinson's Poetic Spirituality

> *"Faith" is a fine invention*
> *When Gentlemen can see —* (Fr202; J185)
>
> One finds prayerful utterance throughout
> Dickinson's poems.
> — Jane Donahue Eberwein, *Dickinson:*
> *Strategies of Limitation*
>
> *Cotton Mather would have burnt her for a witch.*
> — Allen Tate, "Emily Dickinson"

STUDYING EMILY DICKINSON in cultural context brings her "flood subject" of immortality (and all of the spiritual motifs associated with it) into focus. One does not spend much time with Dickinson's poetry before realizing that it is infused with rich and complex spiritual themes — themes that have commanded the exclusive attention of several Dickinson scholars — hence the need for this separate chapter.

Dickinson's Spiritual Sensibility: Tradition and Innovation

Elisa New, in her 1993 book *The Regenerate Lyric: Theology and Innovation in American Poetry*, building from Yvor Winters's theory that American poetry is essentially about "human isolation in a foreign universe" (qtd. New 2), regards American poetry "as the religious center of an already religiocentric literature," fueled by "an experimental Calvinism not so easily dislodged by Unitarian, Transcendentalist, or Romantic forces" (2). If "Puritanism released the energy of uncertainty," as John Robinson states in *Emily Dickinson: Looking to Canaan* (1986: 36), then Dickinson uses that energy to stage a drama of the soul as it struggles to bridge the unbridgeable gulf between the reality of death and the promise of salvation for the undisclosed elect.

As a matter of principle, Dickinson's earliest academic critics generally overlooked or underplayed the influence of cultural forces, including religious ones, upon Dickinson's art (Allen Tate being an exception). But as Alfred Habegger writes in his biography, "One of the biggest mistakes we make with Dickinson is to detach her from the religious currents of the 1850s, without which she could not have become herself" (310). I suppose one could counter-argue that it would be a mistake only if the *primary* goal is to situate Emily Dickinson in American culture rather than to illuminate her intrinsic poetic artistry. In any case, as Habegger suggests, perhaps the most important of the religious currents of Dickinson's day "was the growing tendency within orthodoxy to question the primacy, even the necessity, of a rationally articulated faith" (310).

According to Habegger (311–13), two major Protestant thinkers of the period were associated with this new theological questioning: Horace Bushnell and Edwards A. Park. Bushnell, perhaps the most intellectual and innovative theologian of his time, reflected on the inherent shortcomings of speech in *God in Christ* (1849). "Words are at best 'hints, or images'; ultimate truth must be approached through repeated *poetic attempts*" (310; emphasis added). Habegger points out, intriguingly, that Dickinson's poems "sometimes express a kind of Bushnellian relief at the abandonment of propositional analysis, the 'easing' turn from theology to art" (311). He cites as a case in point Fr797B; J988:

> The Definition of Beauty is
> That Definition is none —
> Of Heaven, easing Analysis,
> Since Heaven and He are one.

Bushnell wished to fuse spiritual life with aesthetic life. Indeed, if we look at some of his essays, such as "Preliminary Dissertation on the Nature of Language as Related to Thought and Spirit," we come upon assertions like this: "The scriptures of God, in providing a clothing for religious truth, have little to do with mere dialectics, much to do with the freer creations of poetry" (*Selected Writings*, 51). When Philip F. Gura, writing on the relationship between language and theology in *The Wisdom of Words: Language, Theology, and Literature in the New England Renaissance* (1981), notes that Bushnell wanted people "to pierce the rotten diction that clotted most religious controversies and to realize that the truest apprehensions of religion were those that consisted of an aesthetic understanding, not merely an assent to emotionally barren dogma" (58), he could just as well be writing about Emily Dickinson.

In a similar vein, Edwards Park argues that religious truths cannot be captured by abstract terms of logic but "can be approximated only by symbol and hyperbole" (312). "No contemporary thinker," Habegger says, "came closer than the liberal Trinitarian Bushnell to formulating the linguistic rationale for Dickinson's poetic vocation" (311).

One of the first academic critics to pay close attention to Dickinson's religious milieu was Allen Tate. In "Emily Dickinson" (1932) Tate points out that Puritan theocracy "permeated, as it could never have done in England, a whole society. It gave final, definite meaning to life.... It gave — and this is the significance for Emily Dickinson ... an heroic proportion and a tragic mode to the experience of the individual" (17). Like her theological forebears Jonathan Edwards and Cotton Mather, Emily Dickinson attains, in Tate's view, "mastery of the world by rejecting the world." Moreover, with regard to the enemy that was nature, Tate argues, Dickinson scrutinized the character of this enemy more deeply than the others. Her symbol for nature, was death, and her weapon against death was the "dumb-show of the puritan theology led by redemption and Immortality" (20).

If Tate portrays Dickinson as a Puritan rebel, Sister Mary James Power in her 1943 monograph *In the Name of the Bee: the Significance of Emily Dickinson* portrays her as a Catholic mystic, a notion first suggested by Kathérine Brégy in her essay, "Emily Dickinson: A New England Anchoress" (1924; see Lubbers 179).[1] "It delights us to find ... that the substance of Emily's creed was that of the Angelic Doctor: Love," Power writes, and she quotes, as an example of Dickinson's "translation of his Purpose," Fr980, J917:

> Love — is anterior to Life —
> Posterior — to Death —
> Initial of creation, and
> The Exponent of Earth —[2]

However, much of what Power calls attention to in Emily Dickinson's poetry seems more non-denominationally Christian than Catholic — she argues, for example, that Dickinson enjoyed a "delightful intimacy with the Supreme Ruler of the Universe" (10), which she finds suggested in the poem "It was too late for Man" (Fr689; J623):

> It was too late for Man —
> But early, yet, for God —
> Creation — impotent to help —
> But Prayer — remained — Our Side
>
> How excellent the Heaven —
> When Earth — cannot be had —
> How hospitable — then — the face
> Of our old neighbor, God —

---

[1] Neither Lubbers nor other critics before 1960 have treated Power's study adequately, hence my calling attention to it here.

[2] Power actually quoted the version of the poem wherein the editors substituted "breath" for "Earth" — the version used in editions published between 1896 and 1937.

Power adds in her concluding reflections that "renunciation had . . . not only chastened [Dickinson's] natural love but sublimated it. Her response to sacrifice had supernaturalized the natural in her heart" (138).

Power is most convincing when she addresses Dickinson's idea of the sacramental in nature:

> Symbols of the Sacraments she did see around her, for, like Gerard Manley Hopkins, she sensed news of God in everything. Those days of sudden mildness in October . . ., Emily looked upon significantly as 'the sacrament of summer days' [Fr122; J310], outward signs reminding her of the Sacrament of Love of which she would eagerly partake: the consecrated bread and the immortal wine. (31)

It is tempting to regard Power's study as the heartfelt but unwarranted effort of a Catholic nun to present Dickinson as a Catholic poet, but I do not see that as the case — at least, not as Power's primary objective. I would argue instead that she is calling attention to the way in which Dickinson appropriates Christian symbolism of a particularly Catholic nature to suit her artistic purposes. Unlike Hopkins, Dickinson does not envision the world or the human soul from a consistently Catholic viewpoint throughout her oeuvre. Reading Power's study, then, is rewarding because it calls attention to a facet of Dickinson's complex spiritual vision we might not otherwise detect.

More recently, Angela Conrad in her book *The Wayward Nun of Amherst* (2000) places Dickinson in the context of medieval Catholic mysitcal women such as Hildegard of Bingen and Catherine of Siena. Because they claim intimate contact with the Divine, Conrad states, these Catholic mystics are able "to avoid the forbidden category of rationalism. . . . The ecstatic life sanctifies and elevates their message" (xiv).

Similar to Tate's perception of Dickinson as a Puritan rebel is Thomas H. Johnson's in his 1955 *Emily Dickinson: An Interpretive Biography*.[3] Johnson cites Dickinson's "resentment against the dogmas in which she had been trained" (234) — for example, the doctrine of infant damnation — as is evident in poems like "Far from Love the Heavenly Father / Leads the Chosen Child, / Oftener through Realm of Briar / Than the Meadow mild . . ." (Fr1032; J1021) and "How happy is the little Stone / That rambles in the Road alone, / And doesn't care about careers / And Exigencies never fears — . . . Fulfilling absolute Decree / In casual simplicity" (Fr1570B; J1510). As Johnson notes of this latter poem's concluding lines,

---

[3] The works of Tate, Johnson, Whicher, and Chase, although published before 1960, need to be discussed here because they lay the groundwork for important later studies by Gelpi and others.

Dickinson is ironically suggesting "that inanimateness alone can be 'happy,' because it alone fulfills absolute decree" (235).

It is interesting to compare Johnson's perspective with that of Dickinson's earlier biographer, George Frisbie Whicher, who, writing in 1938, sees the poet as shaping precepts from Scripture and the Puritan tradition simply for artistic purposes rather than being shaped by them. Even though Dickinson, like most New Englanders of her day, was "saturated in the Bible from early childhood," Whicher argues that she nonetheless "delighted to rearrange [Biblical passages] to suit her private occasions. . . . She took liberties that would have shocked an earlier Puritan. The sayings of Holy Writ were not sacred to her unless they proved true when tested by her own experience" (154).

Dickinson's "experimental Calvinism" — to use Elisa New's useful term (which is not as oxymoronic as it sounds!) — can also be discerned in the way she appropriates divine grace. Richard Chase observes in his 1951 book *Emily Dickinson*, she uses words like "glory" or "dominion" to convey divine grace (for instance, in poems such as "Glory is that bright tragic thing / That for an instant / Means Dominion," Fr1700; J1660). Chase notes that for Dickinson "Dominion" "is a resonant word. Its emphasis is particularly Puritan, since the Puritans stressed, above all God's attributes, His sovereignty. By derivation the word is related to 'domestic,' and in the words 'dominion' and 'home' one discerns the particular kind of regeneration which our poet conceives as being immediately bequeathed by grace" (148). I find this to be a major insight into Dickinson's poetic vision. Her ability to find in religion and mythology domestic analogues — in Chase's words, "to invest the domestic lot of women . . . with a structure of imaginative meaning" (150) is unparalleled in American literature.

Tate, Whicher, Chase, and Johnson set the stage for Albert J. Gelpi's perceptive study, *Emily Dickinson: The Mind of the Poet* (1965). Gelpi calls attention to the peculiar modern flavoring Dickinson gives to conventional Puritan notions of human depravity by extracting strength from them, as we see in lines like "The stimulus of Loss makes most Possession mean" from a letter to Sue written in 1871 (L364), and "Satisfaction — is the Agent / Of Satiety — / Want — a quiet Comissary / For Infinity —" (Fr984; J1036). "In other words," Gelpi explains regarding this poem, "man's littleness was, in a strange way, the condition for his greatness, and his limitations pointed him toward infinity" (71). In this context, according to Gelpi, Dickinson seems more modernistic in her thinking than Emerson, "who would have found [such thinking] morbid" — coming closer in spirit to Nietzsche, who "defined the tragic sense as the assertion of the will to live in the face of death and the *inexhaustible joy* which that assertion releases" (71, 72; emphasis added).

Building upon the Dickinson-as-Puritan-renegade premise, Karl Keller (1979) cleverly characterizes Dickinson's use of Puritan teleology "as a ground to dance on" (7). What is more, Dickinson's spirituality-probing dance is a macabre one — the dance of an artistic consciousness that expresses, at one time or another (and sometimes simultaneously), bafflement and wit, rebelliousness, anguish, terror, childlike petulance and sublime mysticism. Keller compares Dickinson to her Puritan predecessor Anne Bradstreet, and in doing so helps us acquire a keener sense of Dickinson's indebtedness to, as well as rebellion against, her Puritan heritage. It instilled in her "the devotional need to discover her self," the means by which "she advances to her glory, which (ultimately) is a glory of language" (28). Moreover, Puritanism encouraged rebellion, as Dickinson herself recognized in a letter to Josiah Holland: "Unless we become as Rogues, we cannot enter the Kingdom of Heaven" (L715; qtd. Keller, 29).

Dickinson as Unorthodox Christian Mystic

Louise Bogan, in her 1963 article "A Mystical Poet," takes a somewhat different stance toward Dickinson's spirituality. Although Bogan regards Dickinson as possessing "deeply religious feeling," she notes that that feeling is unorthodox, "outside the bounds of dogma." Bogan identifies Dickinson's particular brand of spirituality, her "power to say the unsayable — to hint of the unknowable" — with the power of the seer. According to Bogan, Dickinson's "lyrical notation is so precise, so fine and moves so closely in unison with her mind, that she is continually striking out aphorisms, as is usual in mystical writing from Plotinus to Blake" (143). Bogan's observations hark back to one of the earliest substantive critical commentaries on record, Martha Hale Shackford, in her essay, "The Poetry of Emily Dickinson," published in *The Atlantic Monthly* in January 1913,[4] calls attention to Dickinson's essential mystical spirituality:

> The poems taken in their entirety are a surprising and impressive revelation of poetic attitude and of poetic method in registering spiritual experiences. . . . Hers is the record of a soul endowed with unceasing activity in a world not material, but one where concrete facts are the cherished revelation of divine significances. (80, 81)

Along with a spirituality-probing "dance," however, one can discern throughout Dickinson's poetic canon a profound grappling with doctrine. Shira Wolosky, amplifying and qualifying David Porter's assertion that

---

[4] Reprinted in *The Recognition of Emily Dickinson: Selected Criticism since 1890*, ed. Caesar R. Blake and Carlton F. Wells (Ann Arbor: U of Michigan P, 1968).

Dickinson appropriated hymn meter as "a constant occasion for irony" (1966: 55), makes this important observation:

> A surprising number of Dickinson poems seem written in direct response to particular Watts hymns.[5] ... [Her] relation to Watts is not simply parodic. The hymnal frame of so much Dickinson verse asserts a genuine and profound effort to accept doctrines that she cannot, however, help but question, leading her in turn to question her own doubts. (Wolosky 1988: 215)

Wolosky then shows how particular poems "rais[e] questions concerning the relation between hymnal figures and the truths they are meant to convey ... [working] in two directions — from theology to tropes and from tropes to theology," thereby revealing the way in which the hymnal figures and tropes "not only express but even structure the doctrines they assert" (215). Dickinson's "Faith is the Pierless Bridge" (Fr978; J915), is a good example of this raising of questions by moving from tropes (faith as evidence; faith as a bridge not needing support) to the underlying theology. Here is Watts's hymn:

> Faith is the brightest evidence
> Of things beyond our sight;
> Breaks through the clouds of flesh and sense,
> And dwells in heavenly light.
>
> It sets times past in present view,
> Brings distant prospects home —
> Of things a thousand years ago
> Or thousand years to come.
>
> By faith we know the worlds were made,
> By God's almighty word;
> Abra'am to unknown countries led,
> By faith obey'd the Lord.
>
> He sought a city fair and high,
> Built by th'eternal hands;
> And faith assures us, though we die,
> That heavenly building stands.

---

[5] *The Psalms, Hymns, and Spiritual Songs of the Rev. Isaac Watts, D. D.* (1834).

And here is Dickinson's "troping" of Watts's hymn:

> Faith is the Pierless Bridge
> Supporting what We see
> Unto the Scene that We do not
> Too slender for the eye.
> It bears the Soul as bold
> As it were rocked in Steel
> With Arms of Steel and either side —
> It joins — behind the Veil
> To what, could We presume
> The Bridge would cease to be
> To Our far, vacillating Feet
> A first Necessity.

Both of these poems put forth definitions of faith taken from Hebrews 11 as a pathway from the visible to the invisible, Wolosky explains. But whereas Watts focuses on the objects of faith and how they reveal an image of heaven, Dickinson focuses on the phenomenon of faith itself, "the fact that it supports the soul, its status as means" (219). The image of a pierless bridge is as vivid as it is paradoxical, transcending any kind of rational definition of faith. Eberwein also observes that this poem sets a complex metaphor equal to a logical definition, and in so doing finds "a way to articulate a mystery" (1985: 146).

The Influence of Transcendentalism on Dickinson

To what extent did Emersonian Transcendental Romanticism influence Dickinson's Puritan-Calvinist worldview? Charles Anderson, citing "Essential oils are wrung —" (Fr772; J675), explains that "Poetry and perfume are not natural products 'expressed by Suns alone.' They are manufactured by man's cunning artifice" (1960: 66). According to Anderson, such a view contrasts dramatically with the Transcendentalists' theory of composition. Emerson, for example, captured this idea of organicism by asserting that poems should grow like corn or melons in the sun (66). William R. Sherwood goes a step further in *Circumference and Circumstance* (1968), noting that Dickinson's finding the spirit of God manifest in the natural world recalls the Puritan rather than the Emersonian Transcendentalist tradition:

> ... Emily Dickinson never made Emerson's leap in logic from the premise that God operates in nature to the conclusion that God and nature were identical. Early in her career she had tested this hypothesis and discarded it. And at no time did she share the transcenden-

talists' egalitarian belief that the ability to read the book of nature was
an attribute of the species and not a grant by the divine. (194)

Actually, as Cynthia Griffin Wolff makes clear in her 1986 intellectual biography, *Emily Dickinson,* Dickinson undermined the Puritan vision of nature as readily as the Romantic one. Dickinson dutifully reads the Book of Nature — a Calvinist directive designed to provide the scrutinizer with an intimate sense of God's workings in the world — but uncovers "a system of falsehoods" (283). Alluding to "Some things that fly there be —" (Fr68; J89), Wolff calls attention to the poem's cryptic and desolate last three lines: "There are that resting, rise. / Can I expound the skies? /How still the Riddle lies!" — noting that Christ, who had assured us that those resting would rise, is gone, and because the speaker finds it impossible to "'expound the skies' . . . the promise of Resurrection lies 'still' — corpse-like." Wolff adds: "Is the 'Riddle' the all-too-real dead body, waiting to be magically resurrected from decay into that new life? How . . . lifelessly it lies in the ground! Is the 'Riddle' the promise of Redemption? How . . . persistently and enduringly, it 'lies' and deludes us!" (289).[6]

Wendy Martin, in her *An American Triptych: Anne Bradstreet, Emily Dickinson, Adrienne Rich* (1984), gives an even more thorough point-by-point contrast between Emerson and Dickinson:

> Dickinson perceives the universe in terms of patterned wholes, as resonating fullness rather than sequential opposites; there is no need for the dialectic of unity and variety; no need to strive to "attain the universe," as Emerson writes in *Representative Men* and *Nature.* . . . Emerson believes in limitless possibility; Dickinson is concerned with unfolding moments. While Emerson struggles to rise above nature, Dickinson remains grounded. . . . For Emerson, death is "the reality that will not dodge us," but for Dickinson it is the cessation of life: "That it will not come again / Is what makes life so sweet" (Fr1761; J1741). (122)

Martin even sees Emerson and Dickinson as representing "two modes of consciousness, the linear and the holistic respectively" — a dichotomy I find rather too limited to be useful. While it is true that, as Martin says,

---

[6] For a discussion of the way Dickinson's spirituality encompasses not only evangelical Christianity but also British and American late Romanticism, including the "natural religion" of scientist-theologians such as Edward Hitchcock (president of Amherst College, where he was also professor of geology, and the author of books such as *The Religion of Geology,* 1851), see Richard E. Brantley, *Experience and Faith: The Late-Romantic Imagination of Emily Dickinson* (2004). Brantley writes: "As Dickinson triangulates the open mind, pure soul, and warm heart of Anglo-American sensibility, she generates Romantic meaning and finds Romantic truth" (21).

Dickinson "regarded the unfolding present as infinite" — an "unbounded, nonlinear, timeless mode [which] parallels the phenomenon of egolessness or being outside of oneself — literally, ecstasy" (122–23), as is evident in "Take all away from me, but leave me Ecstasy" (Fr1671B; J1640), Emerson also exhibits many ecstatic moments. Consider, for example, the words immediately preceding the oft-caricatured "transparent eyeball" passage from *Nature* (1836), for example: "Standing on the bare ground, — my head bathed by the blithe air, and uplifted into infinite space, — *all mean egotism vanishes*" (193; emphasis added). Or consider this passage from "Circles" (1841): "Our life is an apprenticeship to the truth, that around every circle another can be drawn; that there is no end in nature, but every end is a beginning . . . There are no fixtures in nature. The universe is fluid and volatile." (302). These are scarcely the words of a linear thinker.

Rogue Preachers

Yet another way of looking at Dickinson's relationship to New England Puritanism is to consider its own "romantic" tendencies taking place in the mid-nineteenth century. We know through her letters that Dickinson was fascinated by preachers who dared to break away from orthodox Calvinist strictures. David S. Reynolds, in *Beneath the American Renaissance* (1988), a richly detailed survey of the subversive undercurrents in nineteenth-century American culture, observes that "[m]any of the central tensions in Emily Dickinson's poetry result from the collision between the old and the new sermon styles" (31). Reynolds calls attention to the fact that the young Emily and her brother Austin had to sneak-read books that dared to depart from rigorous adherence to the faith, as their father forbade them. One such book was Longfellow's novel, *Kavanagh* (1849), about an imaginative, handsome young preacher who replaces one not nearly as dynamic. Reynolds notes that Dickinson mentioned the novel frequently in her letters, because she felt a kinship with Alice Archer, the novel's heroine, a somber, dreamy girl who expresses her infatuation for Kavanagh in poetic visions, similar to the way that Emily herself "may have been driven to a kind of poetic frenzy by her unrequited passion for a real-life Kavanagh, the real-life Rev. Charles Wadsworth" (31). Reynolds's characterization of Dickinson's probable response to Wadsworth makes excellent sense: if indeed she felt any sort of passion for Wadsworth, it was a *sublimated* passion, one that she channeled into her art. As with her spiritual experiences in the larger sense, absence and denial strengthened her rather than debilitated her.

Another way to characterize Dickinson's attraction to Wadsworth is to regard her approach to religion as a "toughminded and resolutely determined 'irreverence,'" which is how Benjamin Lease regards it in his 1990 *Emily Dickinson's Readings of Men and Books: Sacred Surroundings* (4). It is also quite likely that Dickinson had heard the Rev. Wadsworth preach at the Arch Street Presbyterian Church when she visited Philadelphia in 1855 as guests of her old Amherst friends the Colemans (Lyman Coleman had been the Principal of Amherst Academy when Emily was a student there). She might also have had access to his published sermons, occasionally published in pamphlet form.

One of Wadsworth's sermons, "The Gospel Call," contains an italicized passage from Revelation 22:17, which, according to Benjamin Lease, is one that "Emily knew and loved" (6):

> ... the Church below, Christ's witness unto the world ... cries, "Come, come!" and the Church above, with the rustling of white robes and the sweeping of golden harps, cries, "Come, come!" And the angels of heaven, lo! rank above rank, the immortal Principalities, as they circle the eternal throne, they have caught up the sound and cry, "come, come!" ... "*And the Spirit and the Bride say, Come; and let him that heareth say, Come; and let him that is athirst come,* and whosoever will, let him take the water of life freely!"

Lease speculates that poem Fr381; J431 might be a direct response to this sermon, or to Wadsworth himself: "Me — come! My dazzled face / Is such a shining place! . . ."

Liberal, imaginative (that is, Romantic) sermonizing permeated New England life. "To understand a great and good being," William Ellery Channing reasoned in his 1828 sermon "Likeness to God," "we must have the seeds of the same excellence . . . God becomes a real being to us in proportion as His own nature is unfolded within us" (55). In the young America of Channing's day, with the memory of British tyranny still a part of the collective psyche, it is not surprising that Unitarianism took root, and that more rigorous Trinitarian sects such as Calvinism would acquire new life through more daring and imaginative interpretations of doctrine. Channing's declaration that "We cannot bow before a being, however great and powerful, who governs tyrannically" ("Unitarian Christianity," 39) was echoed by the younger generation of preachers who sought to reconcile spirituality with imagination. These included Henry Ward Beecher, who delivered a lecture titled "Imagination" in Amherst in 1851, and Edwards A. Park whom Dickinson heard give a sermon on Judas, as evidenced by her mention of him in a letter to Austin dated November 21, 1853 (L142):

> We had such a splendid sermon from that Prof Park — I never heard anything like it, and dont expect to again, till we stand at the great white throne ... The students and chapel people all came, to our

church, and it was very full, and still — so still, the buzzing of a fly would have boomed like a cannon. And when it was all over, and that wonderful man sat down, people stared at each other, and looked as wan and wild, as if they had seen a spirit, and wondered they had not died. How I wish you had heard him. (ref. Reynolds 32; Leyda I, 287; Habegger 312)

Emily Dickinson's Conversion Experience

As scholars have shown, not only did energetic and innovative religious expression permeate New England life, it permeated Emily Dickinson's personal life, although critics disagree as to the manner and degree of its influence on her art. Writing in 1968, William R. Sherwood goes so far as to claim that her outpouring of poems in 1862 represented nothing less than a religious conversion —

> and that it was precisely the variety of conversion that both her inclinations and her traditions had prepared her for and against which she had fought so vigorously at Mary Lyon's Seminary . . . in 1848. What happened to her in 1862 . . . was what all true Puritans, Edward Dickinson included, wanted to happen to them: to discover that one had been elected to receive the grace of God. (138)

Emily Dickinson's conversion had been prefaced for a dozen years or more, in other words, by resistance and rebellion against what she had referred to in a letter to Higginson as an "Eclipse" she saw the rest of her family addressing (L261) — that is, praying to a God they think they know, whose nature is obscured, ironically, by pre-established opinion. Sherwood calls attention to several poems from 1862 that embody this conversion experience. Consider "Like Flowers, that heard the news of Dews / But never deemed the dripping prize / Awaited their — low Brows —" (Fr361; J513), which sets up an extended analogy between the unexpected gifts of grace in nature in the first four stanzas — triplets, intriguingly, quite uncommon for Dickinson, as if she is alluding to the Trinity[7] — and the unexpected gift of heavenly grace in human life in the concluding stanza:

> The Heaven — unexpected come,
> To Lives that thought the Worshipping
> A too presumptuous Psalm —

---

[7] Cf. "These are the days when birds come back" (Fr122; J130), also a poem about faith.

The conversion experience is described even more intensely and intimately in "To my small Hearth His fire came — / And all my House aglow / Did fan and rock, with sudden light — . . ." (Fr703; J638).

Sherwood also regards the so-called "marriage poems" as religious in essence, pointing out that it is not unusual to use secular marriage or coronation rituals to represent the soul's conversion. Many passages from the Book of Revelations could have suggested these images; they were the customary tropes that Puritan culture used to represent salvation (148).

Jane Donahue Eberwein (1985) sees Dickinson's body of work as embodying a quest "spanning the cavernous gap between limitation and boundlessness" — recognizing this quest "as an implicitly religious action" (17). The quest takes the shape of an ongoing drama in which the protagonist — an anti-hero of sorts ("the wren, the gnat, the slightest figure in the house" [19]) seeks empowerment from its limitation, rather than in spite of it. In what Eberwein refers to as Dickinson's "habit of renunciation" — a movement *away* from selfhood, from autobiographical construction, we discover a poet whose intense probing, defining, and re-defining of the mortal sphere has the effect of heightening her sense of the "Not-Me," to use Emerson's language. Eberwein conceives a category of Dickinson's poems she calls "prayer-poems," by which she means not just poems about praying, as in "I prayed at first, a little Girl" (Fr546; J576) — which can be seen as conveying the poet's own progression from naïve childish praying to the much more intense and probing prayers of her adulthood — but poems that are themselves prayers. Examples of the latter include the satiric "Papa above!" (Fr151B; J61) and especially "My Maker — let me be / Enamored most of thee — / But nearer this / I more should miss —" (Fr1463C; J1403). Eberwein writes, "she was ironically praying for the chance to retain a circumferential barrier between herself and God even while keeping a sort of communication open" (258). Eberwein ultimately regards all of Dickinson's poems as prayers:

> If one discounts the apparatus of prayer and looks instead to its substance, one finds prayer utterance throughout Emily Dickinson's poems — especially her thankful celebrations of life, consciousness, and beauty, her reflections on evanescence and eternity, her probings at circumference to communicate with the force beyond it. (259)

Eberwein quotes Richard B. Sewall's speculation that Dickinson "wrote her poems in much the same spirit that her devout contemporaries prayed in" (Eberwein 259), adding that in so doing Dickinson was "performing a daily ritual of spiritual redirection and refreshment."

Critical attention to Dickinson as a spiritual poet (in the sense that her grappling with human situations can be characterized as spiritual — which in one sense makes her more of a *meta*-spiritual poet) continues to this day, rivaling and sometimes interacting with textual, feminist, and cultural-context scholarship. Three book-length studies, published within the past ten years, fall within this approach: Roger Lundin's *Emily Dickinson and the Art of Belief* (1998), James McIntosh's *Nimble Believing: Dickinson and the Unknown* (2000), and John Delli Carpini's *Poetry as Prayer: Emily Dickinson* (2002).

Lundin considers Dickinson to be "one of the major religious thinkers of her age" (3) — not just because of her deep knowledge of the Bible and Christianity, or her adaptation of the church hymn as the basic template for her poetry — but because she "comprehended more fully than most people in her day how much the human mind contributes to the *process* of belief" (emphasis added). Lundin approaches Dickinson's life as a kind of pilgrimage from the "naïve blind faith" of childhood through her struggles to reconcile faith with reason, along the way "trac[ing] the trajectory of God's decline" (4) in an age when Charles Lyell and Charles Darwin were revolutionizing ideas of time, of the natural world, and most of all of human beings as biological organisms that were no longer special creations apart from the rest of life. One can see evidence of the way the new sciences were undermining traditional faith in poems like "So much of Heaven has gone from Earth / That there must be a Heaven" (Fr1240; J1228). Dickinson, then, in Lundin's view, "considered the central human dilemma to be a problem of knowledge rather than a matter of the will.... [S]he came to regard ignorance as a greater problem than sin." In this regard she resembled the Romantics. However, Lundin goes on to explain, "Dickinson could not accept the romantics' optimism about the self" — about the limitations of mortal being — and quotes Gelpi's memorable description of Dickinson's "peculiar burden," which was "to be a Romantic poet with a Calvinist's sense of things; to know transitory ecstasy in a world tragically fallen and doomed" (Gelpi 1965: 91; qtd. Lundin 25).

McIntosh, by comparison, wishes to approach the poet's "religious imagination in its dynamic diversity" (35); he is more concerned with the psychological complexities of Dickinson's "nimble believing" — a kind of Keatsian negative capability whereby the poet keeps her spirituality alive by ironically subjecting it to challenges, by generating uncertainties, by confronting the terrifying unknown rather than settling for unchallenged and predetermined but comforting certitude. According to McIntosh, "Dickinson's preoccupation with the unknown is pervasive in her work" (124). This can be seen in poems such as "This World is Not Conclusion," in which the "narcotic" of conventional piety (the rolling hallelujahs with which the speaker has been inundated) "cannot still the Tooth" of skepticism, of reason and empirical science "that nibbles at the soul" (Fr373; J501), and most disturbingly, perhaps, in Fr1404; J1382:

> In many and reportless places
> We feel a Joy —
> Reportless, also, but sincere as Nature
> Or Deity —
>
> It comes, without a consternation —
> Dissolves — the same —
> But leaves a sumptuous Destitution —
> Without a Name —[8]

"In this peaceful meditation," McIntosh writes, "the speaker accepts her own predicament as a transient and ignorant creature. . . . A person made bereft of joy becomes destitute. Yet the memory of joy's temporary presence and dissolution is 'sumptuous,' compensating for joy's loss" (140). This, I would add, is Dickinson the Christian existentialist, demonstrating a "paradox of faith," as Kierkegaard describes it in *Fear and Trembling* (1843): "Faith . . . is not an aesthetic emotion but something far higher, precisely because it has resignation as its presupposition; it is not an immediate instinct of the heart, but is the paradox of life and existence" (58).

John Delli Carpini's *Emily Dickinson: Poetry as Prayer* (2002) is an attractively illustrated little book that approaches Dickinson's poetry as essentially spiritual, and for that reason it aims to help the reader "be more attentive to God's breath within [one]" — here Carpini deliberately echoes the Latin origin of "spiritual" (*spiritus*), meaning breath or wind (1). "Her poems," Carpini explains, "can be a stimulus to prayer," which in turn can intensify "our relationship with God" (7).

Considering Carpini's stated purpose, one might expect an artificial picking and choosing of poems that would obscure Dickinson as the bold questioner of Christian doctrine that she was — but Carpini is quite aware of her larger aims and does not shy away from poems such as "I know that He exists. / Somewhere — in Silence," acknowledging that in her quest for God she sometimes did not find what she was looking for:

> Although there were times of disillusionment and discontentment on this great religious odyssey, she worked at finding meaning in the seemingly ordinary events of her day. And sometimes, when she looked, God was recognizable, although silent and invisible. (65)

Carpini, like McIntosh, acknowledges Dickinson's ability "to live each day within the mystery of unknowing" (66) — a demonstration of faith, "her most valued possession," according to Carpini: "Faith allayed her fears and helped her to surrender her anxiety to a Presence that she felt kept a watch-

---

[8] Compare McIntosh's reading of this poem with that of Susan Howe; see chapter 8.

ful and providential eye on her" (98). He cites "My faith is larger than the Hills" (Fr489, J766) as an example. In this little poem, the speaker asserts that her faith is so immense that it endures beyond the inevitable decay of the world by "tak[ing] the Purple Wheel / To Show the Sun the way —" that is, by asserting that the power of faith exceeds even cosmic forces of nature such as that of the sun.

Several recent articles have provided additional insights into Dickinson as a spiritual poet. Rowena Revis Jones, for example, in "A Taste for 'Poison': Dickinson's Departure from Orthodoxy" (1993) shows how Dickinson's "humanizing" of Christ shared much with Theodore Parker's in his *The Two Christmas Celebrations* (1859) — a copy of which Dickinson received as a gift from Mrs. Samuel Bowles — and the "poison" (that is, Parker's unorthodox views) it was supposed to be. "I heard that he [Parker] was 'poison,'" Dickinson wrote in her thank-you letter. "Then I like poison very well" (L213). Parker, whose liberal approach to Christianity had been rejected even by the Unitarians, proclaimed that Jesus Christ offered the most complete revelation to date of what human beings are capable of becoming. Jones argues that Dickinson's warm and lasting friendship with the Bowleses suggests she shared an interest in their "Parkerist" approach to Christianity. Indeed, Samuel Bowles had argued that "the simple philosophy of the Gospel" could be understood by anyone, and deplored the "dry and disgusting lore of theological schools."[9] Jones then demonstrates the way in which several of Dickinson's poems reflect this credo. In "God is a distant — stately Lover —" (Fr615; J357), for example, "Christ attracts [the speaker] more consistently than does the one he was sent to reveal" (55):

> God is a distant — stately Lover —
> Woos, as He states us — by His Son —
> Verily, a Vicarious Courtship —
> "Miles", and "Priscilla", were such an One —
>
> But, lest the Soul — like fair "Priscilla"
> Choose the Envoy — and spurn the Groom —
> Vouches, with hyperbolic archness —
> "Miles". And "John Alden" were Synonyme —

Jones concludes that, like Theodore Parker, Samuel Bowles, and Thomas Wentworth Higginson (the latter of whom was an ordained Unitarian minister) "Dickinson too rejected the 'old' doctrines. Like them, she found in Christ a chiefly human figure who served as a model of charity and a source of courage" (61). Jones, it should be noted, wrote her doctoral

---

[9] George Merriam, *The Life and Times of Samuel Bowles;* qtd. Jones, 1993, 51.

dissertation on Dickinson's conception of immortality.[10] Jones's article approaches the poet's thought in terms of the religious and philosophical views of the period. It emphasizes the internal conflict Dickinson experienced between the promise of an afterlife and the guilt she harbored regarding her ambivalence toward Calvinist doctrine.

Mention should also be made of Jones's 1982 article on the role of Puritan doctrine in Dickinson's formal education, "The Preparation of a Poet: Puritan Directions in Emily Dickinson's Education." In it Jones argues that as result of the Puritan project of cultivating the minds of women as well as of men a more widespread recognition of women's intellectual potential was achieved — as well as greater insight into the ways higher learning and religious faith could interact.

In her 1993 essay, "'Arguments of Pearl': Dickinson's Response to Puritan Semiology," Joanna Yin shows yet another facet of the poet's departure from the religious conventions of her time, and also nicely demonstrates how a spiritual perspective can meld with a feminist one. Yin shows how Dickinson exposes the Calvinist code of gender hierarchy as laid out in John Calvin's *Institutes of the Christian Religion* (1536), which in turn draws upon scriptural authority, specifically 1 Corinthians 11:3, and Ephesians 5:22–23, which establish the husband not only as head of the household, but head of the woman, paralleling Christ as head of the man.

Yin points out the way the Nietzsche of *On the Genealogy of Morals* (as later the Foucault of *The Archaeology of Knowledge*) excavates "foundations" of truth to uncover layers of ungrounded meanings imposed by some group who had power at some time in the past, thus revealing (in Nietzsche's case) "that there are no moral laws but only interpretations of moral phenomena" (Yin 66). She sees Dickinson as performing a similar archaeology on Puritan/Calvinist theology that is reflected by a sign system that ensures Christ's glorification on earth and lures his followers "toward an uncertain eternity in heaven" (67). As a case in point, Dickinson uses the emblem of the butterfly in "My Cocoon tightens" (Fr1107; J1099) — which a Puritan, Yin points out, would consider to be "a sign of both the risen Christ and the Puritan believer regenerated into eternity" as an occasion "to parody Puritan semiology" (68):

> My Cocoon tightens — Colors teaze —
> I'm feeling for the Air —
> A dim capacity for Wings
> Demeans + the Dress I wear —   +Degrades

---

[10] "Emily Dickinson's 'Flood Subject': Immortality," Northwestern University; *Dissertation Abstracts* 21 (1960): 1554–55.

> A power of Butterfly must be —
> The aptitude to fly
> Meadows of Majesty concedes +   +implies
> And easy Sweeps of Sky —
>
> So I must baffle at the Hint
> And cipher at the Sign
> And make much blunder, if at last
> I take the clue divine —

"In this poem," Yin explains, "Calvinist semiotics prompts the butterfly's aspiration and consequent misery. The hopeful pupa is left cocoon-bound, its temporary home more a prison than a comfort, as she . . . baffles and blunders in the excruciating process of trying to read 'the Sign.' There is no promised rebirth or regeneration" (69).

Yin next shows how Dickinson reworks Calvinist precepts relating to the ideal conduct and role of women in the "father's house." Using "You'll know Her — by Her Foot —" (Fr604; J634), Dickinson describes a female robin "who is both subordinate and empowered": the first five stanzas of the poem "stress the dainty smallness of the robin" (75), but in the concluding two stanzas the focus shifts from the image of the robin to the voice of the robin — to show that the robin not only has learned to find its voice, but has learned to produce songs of "Pearl" — songs that are also self-asserting arguments: "You'll know her — by Her Voice — / At first — a doubtful Tone — / A sweet endeavor — but as March / To April — hurries on — // She squanders on your Ear / Such Arguments of Pearl — . . ."

Like the seventeenth-century metaphysical poets, especially George Herbert, Emily Dickinson reworked scriptural themes to serve her artistic objectives. But as Diane Gabrielson Scholl argues in her 1994 article "From Aaron 'Drest' to Dickinson's 'Queen': Protestant Typology in Herbert and Dickinson," their respective aims were dramatically different. Whereas Herbert's Old Testament heroes like Aaron are recast into Christlike penitents, Dickinson's heroines — like her queen in "A Wife — at Daybreak I shall be —" (Fr185B; J461) or "I'm ceded — I've stopped being Their's" (Fr353; J508) are seen as initially penitent, but by the end of the poems break free of subservience. Thus, Scholl observes, the speaker of "I'm ceded," who at the beginning of the poem "most resembles Christ in her relinquishment of past earthly ties and in the magnitude and enormity of her choice" (12), is transformed from a "half unconscious Queen —" to a fully-conscious one, "[w]ith Will to choose, or to reject."

Both Herbert and Dickinson effect a "fundamental tension between Scripture and poetry" (13), Scholl explains; but whereas Scripture for Herbert becomes a garment to be donned, in Dickinson, the scriptural garment becomes secularized, almost playful. We see this occurring in "He ate and drank the precious Words — / His Spirit grew robust — / He knew no more that he was poor, / Nor that his frame was Dust —"; but then a transformation occurs in the last four lines: "He danced along the dingy Days / And this Bequest of Wings / Was but a Book — What Liberty / A loosened Spirit brings —" (Fr1593; J1587).

Another way to look at Dickinson's grappling with scriptural themes is to see it as paralleling the way Scripture itself grapples with the human confrontation with the Divine. This is the focal point of Richard S. Ellis's study, "'A Little East of Jordan': Human-Divine Encounter in Dickinson and the Hebrew Bible" (1999). Ellis asserts that both Dickinson and the Hebrew Bible "articulate the human-Divine encounter in language riddled with paradox, wordplay, and shifts of perspective fluctuating . . . between hierarchy and intimacy, transcendence and immanence, abstraction and sensation — all of which have the effect of creating multiple, often contradictory interpretations" (36). Ellis regards Dickinson's depiction of Jacob wrestling with the angel at Peniel (Fr145B; J59) as "a narrative emblem for these techniques and a concrete point for comparison between Dickinson and the Hebrew Bible" (36–37). The Genesis story of Jacob's wrestling match, up to the point where he demands a blessing from the adversarial angel (actually "a man" according to the King James version, 32:24), serves to prefigure the reconciliation with Jacob's brother Esau and prepare the way for the settling of Israel, which is also the name that the angel confers upon Jacob (32:29). Dickinson, as Ellis points out, erases this drama of sibling rivalry and replaces it with one that highlights "the individual's nakedness before existence, which is both a curse and a promise of freedom" (39). Ellis, a professor of Judaic and Near Eastern Studies, then draws close parallels between Dickinson's use of paradox and wordplay and that of "the Rabbinic interpretive tradition":

> A primary spiritual injunction is to wrestle with the text, to splinter the text into sparks of new meanings by applying exegetical principles such as alternate vocalizations and punctuations, rearrangements of letters, and thematic linking of noncontiguous passages via related consonantal roots. According to the Rabbis, wordplay is the trace of God's breath in the text. In playing with the text, the reader becomes God's partner. (48)

In her most recent examination of Dickinson's use of Calvinist themes, "'Where — Omnipresence — fly?' Calvinism as Impetus to Spiritual Amplitude," published in 2005, Jane Donahue Eberwein calls attention to the poet's concern for conveying spiritual "amplitude," using the "theological vocabulary" of her time to register "a sense of life played for high stakes and on a sublime scale" (14). Eberwein quotes the opening lines of Fr743; J721 as a case in point: "Behind Me — dips Eternity — / Before Me — Immortality — / Myself — the Term between —." Dickinson finds ways of appropriating key Calvinist terms such as "grace" and "glory" — terms, as Eberwein notes, that also figured significantly in the Calvinist poet Edward Taylor's work — to embody "earthly intuitions of heaven" (15), as we see in the first stanza of Fr429; J420: "You'll know it — as you know 'tis Noon — / By Glory — / As you do the Sun — / By Glory — . . ." In other poems, however, Eberwein is quick to point out, Dickinson qualifies such intuitive celestial envisioning, as in Fr1700; J1660, in which "Glory" is now defined as "that bright tragic thing / That for an instant / Means Dominion —." Moreover, as an additional example of expressing spiritual amplitude, Dickinson uses theological vocabulary to create, as Wendy Martin has observed in her entry on Dickinson for the *Columbia Literary History of the United States* (1988), "a cosmology in which consciousness functions as the soul [and in which] ecstasy is the equivalent of grace" (623; qtd. Eberwein 15).

Just as importantly, Eberwein points to Dickinson's efforts to take advantage of "the liberalizing tendencies in Christian thought" prevalent even in Trinitarian-oriented Western Massachusetts. Examples include the poet's "Unitarian tendency to [represent] Jesus as fellow human sufferer rather than divinity," and her Transcendentalist tendency to respond "rapturously" to natural phenomena, as in the concluding stanza of "By my Window have I for Scenery" in which the speaker suspects that immorality

> Was the Pine at my Window a "Fellow
> Of the Royal" Infinity?
> Apprehensions are God's introductions —
> To be +hallowed — accordingly —   +Extended inscrutably —
>   (Fr849; J797)

In his 2004 study, *Experience and Faith: The Late Romantic Imagination of Emily Dickinson,* Richard E. Brantley notes the way Dickinson oscillates between the experience of faith and the faith of experience (27). Like the "scientist of Faith" from line 12 of Fr1261; J1241, Dickinson's speakers "look before they leap," Brantley writes. "As they induce hope after hope, they put even their doctrine of immortality to the test of their experience" (24).

A renegade spiritualist is Emily Dickinson, to be sure — one whose attitude toward God, in Bettina Knapp's words, "was neither complacent nor confident. On the contrary, it was marked with contention, defiance, and continuous oscillation" (128). God is the aching tooth "that nibbles at the Soul," as she concludes "This World is not Conclusion" (Fr373; J501). What greater testament of faith could we possibly have?

Eberwein, whose scholarship has focused mainly on the spiritual aspects of Emily Dickinson's life and work, cautions us in her 1998 article "Dickinson's Local, Global, and Cosmic Perspectives" not to misconstrue Dickinson's "spirited contempt for 'Soft — Cherubic Creatures' among the 'Gentlewomen' she observed" (Fr675; J401) because "she drew strength from a network of female friends and the sentimental women's culture of her time" (38). Eberwein's point, I believe, can be extended to include Dickinson's religious milieu: she drew strength from the revivalism that had energized life in the Connecticut Valley at least since the time of Jonathan Edwards and the Great Awakening. Critics like Eberwein, New, Reynolds, and Wolff have shown us how a great poet is nurtured by the cultural traditions she artistically critiques.

Dickinson can be characterized as a spiritual poet; the spiritual motifs permeating her work, letters as well as poems, suggest that she was completely connected to her cultural milieu, despite her being a recluse. On the other hand, she used spiritual motifs much as a painter uses pigment, not so much to assert a belief or meditate upon a doctrine of faith as to see how the motif might be played out poetically. "Let us imagine, for sake of argument," Dickinson seems to be saying, "that a speaker thinks of God as 'a distant, stately lover' (Fr615; J357); or that a speaker says of God that 'He strained my faith — / Did he find it supple?' (Fr366; J497); or that a speaker shares her ambivalent experience of God as both divine authority and mortal lover by proclaiming 'I gave myself to Him —' (Fr426; J580)." In other words, one can argue that Dickinson is not merely a spiritual poet but a poet who devises scenarios in which spiritual conflicts are played out, thus allowing us to acquire a deeper understanding of the interplay between the supernatural and the natural.

7: Scholarship on Archetypal and Philosophical Themes in Dickinson's Poetry

> *September's Baccalaureate*
> *A combination is*
> *Of Crickets — Crows — and Retrospects*
> *And a dissembling Breeze*
> . . .
> *That makes the Heart put up its Fun*
> *And turn Philosopher.*
> (Fr1313; J1271)
>
> *The central paradox of Dickinson's thought — her awareness that the ratio of actual loss to visionary gain formed the controlling, measurable condition of existential life — ultimately energized her thought itself, made her quest vital and meaningful.*
> — Greg Johnson, *Emily Dickinson: Perception and the Poet's Quest* (1985)
>
> *Her agon was waged with the whole of tradition, but particularly with the Bible and with romanticism.*
> — Harold Bloom, introduction to *Modern Critical Views: Emily Dickinson* (1985)

TO PERCEIVE A LITERARY WORK FROM an archetypal perspective is to disregard the author as an "isolate self" — to use Frank Lentricchia's term from *After the New Criticism* (1980) — in order to foreground the author's universal patterns of thought, or the Jungian "collective unconscious." Such universal patterns or archetypes are what, presumably, have given rise to the ancient myths. Myth, according to Northrop Frye in his landmark *Anatomy of Criticism* (1957) "is the imitation of actions near or at the conceivable limits of desire" (136). For Frye any school of criticism that searches for "a limiting principle in literature . . . is mistaken" (17). Of course he has in mind the formalists, who regard the work of art under scrutiny as a self-contained, complex aesthetic system. A formalist, he argues, has "no conceptual framework: it is simply his job to take a poem into which a poet has diligently stuffed a specific number of beauties or effects, and complacently extract them one by one, like his prototype Little Jack Horner (17–18).

Such criticism Frye terms "centripetal": it keeps the subject of study — the literary work in question — at the center. But criticism for Frye, as he writes in his 1963 *Fables of Identity,* must be "centrifugal": the literary work should move us toward universals, toward the galaxy of archetypes (9).

To expound his system of archetypal meaning, Frye identifies three major types of imagery: the apocalyptic, the demonic, and the analogical. The apocalyptic world, for example, posits categories of reality in the varieties of human desire, as shown by the forms they assume under the work of human civilization (*Anatomy of Criticism,* 141). Frye explains:

> The form imposed by human work and desire on the *vegetable* world ... is that of the garden, the farm, the grove, or the park. The human form of the *animal* world is a world of domesticated animals, of which the sheep has a traditional priority in both Classical and Christian metaphor. The human form of the mineral world, the form into which human work transforms stone, is the city. The city, the garden, and the sheepfold are the organizing metaphors of the Bible and of most Christian symbolism, and they are brought into complete metaphorical identification in the book explicitly called the Apocalypse or Revelation, which has been carefully designed to form an undisplaced mythical conclusion for the Bible as a whole. (141)

Demonic imagery, the second form of archetypal meaning, evokes the realm of the nightmare, the scapegoat, bondage, pain, and confusion. This world consists of the demonic divine: "the vast, menacing ... powers of nature as they appear to a technologically undeveloped society," and the demonic human: "a society held together by a kind of molecular tension of egos, a loyalty to the group or the leader which diminishes the individual" (147). Analogical imagery, finally, presents idealized worlds. In romance, heroes demonstrate bravery, heroines beauty, and villains malice, while the difficulties of ordinary life are given short shrift (151).

So what does an archetypal study of Emily Dickinson's poetry yield? Frye's own essay on the poet, "Emily Dickinson," from *Fables of Identity,* unfortunately offers little more than a summary. After devoting half of the essay to an overview of her life, he focuses on what he calls her multivocal "drama of life, death, and immortality, of love and renunciation, ecstasy and suffering," which she created out of the "tiny incidents" of her own experience. But, Frye cautions, to read these poetic dramas as "biographical allegory where we ought to be reading poetry is precisely the kind of vulgarity that made her dread publication" (198). What we see in the poetry most of all, he argues, is a religious experience that begins in Christianity and extends outward toward paganism, driven by "circumference" or "awe" — Dickinson's metaphors for human consciousness in direct confrontation with the most fundamental aspects of existence —

"flood subjects," to use another of her metaphors. "Awe," asserts Frye, "is not a dogmatic God, and is tolerant enough to satisfy not only the poet's Christian longings but the paganism that makes her feel that there ought to be a god for every mood of the soul and every department of nature." He cites the concluding stanza of "Because that you are going / and never coming back" as a case in point:

> If "All is possible with him"
> As he besides concedes,
> He will refund us finally
> Our confiscated Gods —
> 		(Fr1314; J1260)

Frye notes, too, that Dickinson even identifies the God that is awe as female: "I always ran Home to Awe when a child. . . . He was an awful Mother, but I liked him better than none" (210) — an important observation that Frye ought to have explored further in the context of the Mother Archetype.[1] Be that as it may, he shifts attention to Dickinson's "Awe" as her equivalent of the Holy Spirit, which, as he points out, is "symbolized in the Bible by two of her favorite images, the bird and the wind." Frye rather cleverly equates Dickinson's poet with Noah, "sailing the flood of experience," and the Holy Spirit with the dove who delivered the news of land not only to Noah but to Christopher Columbus — as we see in the second stanza of "Once more, my now bewildered Dove" (Fr65; J48):

> Thrice to the floating casement
> The Patriarch's bird returned —
> Courage! My brave Columbia!
> There may yet be *Land!*

Roland Hagenbüchle, in his commentary on archetypal/myth criticism (1998) calls attention to Frye's combination of "hermeneutic interpretation with a fascinating model of literary history." Frye's breakdown of literature into five modes — mythic, romantic, high mimetic, low mimetic, and ironic — Hagenbüchle writes, "could usefully be drawn upon to characterize Dickinson's style and to place the poet in her cultural milieu"

---

[1] See, for example, "Psychological Aspects of the Mother Archetype," in which Jung explores such paradoxical elements of the mother archetype as, on the one hand, "the magic authority of the female" and "the wisdom and spiritual exaltation that transcend reason" and on the other as "anything secret, hidden, dark; the abyss, the world of the dead, anything that devours, seduces, and poisons, that is terrifying and inescapable like fate" (16).

(362). Hagenbüchle then singles out Albert Gelpi's *The Tenth Muse* (1975) for its compelling depiction of what Gelpi calls "the lifelong contention of eros and psyche" in Dickinson's and Whitman's poetry (qtd. Hagenbüchle 362).

According to Gelpi, the animus has an ambiguous nature in Dickinson: "This figure appears at once as God, lover, demon, and death, 'the masculine "other" filling what her female nature' both 'lacked and feared'" (Gelpi 251). Gelpi points out that in contrast to Emerson, who in his essay "Circles" (1844) lays out a neo-Platonic system whereby "[t]he eye is the first circle; the horizon which it forms is the second; and throughout nature this primary figure is repeated without end" (296), Dickinson's circles represent a human consciousness exploring its own nature and its relation to the world (269). He cites the following poem to illustrate:

> Time feels so vast that were it not
> For an Eternity —
> I fear me this Circumference
> Engross my Finity —
>
> To His exclusion, who prepare
> By Processes+ of Size   +Rudiments — * [By] Prefaces
> For the Stupendous Vision+   +volume
> Of His Diameters —
>   (Fr858; J802)

Here, as Gelpi explains, "[t]he figure is a series of concentric circles in which the poet is the finite center surrounded by the sweep of Time, which is in turn encompassed by . . . Eternity. . . . Paradoxically, eternity makes time bearable by confining it to a circumference which allows the individual to establish herself within it as a center for the time-space experience. . . . Containment not only proves positive but necessary" (270).

Dickinson as Carlylean Poet-Hero

As one who "Distills amazing sense / From ordinary Meanings" (Fr446; J448), the poet possesses extraordinary power, a conviction Emily Dickinson expressed explicitly in a note to Susan Dickinson in 1878 that Gary Lee Stonum calls attention to in *The Dickinson Sublime* (1990: 53):

> Cherish Power — dear —
> Remember that stands in the Bible between the Kingdom
> and the Glory, because it is wilder than either of them.
>   (L 583)

As part of his rebuttal against those scholars who, like David Porter, regard Dickinson as "a poet without a project," possessing "no subject because she had no scheme, philosophical or poetical" (Porter, 1981: 152–53), Stonum invokes the Carlylean poet, whose powers render her more deserving of the title "Monarch" or "Queen." After all, they possess the mythic Zeus-like power to stun the world with "Bolts of Melody" (Fr348; J505). "Both Carlyle and Dickinson," Stonum writes, "imagine poetic greatness as the pictorial disclosure of the authentic and harmonious meanings otherwise hidden in nature. But whereas Carlyle stresses the poet's eye as a synecdoche of his rare and grand powers, Dickinson's concern is with the *effect* of poetry, not its production" (13; emphasis added). Just as importantly, the poet's relationship to her audience is never neutral; "it is always a power relation and hence always potentially charged with the affects of power: anxiety, resentment, exultation, and so on" (15). Moreover, Dickinson's distinctive style, rather than, as Porter has it, "pull[ing] away from reality by its eccentricity, refusing to mirror that reality in a straightforward, unambiguous way" (1981: 75), or representing "a reality that can be projected only in the world of language ... and not representation in the world" (120–21), is according to Stonum "part of a larger rhetoric of stimulus. It is meant to cherish a power that extends considerably beyond the author's direct control" (67). In other words, Dickinson's poetry embraces the sublime. Unlike Emerson and Thoreau, who wish to recover the symbolic power of words by re-invoking their original meanings, Dickinson "works to denaturalize the available symbolic resources of our condition and culture" (92), and in so doing privileges the poet's power to reshape language over her ability to mediate between language and nature.

Power Archetypes in Dickinson

Dickinson's wielding of archetypal themes of power is the key concern of Camille Paglia. In *Sexual Personae: Art and Decadence from Nefertiti to Emily Dickinson* (1990) her highly charged defense "of the unity and continuity of western culture," Paglia augments Frye's and Gelpi's approaches to Dickinson's poetry by calling attention to its daemonic, mythic energy. The forces of nature trump any human efforts to tame daemonic sexual energy into civil non-hierarchical behavior. "Sex is a far darker power than feminism has admitted," Paglia stresses (3). Thus, Emily Dickinson becomes, for Paglia, "the female Sade" (624). Her "high condensation and riddling ellipses," her hymn-measure, "warped and deformed by a stupefying energy"; her words "are rammed into lines with such force that syntax shatters and collapses into itself." For Paglia, such syntax reanimates long dormant pagan energies. As "a pioneer among women writers in renouncing genteel good manners" (634) Paglia's Emily Dickinson opens the top of the skull of a society oppressed by religion to release the brain's startling and autonomous power:

> Dickinson's brain has a will of its own: "If ever the lid gets off my head / And lets the brain away / The fellow will go where he belonged / Without a hint from me" (Fr585; J1727). The skull seems trepanned, like a cookie jar. The brain, as masculine intellect, escapes like a canary from a cage or a firefly from a bottle. We see a Late Romantic rebellion of part against whole, the brain boldly abandoning its master, like Gogol's nose or Gautier's mummified foot. (625)

Consistent with her ongoing battle against feminism is Paglia's insistence that "it is a sentimental error to think Emily Dickinson the victim of male obstructionism. Without her struggle with God and father, there would have been no poetry" (653). Of course, that does not prove the *absence* of "male obstructionism" — only that Dickinson never was victimized by it, insofar as her artistic integrity was concerned. In the end, Paglia projects more of a feminist sensibility than she cares to admit: "Dickinson was a woman of abnormal will. Her poetry profits from the enormous disparity between that will and the feminine social persona to which she fell heir at birth." Even so, "her sadism is not anger, the a posteriori response to social injustice. It is hostility, an a priori Achillean intolerance for the existence of others, the female version of Romantic solipsism" (653).

Harold Bloom is similarly staggered by the energy Dickinson compresses into her poems. Singling out "From Blank to Blank" (Fr484; J761), Bloom in *The Western Canon* (1994) exclaims, "To pack this much into forty-one words and ten lines ought not to be possible" (293):

> From Blank to Blank —
> A Threadless Way+   +Course
> I pushed Mechanic feet —
> To stop — or perish — or advance —
> Alike indifferent —
>
> If end I gained+   +reached
> It ends beyond
> Indefinites disclosed —
> I shut my eyes — and groped as well
> 'Twas lighter+ — to be Blind —   +firmer

"This minute gnome of a lyric," Bloom writes with typical sweeping exuberance, "takes us all the way from Theseus, archetype of the ungrateful hero, who abandons the woman who gives him the thread to the labyrinth, to Milton, who dominates male poets' use of his metaphor of the universal blank that nature presented to his blindness" — and that's just in the first stanza. In commenting on the second stanza Bloom evokes Emerson and "the ruin or blank that we see in nature being that of our own eye" (293) — a trope, Bloom supposes, that Dickinson uses to express poetic crisis. But then we have "The Tint I cannot take — is best —" (Fr696; J627):

> The Tint I cannot take — is best —
> The Color too remote
> That I could show it in Bazaar —
> A Guinea at a sight —
> . . .
> The Moments of Dominion
> That happen on the Soul
> And leave it with a Discontent
> Too exquisite — to tell —
> . . .

Bloom sees this poem as a statement of Dickinson's poetics, "at once Emersonian and counter-Emersonian, a new and wholly personal Self-Reliance and a grand unnaming, an act of negation as dialectical and profound as any essayed by Nietzsche or Freud" (304–5); in fact Bloom places the poem side by side with a passage from Nietzsche's *Will to Power* aphorisms:

> We want to hold fast to our senses and to our faith in them — and think their consequences through to the end!
> The existing world, upon which all earthly living things have worked so that it appears as it does (durable and changing slowly), we want to go on building — and not criticize it away as false!
> (from section 1046; qtd. Bloom, 305)

Dickinson's "Tint" poem, Bloom concludes, emphasizes "what cannot be taken, an ungraspable secret, a trope or metaphor not to be expressed" (305).

Dickinsonian Gothic

According to Paglia, the gothic "is a style of claustrophobic sensuality. Its closed spaces are daemonic wombs" (265). Arising out of forerunners like *The Faerie Queen, Paradise Lost,* and *Faust,* Paglia says, the Gothic novel came into being in 1794 with *The Mysteries of Udolpho* by Anne Radcliffe, an unusual example of a woman fashioning an artistic style (265), and makes the strongest impact on Romanticism with Matthew Gregory Lewis's *The Monk* in 1796 (265–66). Daneen Wardrop, by contrast, in

Emily Dickinson's Gothic: Goblin with a Gauge (1996) gives Dickinson's gothic a gendered reading:

> The female gothic asks ... How hard does a culture work to domesticate female texts so that women are relegated to the status of dolls who are animate and inanimate at the same time? How does a repressive society transform those "dolls" to ... victims of uncanny repression. How might Olympia [the mechanized doll in E. T. A. Hoffman's story "The Sandman," which Freud critiques in his essay, *Das Unheimliche* ("The Uncanny")], find her voice from her position, locked in the poetic absurdity of the prefix *Un-*, which stipulates paradox? Entrapped, Olympia finds herself constituted in the repression from which the theory of the uncanny arises. The Dickinson gothic embodies that psycholinguistic entrapment, as Dickinson locks us in language predicaments again and again. What if, in looking at the Dickinson text, we were to animate Olympia? Female gothicism works assiduously to negotiate the dilemma. (xv)

Wardrop begins her analysis of Dickinson's gothicism by focusing on the theme of the haunted house — "the primary gothic scene, whereby some unknown force may gain access from the outside, or the heroine may be imprisoned on the inside" (23). Hauntedness is Dickinson's artistic ideal, as her oft-quoted proclamation to Higginson asserts ("Nature is a Haunted House — but Art — a House that tries to be haunted"; L459a). Next on Wardrop's agenda is the theme of the wedding, which "offer[s] a profound gothic hesitation in terms of temporal suspension" (54). It is interesting to compare Wardrop's reading of the wedding poems with that of William H. Shurr (1983), who interprets Dickinson's entire fascicle sequence as the literal chronicle of a betrothal, marriage, and separation.

Gothicism, of course, possesses a deeply sexual aspect. Descending into the darkest, dungeon-like regions of the human psyche, we inevitably meet up with the libido. Wardrop casts gothicism, using G. R. Thompson's expression, as Romanticism's "dark twin,"[2] which "thrives at the conflux of the sacred and the profane," pivoting on intense experiences such as rapture, which can be both spiritual and carnal. This is an ambivalence that Dickinson captures in "The Thrill came slowly" (Fr1528; J1495), in which spiritual rapture, through Biblical history, is transmuted into a "ravished Holiness" in the concluding line. For Wardrop, rapture beholds a ravaged holiness, which gives rise to the gothic moment (12). Moreover, for Dickinson's gothic heroine, sex is often inevitably linked with

---

[2] "Romanticism and the Gothic Tradition," in *The Gothic Imagination: Essays in Dark Romanticism*, ed. G. R. Thompson (1974); cited by Wardrop, 11.

pain or death (70); she also "internalize(s) phallogocentric dread" (71). Wardrop cites the following poem as an example of this:

> I breathed enough to take the Trick —
> And now, removed from Air —
> I stimulate the Breath, so well —
> That One, to be quite sure —
>
> The Lungs are stirless — must descend
> Among the cunning cells —
> And touch the Pantomime — Himself,
> How numb,+ the Bellows feels!   +cool —
> (Fr308; J272)

"Not accidentally," observes Wardrop, "at the same time that the poem describes a woman's experience of numbness at owning a body in a man-centered world, it describes the experience of being unable to speak. The same 'Cells' that render her a female body in a patriarchal society have imprisoned her so that she feels she cannot express herself" (72).

Another fundamental characteristic of gothicism Wardrop identifies in the poems is what she calls "dissociative seeing ... perceptions of the unreal alongside perceptions of the ordinary in order to elicit uncertainty" (96). Dickinson's symbol of the veil functions effectively in this context:

> Dickinson's veil forms a translucency behind which she works out quandaries that include fantastic corollaries to her religious impulses, admissions of the fear of sex in a patriarchal society, and a gothic relationship with the printed word.... The veil condenses the vale-vail-veil possibilities of the word into the particularly female accoutrement most usual for brides, nuns, and mourners. (97–98)

Wardrop finally shows how Dickinson's gothic sensibilities invoke postmodern concerns with language. She suggests that we might regard deconstruction as an essentially gothic subgenre in the sense that its main objective is to get us to notice the supernatural character of language (154). Whereas in conventional discourse the goal of the writer or speaker is to minimize the gap that inevitably exists between signifier and signified, the opposite is often the case in poetic discourse. Dickinson, through her linguistic and semantic inventiveness, heightens awareness of that gap — a gothic impulse to generate the uncanniness that lurks at the very heart of language, of reality itself.

Dickinson's Ironic Quest Voyagers

"What Liberty / A loosened spirit brings —," Dickinson's speaker proclaims at the end of "He ate and drank the precious Words —" (Fr1593; J1587). In a poem that conceives of art as sacrament (hence the metaphor of Holy Communion), Dickinson appropriates the religious quest to seek union with God to her own quest, which is to venture out "upon Circumference" (Fr633; J378), not to break free of the world that yokes her to mortal life (the ideal of a religious quest) but to explore all of the possibilities that existence has to offer. Dickinson does not so much adopt art as her religion, as some would have it, as she erases the distinction between art and religion. The Christian Heaven does indeed exist for her, but it "is what I cannot reach!" (Fr310; J239).

Dickinson's stature as a quest poet comes into sharp focus when she is compared with the other great quest poet in American literature, Walt Whitman. In Agnieszka Salska's 1985 study, *Walt Whitman and Emily Dickinson: Poetry of the Central Consciousness,* the two poets illuminate each other's similar yet different poetic journeys. In both poets, Salska argues, "the self is central"; for that reason all experiences can only be perceived subjectively (36). Whitman's self is a "kosmos" ("Song of Myself" 34:1) that seeks identity with all that surrounds it. Moreover, that self, or soul is never distinct from the body ("Song of Myself" 48:1), never a limiting factor. On the contrary, as Salska notes, "it is a marvelous agent activating the soul" (41). Whitman's journeys, moreover, "provide opportunities for [the soul's] enlargement" (41), transcending containment or ultimate definition:

> People I meet, the effect upon me of my early life or the ward and
>   city I live in, or the nation,
> The latest dates, discoveries, inventions, societies, authors old and new,
> My dinner, dress, associates, looks, compliments, dues
> . . .
> These come to me days and nights and go from me again,
> But they are not the Me myself
>   — "Song of Myself," 4:2–4; 8–9

Dickinson's self, by contrast, remains isolated. Hers is the "happy . . . little Stone / That rambles in the Road alone, / And doesn't care about careers / And Exigencies never fears —" (Fr1570B; J1510). But there's a more ominous dimension of the self as well: its hidden nature, which seems more like the powers that are beyond human understanding (54) — a facet, to use Gary Lee Stonum's term, of the Dickinson sublime.

> Ourself behind ourself, concealed —
> Should startle most —
> Assassin hid in our Apartment
> Be Horror's least.
> . . .   (Fr407; J670)

A liberated self, for Emily Dickinson, then, exists within the confines of the body:

> No Rack can torture me —
> My Soul — at Liberty —
> Behind this mortal Bone
> There knits a bolder One —
> . . .   (Fr649; J384)

Dickinson as Poet-Philosopher

Many critics writing extensively about Dickinson call attention to her philosophical ideas, as so many of her poems grapple with epistemological or metaphysical questions. A few critics, however, have studied her exclusively as a philosophical poet: Gelpi in *The Tenth Muse* (1975), Inder Nath Kher in *The Landscape of Absence* (1974), Greg Johnson in *Perception and the Poet's Quest* (1985); Christopher E. G. Benfey in *Emily Dickinson and the Problem of Others* (1984), and Ben Kimpel in *Emily Dickinson as Philosopher* (1981).

For Inder Nath Kher, even though Dickinson exhibits a keen awareness of her cultural milieu, to study her poetry from such a perspective (or as Kher puts it, from "within the confines of American history and culture") would be "to minimize the range of her poetic perspective" (4–5). Adopting Charles Anderson's goal of limiting the scope of analysis to the poems themselves, Kher gives special attention to the "metaphoric-metamorphic structures of [Dickinson's] art" (1), approaching the poetry "as one long poem of multidimensional reality." Kher also characterizes Dickinson's poetry as an "existentialist-romanticist vision of multidimensional reality" (2, 5) and as a "primordial metaphor" (7). Examples occur in poems that enact the myth of the eternal return, as in "The Dandelion's pallid tube / Astonishes the Grass, / And Winter instantly becomes / An infinite Alas — / The tube uplifts a signal Bud / And then a shouting Flower . . ." (Fr1565; J1519). Such an archetypal image of spring's resurrection from the depths of winter becomes emblematic of the way individual experiences — ecstasy, anguish, pain, the inexorable movement of time — become part of a larger mythic drama. With regard to the latter, for example, Dickinson's vivid sense of the moment comprises experience of the eternal, mythic moment of consciousness (24) as we see in "Forever — is composed of Nows — / 'Tis not a different time — / Except for Infiniteness — / And Latitude of Home — ... (Fr690; J624). What Kher perceives in Dickinson, then, is most unlike Paglia's Sadean late Romantic decadence: a kind of mythic existentialism whereby timeless archetypes are subsumed by the poet's temporal entrapment.

Temporal entrapment? Greg Johnson, In *Emily Dickinson: Perception and the Poet's Quest* (1985), takes a different view. Emily Dickinson, Johnson feels, "was clearly engaged in a kind of mythmaking . . . a mythologizing of self through which she made her life the literal and symbolic center of her poetry" (2). Being a "quest poet," however, even in Dickinson's interiorized universe, is fraught with paradox. Dickinson's personae quickly discover any quest for transcendence to be illusory, as in "Before I got my eye put out / I liked as well to see" (Fr336; J327), which, as Johnson suggests, "contrasts two kinds of perception — visual and intuitive" (49). The idea reappears in "What I see not, I better see —" (Fr869; J939). The paradox does not end here, though. The privileging of intuitive vision and inward-directed questing brings no easy resolution in Dickinson's complex existential worldview. As Johnson makes clear, Dickinson's personae never become oblivious to the harsh realities of mortal life in which love is withheld, heaven is forever out of reach, and happiness is eclipsed by despair. Dickinson reflects on this state of being in the following poem:

> Had I presumed to hope —
> The loss had been to Me
> A Value — for the Greatness' Sake —
> As Giants — gone+ away —   +claimed
>
> Had I presumed to gain
> A Favor so remote —
> The failure but confirm the Grace
> In further Infinite —
>
> 'Tis failure — not of Hope —
> But Confident+ Despair —   +diligent resolute
> Advancing on Celestial Lists —
> With faint — Terrestrial power —
>
> 'Tis Honor — though I die —
> For That no Man obtain
> Till He be justified by Death —
> This — is the Second Gain —
>   (Fr634; J522)

Confident despair: even when experiencing this most debilitating of emotions, the speaker manages to detach herself from it in order to recognize its existential necessity to living one's life as a mortal on earth. That in itself qualifies, says Johnson, as one of Dickinson's "numinous moments" (61).

"Numinous" is how Dickinson's perception might best be described, rather than philosophical or systematic. Dickinson, for Thomas W. Ford, as for George Frisbie Whicher, Richard Chase, and Charles R. Anderson before him, "was not a well-organized thinker."[3] In discussing her poems about death, Chase traces the way her "existential awareness of the reality and the 'problem' of death, together with the circumstances of her life, led her to write in the manner she chose." For example, "the sense of urgency and haste running throughout her poetry reflects her acute awareness of the presence of death, ready at any moment to cut her life short. As she told T. W. Higginson, 'Shortness to live has made me bold'" (182).

Another important facet of Dickinson's philosophical vision is introduced by Christopher E. G. Benfey in *Emily Dickinson and the Problem of Others* (1984): her skepticism. Benfey begins with the observation that "Dickinson is preoccupied, even obsessed, with issues of evidence, inference, and knowledge," an analysis that has led some critics to regard her as a skeptic — but Dickinson's brand of skepticism is different from, say, Emerson's or Montaigne's in that even while accepting the skeptic's stance of the unknowability of God, Nature, and other people, she nonetheless "challenges the skeptic ... to live and act according to his claims. She examines the consequences of living certain kinds of skepticism. Finally she suggests that we can relinquish certainty in our relations to others, and yet acknowledge our relatedness to them. She will often call this relation one of 'nearness'" (64). "Split the Lark" seems to convey this thought:

> Split the Lark — and you'll find the Music —
> Bulb after Bulb, in Silver rolled —
> Scantily dealt to the Summer Morning
> Saved for your Ear, when Lutes be old —
>
> Loose the Flood — you shall find it patent —
> Gush after Gush, reserved for you —
> Scarlet Experiment! Sceptic Thomas!
> Now, do you doubt that your Bird was true?
>
> (Fr905; J861)

---

[3] Whicher, *This Was a Poet* (1938), 163; Chase, *Emily Dickinson* (1951), 131; Anderson, *Emily Dickinson's Poetry* (1960), 285. Whicher, Chase, and Anderson all say that she was not a *systematic* thinker — not quite the same as saying she was not a well-organized thinker. See Ford's note 13: 188.

Like the skeptics of the New Testament, of whom Dickinson was particularly fond, as Benfey reminds us (93), she calls attention to the folly of harboring doubt in the face of the bird's music — as much a folly as Philip's and Thomas's doubt when confronting Jesus's resurrection. "The proof they ask for, and receive," Benfey writes, "is the revelation of a mutilated body" (93).

Dickinson's skepticism also has an existentialist character, which becomes apparent when one compares her perception of nature to Emerson's, as Joanne Feit Diehl does in *Dickinson and the Romantic Imagination* (1981): Diehl argues that Dickinson is unable to rely on a central self. When she turns to it, she confronts a consciousness that immediately hides. Experience thus becomes for her a "going through peril," a precarious walk above over the abyss. I would add, however, that Dickinson is not necessarily confessing her own existential angst, but rather creates in her poems dramatic scenarios in which the speakers are experiencing the threat of annihilation.[4]

"Being baffled or perplexed," Ben Kimpel tells us at the beginning of *Emily Dickinson as Philosopher* (1981), is an experience out of which philosophy emerges. All too often, though, philosophers have been tempted, as Kant complained, to speculate "about realities of which *in principle* nothing can be known," characterizing such speculations as "so many unfounded pretensions to enlarge our knowledge" (Kant, *Critique of Pure Reason*, 387; 171; qtd. Kimpel 2). Emily Dickinson shared Kant's impatience for such pretensions, and approaches each realm of human experience — sacrifice; suffering; moral duty; interaction with the natural world, with spirituality, and finally with death and immortality — with uncompromising clarity of thought, compressed into nuggets of poetic wisdom.

With regard to moral duty, for example, Dickinson argues that it cannot be put off:

> "Tomorrow" — whose location
> The Wise deceives
> Though its hallucination
> Is last that leaves —
> Tomorrow — thou Retriever
> Of every tare —
> Of Alibi art thou
> Or ownest where?
>
> (Fr1417; J1367)

---

[4] A premise I argue in my essay "Dickinson's Existential Dramas" (2002).

As Kimpel understands this, the next day is not necessarily accompanied by those duties "which were neglected the day before, and which an alibi can disavow. She is convinced that a mark of moral maturity is an intelligence to acknowledge that there is no . . . shirking of responsibilities" (113).

Dickinson's impulse to share her enlightened state with others represents yet another facet of her moral consciousness. In poems like "We met as Sparks — Diverging Flints / Sent various — scattered ways — / . . . Subsisting on the Light We bore / Before We felt the Dark — / A Flint unto this Day — perhaps — / But for that single spark" (Fr918; J958), Dickinson, according to Kimpel, "is concerned that the light which she treasures for illuminating her life may also enlighten the life of others" (16). In this way she shares Plato's view that enlightened individuals have the moral obligation "to go among people who are without comparable enlightenment" (16), as we see taking place in the famous Allegory of the Cave from book 7 of Plato's *Republic*.

The question that inevitably arises is how we reconcile the Emily Dickinson whose moral consciousness was so keenly articulated with the Emily Dickinson who shut the door on society and did not publish? Kimpel never addresses this matter as explicitly as he might have; but we can forge a hypothesis based on his piecemeal glimpses into her approach to the very act of thought. One of Kimpel's most important insights into Dickinson as a thinker is that she possessed the "capacity to be aware not only of objects external to herself, but also to reflect upon herself as an object of her own thinking" (128). As a thinking being, Dickinson saw herself apart from yet possessing a special relationship with unthinking nature: she felt assured in her capacity for deep thought, which was linked to her pride in what she could do with language (131). This is not the pride of vanity but the pride of knowing what one is capable of achieving, and conveying that knowledge intimately to her "select society."

Kimpel continues to assert that Dickinson, in her self-imposed exile, felt joy at the sights and sounds of that world as they entered her bedroom window, she also "was saddened, and saddened to the extreme of suffering," knowing that she was "immobilized by her own nature to move out to enjoy it and to take part in it" (192). We get a keen sense of this immobility in Fr1450; J1420:

One Joy+ of so much anguish	+sound
Sweet Nature has for me —	
I shun it as I do Despair	
Or dear iniquity —	
Why Birds, a Summer morning	
Before the Quick+ of Day	+ripe * peal * Drum * Flags * step
Should stab my ravished Spirit	* Red * Bells * tick * shouts * Blade

> With Dirks of Melody
> Is part of an inquiry
> That will receive reply
> . . .

Kimpel sees a parallel between this kind of agony and that of the Greek tragedians, who "were so eloquent in pointing out how helpless human beings are as victims of a Fate over which they have no control" (193). I would argue, however, that Dickinson, being fully aware of her nature, wholly accepted it, and was not afflicted by it — certainly not victimized by it, no more than a cloistered nun is victimized by her seclusion, or Boethius by his prison bars.

Understanding Emily Dickinson's archetypal poetics seems to me a necessary corollary to understanding her spiritual poetics. Whereas her Christian spirituality clearly situates her in her New England cultural milieu, her pagan mythic sensibility extends that milieu outward until it embraces all of human civilization across the ages. Also, her mythic sensibilities, coupled with her gothic impulse to destabilize conventional representations of reality, open new possibilities for spiritual perception in a world that typically draws sharp boundary lines between the natural and the supernatural.

8: Reassessing Dickinson's Poetic Project: A Postmodern Perspective

> *We need to interpret interpretations more than to interpret things.*
> — Montaigne, as quoted by Jacques Derrida

> *Dickinson's poetry changes literary theory.*
> — Helen McNeil, *Emily Dickinson* (1986)

> *Rilke writes in one of the* Duino Elegies, *"Strange to see meanings that clung together once, floating away / in every direction —." This is always the way with Dickinson. She is always somewhere else.*
> — Susan Howe, *The Birth-Mark* (1993)

LITERARY CRITICS TODAY not only deconstruct texts but, to paraphrase J. Hillis Miller, show how texts deconstruct themselves — by contradicting their own tacit assumptions that they refer to pre-existent features anchored in the world "out there," that is, to transcendental signifieds. But as Ferdinand de Saussure theorized in his *Course in General Linguistics* (1916; trans. 1959), linguistic signifiers speak to, formulate, or reformulate *mental representations* ("signifieds") of those language signifiers. Abolished was the assumption that words refer to transcendental signifieds — that is, to a universally agreed-upon objective reality. Jacques Derrida in turn argued that signifiers relate only to other signifiers, that "the absence of the transcendental signified extends the domain and the interplay of signification infinitely" (1978: 280).

Dickinson's Words

One of the biggest challenges that Dickinson scholars adopting a postmodern perspective face is that the poet already seems to be doing their job. Emerson blithely proclaims in *Nature* that words are "signs of natural facts" (197); but for Emily Dickinson,

> A word is dead when it is said,
> some say.
> I say it just begins to live
> that day.
>
> (Fr278A.1; J1212)

— a rather straightforward poem by Dickinsonian standards, or so it would seem. In its original context (part of a letter sent to her Norcross cousins) the poem is prefaced with "Thank you for the passage. How long to live the truth is!"[1] — suggesting that words of a powerful poem or of Scripture (or whatever passage she was referring to) endure because of their truth content.

But Dickinson's poem subtly contradicts that thought. A word "begins to live" the moment it is uttered because the rhetorical situation — the particular configuration of speaker, utterance, occasion, and audience — is unique.[2] The speaker-poet deploys a set of signifiers in an effort to construct a unique signified (the poem) that is "anchorless," that does not and *cannot* allude to a transcendental signified. Dickinson understood that the very act of trying to net reality with language pushes reality, like some mythic butterfly, ever farther away.

In *Emily Dickinson: The Modern Idiom* (1981) David Porter also sees Dickinson's words as in effect anchorless — a "withdrawal into words" is the way he phrases it (120). But why "withdrawal" with its negative-stereotype connotations of Dickinson as cowering victim, instead of, say, "venturing forth"? Similarly, Porter regards "the exclusion of interest in circumstantial reality" he finds in Dickinson's writing as "defensive, technically disturbed, closed off" — producing "a reality that can be projected only in the world of language" (120). There's more: Porter regards the "surreal word-world" her poetics generates as "hermetic language" (120), "narcissistic" (121), language "speaking itself," which, "removed from exterior referents . . . becomes almost pure locution" (121). He has in mind especially the conclusion of "I felt a Funeral, in my Brain," when "Space — began to toll, / As all the Heavens were a Bell, / And Being but an Ear, / And I, and Silence, some strange Race / Wrecked solitary, here —" (Fr340; J280).

"I felt a Funeral" typifies for Porter many of Dickinson's poems in which "language orbit(s) away from reality, speaking itself" (122), leaving us to confront only "an interplay of tropes" (122). Even in her most famous poem, "Because I could not stop for Death — / He kindly stopped for me —" (Fr479; J712), Dickinson, according to Porter, in using the "domineering selectional stroke 'stop,' . . . usurps the reality that might

---

[1] The original letter is lost. According to Franklin (1998), Mabel Loomis Todd transcribed the poem from a Norcross transcript, also lost. Because Todd noted that the poem, "Going to them, happy letter!" (Fr277A) had been enclosed with the letter containing "A word is dead," Franklin dates the poem from early 1862.

[2] For further discussion of Dickinson's use of rhetorical strategies in her poetry, see chapter 1.

otherwise be represented in the poem" (124). Porter reinforces his point a moment later by concluding that Dickinson's "severely inward poems could not regard the complicated world in a faithfully detailed way" (125). In other words, Porter's withdrawn poet-victim is also artistically inept.

It seems to me that Porter understands what Dickinson is up to, but like a formalist in postmodernist clothing, cannot permit himself to appreciate it. To a postmodernist the "reality" represented in "Because I could not stop for Death" is no more real than any other reality we represent in language. The only difference is that more conventional representations seem closer to reality because that is the illusion conventional language use creates. Yes, the texts of Dickinson's poems, being "traces of non-specifiable states" (121) can refer only to other texts, other signifieds. But Emily Dickinson would not have it any other way.

Taking a less radical stance on Dickinson's subjectivity, Guy Rotella, in his 1991 book *Reading and Writing Nature*, sees the metaphors in a poem like "There's a certain Slant of light" (Fr320; J258) as being "projected from within" (44). From an Emersonian perspective, our experience of nature is based upon what "is actually there.... Here is the source of Emerson's faith in intuition, and ... the doctrine of self-reliance" (24). Dickinson too has faith in intuition and self-reliance, but her certainties "are certainties of negation. Her skeptical 'Acres of Perhaps'[3] weaken the analogical foundations on which spiritualist and symbolist trust in nature and in God are based" (33).

Dickinson from a Lacanian Perspective

Contemporary critics typically do not take kindly to Freudian literary analysis. In *Dickinson and the Boundaries of Feminist Theory* (1991) Mary Loeffelholz examines the cultural, psychological, and artistic constructions that inform Dickinson's poetics, and in effect demolishes the psychopathology-based scenario that John Cody presented twenty years earlier in *After Great Pain*. Whereas Cody in his psychoanalytic reading of Dickinson's work sees the poet as having taken, in Loeffelholz's words, "a closed psychic economy in which art and language are less-than-abundant recompense for psychic trauma and loss" (8), Loeffelholz applies the lens of Lacanian psychoanalysis to reveal how Dickinson in her poems interrogates the gendered relationships of words to meanings in her society. Thus, in "It always felt to me — a wrong" (Fr521; J597), Dickinson takes

---

[3] From "Their Hight in Heaven comforts not —"; Fr725; J696. See also "Four Trees — upon a solitary Acre — / Without Design / Or Order, or Apparent Action — / Maintain —" (Fr778; J742).

the phallocentric Law of the Father to task in the most influential of contexts, the Holy Bible:

> It always felt to me — a wrong
> To that Old Moses — done —
> To let him see — the Canaan —
> Without the entering —
>
> And tho' in soberer moments —
> No Moses there can be
> I'm satisfied — the Romance
> In point of injury —
>
> Surpasses sharper stated —
> Of Stephen — or of Paul —
> For these — were only put to death —
> While God's adroiter will
>
> On Moses — seemed to fasten
> With+ tantalizing Play   +in
> As Boy — should deal with lesser Boy —
> To prove ability+   +show supremacy
>
> The fault — was doubtless Israel's —
> Myself — had banned the Tribes —
> And ushered Grand Old Moses
> In Pentateuchal Robes
>
> Upon the Broad Possession+   +Lawful Manor
> 'Twas little — He should see —+   +But titled Him — to see —
> Old Man on Nebo! Late as this —
> My+ justice bleeds — for Thee!   +One —
>
>   (Fr521; J597)

Three authorities are engaged in textual play here: Moses, leading his people out of bondage; God, who banishes Moses (and in so doing permits the unruly Israelites to enter the Promised Land), and the female speaker, through whose eyes the great patriarchal forces of Western civilization demonstrate, in Loeffelholz's view, "a bullying scheme of male rivalry, with the Father at the top of the heap" (63). Loeffelholz also notes how the speaker defends Moses' rights not as a contending counterpart of Christ, "but as a fellow author." That is to say, "[h]is own book, the Pentateuch, entitles him to his 'Possession' of Canaan, and that is the right Dickinson would enforce. Her justice 'bleeds' for him: Dickinson herself . . . becomes the alternative Christ figure, redeeming the writers of books in defiance of the Law of the Father" (64).[4] Loeffelholz's reading of this poem combines a formalist's attentiveness to the poem's scriptural allusions — its use of poetic devices, its diction, and so on — with a poststructuralist's effort to situate Dickinson's art in its cultural and ideological context. Hence she turns to Lacan's counter-Freudian system in order to foreground the patriarchal system governing religion and culture in Dickinson's day. In fact, Dickinson herself undertakes this task, but until recently that aspect of her work was muted or ignored, as it fell outside the paradigm of literary study.

Complexities of Lyricism

In her 1979 book *Lyric Time: Dickinson and the Limits of Genre,* Sharon Cameron sets out to probe the very nature of the lyric in terms of the complexities of lyricism that Dickinson works with. In general, Cameron views Dickinson's lyric utterances as "recoil from temporality" (24) — that is, from mortality. "Underneath words and syntax," Cameron explains, "at the primary level of thought, we sense Dickinson's belief that to adhere to the exaction of temporal relationship is to relinquish all hope of the immortality that will replace time itself" (1). Cameron sees Dickinson's syntactic and temporal discontinuities, then, as a way of using language — in this case the medium of lyric poetry — to get a taste of what otherwise lies beyond experience. "To tell the story of the self and its experiences is necessarily to posit a history for that self: a temporal structuring of the elements that comprise its meanings" (44).

Freedom from temporal progression also begets freedom from other conventional means of ordering the world — peeling away definitions from the phenomena they define, for example — so as to probe the underlying essences. Perhaps one of Dickinson's most perplexing lyric strategies is to open a poem with a more or less straightforward definition, but instead of using the definition as a stepping-stone toward understanding the thing defined, the speaker in effect uses the definition to undermine that understanding — or rather, to deconstruct the conventional understanding in order to discover its metaphysical nature, its essence. Cameron uses Fr781; J744 as an example:

---

[4] See also Cynthia Griffin Wolff's reading of this poem in her 1986 biography *Emily Dickinson* (348–49). Wolff notes that Dickinson's God comes across here as "insecure in his authority. It does not suffice the Lord to know that He is almighty. He needed to create us so that He would have some means for affirming His sense of His own importance by taunting humanity with its helplessness before His power."

> Remorse — is Memory — awake —
> Her Parties all astir —
> A Presence of Departed Acts —
> At window — and at Door —
>
> Its Past — set down before the Soul
> And lighted with a Match —
> . . .

The definition in this poem, Cameron writes, "exists for the purpose of dismissing the situation with which it purports to deal" (35). The speaker's definition of remorse calls attention to "the excruciating sense in which we can be inhabited by a past that will not stay still" because remorse reanimates past memories in distractingly condensed, distorted form. The terrible thing about remorse is that it obliterates the real meanings of our experiences and at the same time convinces us that the distortion we are seeing is the true reality (36).

As with definitions, so with narratives. In her chapter titled "A Loaded Gun: The Dialectics of Rage," Cameron calls attention to those Dickinson poems that "tell a story predicated on a dialectic: this life versus the next; the pleasures of love and sexuality versus a more chaste and bodiless devotion; the demands of the self versus their capitulation to the world's otherness. . . . A third voice, intervening in the dialectic . . . is often one of rage" that prevents a resolution to the dialectic (57). Poems that illustrate this dialectical structure include "I got so I could hear[5] his name — / Without — tremendous gain —" (Fr292; J293); "I should have been too glad, I see — / Too lifted — for the scant degree / Of Life's penurious Round —" (Fr283C; J313), and — most famously "My Life had stood — a Loaded Gun —" (Fr764; J754), which has deservedly become a centerpiece of contemporary Dickinson criticism regardless of critical perspective:[6]

---

[5] Dickinson lists two variants for "hear" in this fascicle poem: "think" and "take," with "take" underscored.

[6] For other extended discussions of this crucial poem see John Cody, *After Great Pain* (1971), 399–415); Judith Farr, *The Passion of Emily Dickinson* (1992), 241–43; Albert Gelpi, "Emily Dickinson and the Deerslayer: The Dilemma of the Woman Poet in America," in *Shakespeare's Sisters: Feminist Essays on Women Poets* (1979), 222–50; Jerome Loving, *Emily Dickinson: The Poet on the Second Story* (1986), 45–47; Cristanne Miller, *Emily Dickinson: A Poet's Grammar* (1987), 34–37); Barbara Antonina Clarke Mossberg, *Emily Dickinson: When the Writer Is a Daughter* (1982), 20–23); David Porter, *Emily Dickinson: The Modern Idiom* (1981), 209–17; Adrienne Rich, "Vesuvius at Home: The Power of Emily Dickinson," *Parnassus* 5 (1976): 49–74; Daneen Wardrop, *Emily Dickinson's Gothic: Goblin with a Gauge* (1996), 122–25; and Shira Wolosky, *Emily Dickinson: A Voice of War* (1984), 92–94.

My Life had stood — a Loaded Gun —
In Corners — till a Day
The Owner passed — identified —
And carried Me away —

And now We roam in+ Sovereign Woods —   +the
And now We hunt the Doe —
And every time I speak for Him —
The Mountains straight reply —

And do I smile, such cordial light
Upon the Valley glow —
It is as a Vesuvian face
Had let its pleasure through —

And when at Night — Our good Day done —
I guard my Master's Head —
'Tis better than the Eider-Duck's
Deep+ Pillow — to have shared —   +low

To foe of His — I'm deadly foe —
None stir+ the second time —   +harm
On whom I lay a Yellow Eye —
Or an emphatic Thumb —

Though I than He — may longer live
He longer must — than I —
For I have but the power+ to kill,   +art
Without the power to die —

Like Clark Griffith in his explication of "I started early, took my Dog" (see chapter 1), Cameron begins with superficial readings of the poem, which she then suggests not adequate. In her first reading, she sees the speaker, retrieved by God becomes the agent of God's marksmanship, and the mountains echo her shots. In the second superficial reading, Cameron writes that "if 'Owner' is a term that suggests a deity, 'Master' may suggest a lover (a theory prompted by the 'Master' letters). In this reading, the speaker receives identity when she is carried off by the earthly lover whom she thereafter guards with murderous and possessive fury, anxious to protect him from his enemies and preferring . . . to watch over his bed than to share it with him; preferring, that is, violence to sexuality" (66). But for Cameron the poem does not make much sense as a religious allegory ("the speaker's service to God does not involve the killing of the unrighteous"), nor as one of an erotic relationship, especially in light of the last stanza, which, when taken literally, cannot refer to human beings (who *do* possess "the power to die"). Cameron then builds a more nuanced explication around the premise that "'identity' in the poem is conceived of as violence, just as life is apparently conceived of as rage. The speaker of the poem acknowledges that being alive requires that she accept the power — and in turn the obligation — to commit acts of violence (67).

If not religious allegory, then what? For Cameron, Dickinson's lyrics are essentially non-referential; Dickinson dramatizes the *struggle* of wording existence into being (193). E. Miller Budick, however, sees the poet as engaged in symbolic texturing. Unlike many scholars who discuss Dickinson's symbolism in the context of their respective critical agendas, Budick devotes her 1985 monograph, *Emily Dickinson and the Life of Language: A Study of Symbolic Poetics* to the way Dickinson fashions her own symbolic system. Drawing from such venerable studies of symbolism in literature as Wilbur Urban's *Language and Reality* (1951), Charles Fiedelson, Jr.'s *Symbolism and American Literature* (1953), and Kenneth Burke's *Language as Symbolic Action* (1966), Budick argues that "[i]n its dissociation from society and the world, Dickinson's poetry is . . . a poetry about language"; but while the poems, in Budick's view, are distanced from the world, their "life of language does not exist apart from the larger life of the universe and of God." The life that the language delineates, then, exists on a symbolic plane of Dickinson's own making, and "rejects the symbolic attitudes and methodologies that are part and parcel of New England history, and perhaps also of most philosophical reflection from Plato onward" (30). For example, Dickinson's poems about the soul, "are . . . not simply abstract statements about the dualities of mind that have affected all men in all times. Rather, they are specific judgments rendered against American intellectual origins as they are interpreted by Dickinson" (144). Budick turns to Sacvan Bercovich, who, reflecting in his 1975 book *The Puritan Origins of the American Self* on the Puritan "inner civil war," writes that the Puritan belief in the welfare of one's own soul hinges on the fact that it is in opposition to the self — although, paradoxically, continual attention to self-abnegation is as effective a form of self-improvement as any that typified the Romantics or Transcendentalists (Budick 145; Bercovich, 17, 20). The language of the poem presents a reality that simultaneously excites and terrifies, a reality in which creation and destruction coexist in and through each other (5) — this in reference to "Blazing in Gold and quenching in Purple" (Fr321C; J228).

Dickinson's defiance of genre and conventions of textual production presents a more fundamental problem to contemporary scholars. This is the area Virginia Jackson examines in *Dickinson's Misery: A Theory of Lyric Reading* (2005). Jackson begins by reconceptualizing the idea of lyric in the context of nineteenth-century editorial "packaging" of published texts of lyric poetry. Unlike the socially contingent genres of the novel and the drama, "the lyric emerged as the one genre indisputably literary and independent of social contingency" — a startling irony, given the fact that "[b]y the early nineteenth century, poetry had never before been so dependent on the mediating hands of the editors and reviewers who managed the print public sphere" (7). In other words, Jackson goes on to explain, "the lyric takes form through the development of reading practices in the nineteenth and twentieth centuries that become the practices of literary criticism" (8).

Jackson's goal in *Dickinson's Misery,* then, is to show that what has come to be known as the genre of lyric poetry, traditionally regarded as unmediated, is indeed based on editorial constructs. Early formalists like Cleanth Brooks and Robert Penn Warren in *Understanding Poetry* (1938) tried to erase the old subdivisions of lyric poetry (meditations, odes, songs, and so on) on grounds that they were irrational and arbitrary (Jackson, 10). Emily Dickinson's poetry has been similarly essentialized by the formalist: "The lyric reading practiced by every editor since Higginson has actively cultivated a disregard for the circumstances of Dickinson's manuscripts' circulation. By being taken out of their sociable circumstances, those manuscripts have become poems, and by becoming poems, they have been interpreted as lyrics" (21). From Dickinson's perspective, a change in address can signal a change in genre, just as publicly transmitting a text makes it so, "but that historical process does not mean that the writer originally intended that form of address to make such a difference. What is at stake in establishing the genre of Dickinson's writing is nothing less than its literary afterlife" (125). The battle lines are thus drawn between the traditionalist's efforts to preserve an essential idea of lyric poetry, whereby any anomalies or discontinuities are stigmatized and overthrown, and the efforts of poststructuralists to decenter, to negate ontology, to foreground discontinuity. Frank Lentricchia, in describing Foucault's "Derridean alternative to the totalizing history that wants to draw 'all phenomena around a single center,'"[7] notes that that single center "functions according to the model of a Platonic form: as an essentializing force which, by causing particular texts to become veils covering a hidden ontological realm, robs them of their identity as it annihilates differences" (Lentricchia, 191).

Margaret Dickie, in her *Lyric Contingencies: Emily Dickinson and Wallace Stevens* (1991), also regards Dickinson's lyricism in stark contrast to traditional notions of "lyric," especially the one propagated by American Romanticism as typified by Emerson and Whitman, in which the

---

[7] Foucault, *The Archaeology of Knowledge,* 12; qtd. Lentricchia, *After the New Criticism,* 191.

individual is celebrated as both unique and representative — the latter occurring when lyrics are conventionalized. "The concept of individualism," Dickie writes, "includes a commonality and a sense of partaking in the common that threatens the claim of individuality. Individualism is always spoken with a forked tongue" (18). Dickinson, says Dickie, chose to undomesticate the lyric precisely because, like the hymn, it was "available for subversive expression" (18). Her first order of business was to undercut the romantic ideal of identification; "[w]here Whitman would claim, 'And what I assume, you shall assume . . .' Dickinson could never make that identification, writing rather, "I never felt at Home — Below — / And in the Handsome Skies / I shall not feel at Home — I know —" (Fr437; J413). She is concerned with transience, not transcendence; with existential discontinuity rather than celestial unity. Dickie writes, "[h]er sense is of the always changing self that cannot be described by that Transcendental state beyond activity to which Emerson aspired" (9). Dickie calls attention to an especially fine example of a Dickinson lyric that undermines one of the ideals of lyric poetry, that of establishing a harmonious identification between self and other — in this case between speaker and robin:

> You'll know Her — by Her Foot —
> The smallest+ Gamboge Hand   +finest
> With Fingers — where the Toes should be —
> Would more affront the Sand —
>
> Than this Quaint Creature's Boot —
> Adjusted by a stem —
> Without a Button — I c'd vouch —
> Unto a Velvet Limb —
>
> You'll know Her — by Her Vest —
> Tight fitting — Orange — Brown —
> Inside a Jacket duller —
> She wore when she was born —
>   . . .   (Fr604; J634)

Here we see Dickinson reflecting lyrically on what Dickie calls "the paradox of identity." She goes on to say "[w]hat we see best, we see least well; what we cannot see or refuse to see becomes clearest evidence" (19). Along with the fanciful association of bird with poet triggered by the punning of "foot," Dickinson *widens* the gap between bird and speaker as the speaker tries so valiantly to close it. Dickie writes:

> The bird's foot described as "this Quaint Creature's Boot" is rendered unknowable as either foot or boot when the speaker says it is

"Without a Button — I could vouch —." That testimony guarantees enigma. Without a button it is not a boot, and so the vouching undoes the knowledge that it would confirm.... Like Nietzsche's individual, this bird is something other than its type. (20)

One can argue, of course, that Dickinson is simply extending the idea (if not the ideal) of lyricism, not undermining it — that re-experiencing the spiritual certainties as uncertainties or what is assumed to be knowable as unknowable should also be part of a lyrical-poetical experience; but perhaps such a "neo-lyrical" experience is a product of our postmodern era. In Dickinson's day, the impact on the reader would have been far more discordant, to the point of not being regarded as an aesthetic experience at all.

When a poet does the critic's job, perhaps the best way for the critic to respond is to return the favor, to do the poet's job, so to speak. Susan Howe's *My Emily Dickinson* (1985) is a remarkable example of literary criticism as prose-poetry (Howe is a poet as well as a scholar-teacher), worthy of comparison to the literary criticism of Thomas Carlyle, Oscar Wilde, D. H. Lawrence, and Gertrude Stein. Howe gives us Emily Dickinson from the inside looking out. As one postmodern poet contemplating another, Howe recognizes the way Dickinson "explored the implications of breaking the law just short of breaking off communication with a reader" (11). Like Gertrude Stein, Susan Howe and Emily Dickinson also want to know, "[w]hose order is that inside the structure of a sentence? What inner articulation releases the coils and complications of Saying's assertion?" (11). Howe understands that Dickinson's "self-imposed exile, indoors" was emancipation, not confinement, a behavioral act paralleling an ideological one in which conventional paradigms of order (grammatical, poetical, religious, or otherwise) are abandoned. "Do Emily Dickinson's words flee conventional meaning?, asks Howe. "Define definition" (16). In order for Dickinson to become Dickinson, "free to excavate and interrogate definition," Howe asserts, "the first labor called for was to sweep away the pernicious idea of poetry as embroidery for women" (17).

My Emily Dickinson is most engrossing when we witness Howe's sensibility melding with Dickinson's, as in the following passage that does not just discuss but *embraces* "In many and reportless places" (Fr1404; J1382):

At the center of Indifference I feel my own freedom.... the Liberty in wavering. Compression of possibility tensing to spring. Might and might.... mystic illumination of analogies ... incentive human supposition that any word may mean its opposite. Occult tendency of opposites to attract and merge. *Hesitation of us all,* one fire-baptized soul was singing.

> In many and reportless places
> We feel a Joy —
> Reportless, also, but sincere as Nature
> Or Deity —
>
> It comes, without a consternation —
> Dissolves+ — the same —   +abates * Exhales
> But leaves a sumptuous+ Destitution —   +blissful
> Without a Name —
>
> Profane it by a search+ — we cannot   +pursuit
> It has no home —
> Nor we who having once inhaled+ it —   +waylaid
> Therefore roam.
>
> On this heath wrecked from Genesis, nerve endings quicken. Naked sensibility at the extremest periphery. Narrative expanding contracting dissolving. Nearer to know less before afterward schism in sum. No hierarchy, no notion of polarity. Perception of an object means loosing and losing it. Quests end in failure, no victory and sham questor. One answer undoes another and fiction is real. Trust absence, allegory, mystery . . . No titles or numbers for the poems. That would force order. . . . No outside editor / "robber." Conventional punctuation was abolished. . . . Dashes drew liberty of interruption inside the structure of each poem. (22–23)

Howe gives a distinctly postmodernist flavoring to formalist textual explication. For example, her approach to the first stanza of Fr764; J754 ("My Life had stood — a Loaded Gun —") reads as follows:

> My and me. In this unsettling New England lexical landscape nothing is sure. In a shorter space (woman's quick voice) Dickinson went further than Browning, coding and erasing — deciphering the idea of herself, dissimulation in revelation. Really alone at a real frontier, dwelling in Possibility was what she had brilliantly learned to do.
>
> POSSIBILITIES:
> *My Life:* A Soul finding God.
> *My Life:* A Soul finding herself
> *My Life:* A poet's admiring heart born into voice by idealizing a precursor poet's song.
> *My Life:* Dickinson herself, waiting in corners of neglect for Higginson to Recognize her ability and help her to join the ranks of other published American poets. (76)

I see Susan Howe the poet merging with Susan Howe the critic to create a new synthesis of poetic criticism. Such a "transgression" of genre boundaries would gladden Emily Dickinson's heart.

Dickinson's Seductions

Articulating the problem he sees with some cultural-context approaches to Dickinson, Robert McClure Smith writes in his 1996 *The Seductions of Emily Dickinson* that "[e]ach [critic] assumes that literary text and history can be distinguished as foreground and background and that the devices through which the text refracts or reflects the contextual background are therefore easily observable for the critical analyst" (19). Instead of establishing a historically-based "master narrative" such as the one Betsy Erkkila identifies as a "poetic revolution . . . grounded in the privilege of [Dickinson's] class position in a conservative Whig household" (1992; qtd. Smith, 19), Smith turns to master *texts* which, in Dickinson's historical and geographical milieu, exerted widespread influence. One of the most important of these is Milton's *Paradise Lost,* which Smith calls "the quintessential narrative of seduction," used by Mary Lyon as exam material for the graduating class at Mt. Holyoke Seminary for Women.

> In Milton's epic poem, as in Genesis, Satan is the first tempter of women into sin: he is the epitome of successful seduction. It is Satan's subtle persuasion of Eve, his rhetorical seduction of her, that introduces into the discourse of humanity the possibility of using linguistic signs for the purposes of deception. (26)

Smith reflects on the notion that a poem dramatizing satanic seduction can itself be seductive — a paradox Milton himself recognized — Milton being "the religious poet who found the uses of rhetoric intrinsically satanic" (28).

But how does this relate to Emily Dickinson's poetry? In addition to the likelihood of her necessary immersion in *Paradise Lost* during her year at Mt. Holyoke, and the fact that a copy of *Paradise Lost* was in the Dickinson family library, Smith says, Dickinson "associates a 'calling' to poetry with a dangerous external temptation ambiguously resisted" (29).

Smith next lays out a "poetics of seduction" that he sees operating in Dickinson's canon. Refuting the notion that Dickinson "was primarily an exponent of an art-for-art's-sake aesthetic," Smith argues that the male figures in Dickinson's poems, for example, have recognizable sociohistorical counterparts, so that in a poem like "It was a quiet way" (Fr573B; J1053), Dickinson is adapting "a specific antebellum discourse of seduction" (134):

> It was a quiet way —
> He asked if I was his —
> I made no answer of the Tongue
> But answer of the Eyes —
> And then He bore me on

Before this mortal noise
With swiftness, as of Chariots
And distance, as of Wheels.
. . .

In addition to featuring "an unspecified male figure" of a kind that occupies many of her poems, Dickinson, Smith argues, could be alluding to the antebellum seducer whose seduction, "at least in its fictional representation, was inevitably considered a prefiguring of the seducee's death" (84).

In his chapter on ways of reading seduction Smith notes how the word "seduction" has become a metaphor for the practice of deconstruction, the result of the influence of psychoanalysis in postmodern theoretical discourse (134). Just as psychoanalysis is in a sense a discourse about seduction (for instance, in Freud's patients who were sexually abused as children, which abuse Freud referred to as "seductions," his euphemism for incest; Smith 135), so too can we see Dickinson's poetics evolving from her adapting of "an existing discourse *about* seduction" and that antebellum discourse concerning seduction "was reconstituted by her into a discourse *of* seduction" (136; emphasis Smith's). Smith thus gives a postmodern twist to the psychoanalytic approach to Dickinson's poetry a la John Cody: "[t]he question critical readers need to ask . . . is not what psychoanalysis can teach us about the poet but what the poet can teach us about the workings of psychoanalysis" (136).

Perhaps something similar could be said of postmodernism. Dickinson might be able to teach us more about it than it can teach us about Dickinson.

9: Celebrating Emily Dickinson in Belles Lettres, Music, and Art

> *If fame belonged to me, I could not escape her —*
> — E. D. to Higginson, 7 June 1866

> *... legend won't explain the sheer sanity*
> *of vision, the serious mischief*
> *of language, the economy of pain.*
> — Linda Pastan, "Emily Dickinson" (2000)

EMILY DICKINSON AND HER WORK have served as subject matter for poets and fiction writers, painters, sculptors, and composers going back to the poet's own lifetime. The protagonist in Helen Hunt Jackson's novel *Mercy Philbrick's Choice* (1876) is said to have been modeled after the poet, a friend since childhood.[1] Artistic works based on the poet have proliferated over the decades, yet have only very recently begun to receive serious critical attention. Bibliographic surveys include those by Klaus Lubbers (1968), who comments briefly on poems, novels, and dramas about the poet's life published or produced through 1957; by Carlton Lowenberg, who in *Musicians Wrestle Everywhere: Emily Dickinson and Music* (1992) cites hundreds of musical compositions based on Dickinson's poems; and by Jonnie Guerra, whose "Dickinson Adaptations in the Arts and the Theater," appears in *The Emily Dickinson Handbook* (1998). *Titanic Operas,* an online bibliography of more than 150 published poems about Emily Dickinson, is accessible through the Emily Dickinson Electronic Archives. In the introduction to her *Emily Dickinson: A Bibliography of Secondary Sources, with Selective Annotations, 1890 through 1987,* Jeanetta Boswell omitted what she terms "literary tributes to Dickinson" because "they seemed to say more of the person who wrote them than about Emily Dickinson" (she nevertheless cites poems about Dickinson by Hart Crane and Richard Wilbur). Whether Boswell's assertion is valid or not, I believe that a bibliographic record of creative responses to Dickinson is necessary because such works collectively shed important light on Dickinson's cultural reception.

---

[1] "Set in a western New England village modeled on Amherst, the narrative concerned a woman poet whose 'choice' was not to remarry" (Alfred Habegger, *My Wars Are Laid Away in Books,* 556).

Dramatic Works

Over the decades the Dickinson mystique has spawned several stage plays. For detailed commentary on the plays from the 1930s and 40s — Susan Glaspell's *Alison's House* (1930), Vincent York and Frederick Pohl's *Brittle Heaven* (1935), and Dorothy Gardner's *Eastward in Eden* (1949), see Jonnie Guerra's 1998 essay, "Dickinson Adaptations in the Arts and Theater"; Paul J. Ferlazzo also offers detailed commentary on Glaspell's play, summarizing the central conflict whereby the sister of a deceased poet attempts to destroy the latter's manuscripts, exclaiming "I say she does not belong to the world! . . . And I'll keep her from the world!" (Glaspell, 5; qtd. Ferlazzo 1976, 17).

The most popular play about Emily Dickinson thus far is William Luce's one-woman show *The Belle of Amherst* (1976), which received a Broadway production starring Julie Harris, directed by Charles Nelson Reilly.[2] Luce foregrounds Dickinson's domesticity and her intense feelings. Despite Julie Harris's consummate skill as a stage performer, the play neglects to make sense of a fundamental paradox: why America's most reclusive genius would wish to share her innermost feelings with an audience. Nevertheless, the play skillfully integrates fascinating minutiae from facets of Dickinson's life, even Dickinson's own recipes, several of which have survived,[3] such as her recipe for black cake, which Luce has the poet share with the audience.

From the moment that Luce's Dickinson introduces herself to the audience, we realize that this playwright dug deep for factual details

> My name is Emily Elizabeth Dickinson. Elizabeth is for my Aunt Elizabeth Currier. She's Father's sister. Oh, how the trees stand up straight when they hear Aunt Libbie's little boots come thumping into Amherst! She's the only male relative on the female side. (2)

That last quip comes from a letter Dickinson wrote to Elizabeth Holland in 1876 (L473), and is characteristic of her wit — a wit that Luce fully exploits in his play.

All too soon, however, the play slides into bathos. Emily Dickinson must appear as suffering inside regardless of her outward charm. This to me is symptomatic of popular culture's inability or unwillingness to com-

---

[2] *The Belle of Amherst: A Play Based on the Life of Emily Dickinson*, premiered at the Moore Egyptian Theatre in Seattle on Feb. 25, 1976; it opened on Broadway at the Longacre Theatre on April 28, 1976. The play was published the same year, and produced on television (PBS) in the 1980s.

[3] See *Emily Dickinson: Profile of the Poet as Cook, with Selected Recipes*, compiled by the Guides at the Dickinson Homestead (1976).

prehend (let alone appreciate) the healthy need for an individual artist to sequester herself from the world: surely she had to have been deeply wounded somehow. In a world where many people cannot seem to function without a mobile phone fastened to their jaws, many are dumbfounded by the woman who champions *dis*connectedness and the joys of intellectual independence. Another problem with *The Belle of Amherst* is that, as Guerra points out, Luce makes oversimplified cause-effect connections between Dickinson's becoming a poet and "her 'failure' within the courtship-marriage plot conventionally used to narrate women's lives" (Guerra, 390). Despite these flaws, however, *The Belle of Amherst* has probably stimulated a greater interest in the poet than any biography.

Other one-woman shows crop up in regional theaters now and then. Martha Furey's "Tea with Emily" (2002), which debuted in Edinburgh, is an example. Furey depicts a strong-willed, upbeat Emily Dickinson. However, the playwright (who also plays the role) strains credulity when she has Dickinson preparing to receive two gentlemen callers, Henry David Thoreau and Mark Twain. With a scenario like that, the play might be more accurately billed as a fantasy. Another one-woman show, "Emily Dickinson: The Soul's Society," by Laurette Willis, premiered at Northeastern State University in 1995, starring the playwright.

In 1989 Massachusetts playwright Brian Marsh produced *The Search for Emily*.[4] The play is set in the Dickinson Homestead; the central character, Alice, a playwright in search of the authentic Emily Dickinson, brings the poet face to face with several late-twentieth-century admirers. Marsh's play is worthy of serious attention because its theme is serious: what knowledge must we acquire of a genius like Emily Dickinson before we can say that we truly *know* her? At one point Alice says, "[s]earching for Emily Dickinson in old manuscripts and letters is an experience, certainly. It has kept three generations of biographers furiously busy — each on a separate search for the truth that was Emily. *Their* Emily" (20; emphasis added).

Poetical Works

The first poem we have about Emily Dickinson is a sonnet by one of Dickinson's friends from young adulthood, Emily Ford (née Fowler), daughter of William Fowler, a professor of rhetoric at Amherst, and granddaughter of Noah Webster. According to Richard B. Sewall's 1974 *Life of Emily Dickinson*, when Ford visited Amherst in July 1882 Emily would not see her. After the appearance of the first volume of *Poems* (1890),

---

[4] First presented as a work-in-progress at the Jones Library, Amherst, MA on Dec. 8, 1988; produced professionally at the University of Massachusetts, premiering on July 21, 1989, directed by Timothy Holcomb.

Ford commemorated the snub in her poem, which she sent to the *Springfield Republican,* where it was published in January 1891:

> Eheu! Emily Dickinson!
> Oh, friend, these sighs from out your solitude
>   But pierce my heart! Social with bird and bee,
>   Loving your tender flowers with ecstacy, [*sic*]
> You shun the eye, the voice, and shy elude
> The loving souls that dare not to intrude
>   Upon your chosen silence. Friend, you thought
>   No life so sweet and fair as hiding brought,
> And beauty is your song, with interlude
> Of outer life which to your soul seems crude,
>   Thoughtless, unfeeling, idle, scant of grace;
> For common daily strife to you is rude,
>   And, shrinking, you in shadow lonely stay
>   Invisible to all, howe'er we pray.
>   (qtd. Sewall, 1974: 379)

As Sewall notes, the poem "is unimportant except for one thing: it shows the Myth in action" (379). I would add that the poem also reveals the ire of a spurned friend, one of the "loving souls" who had been devoted to the poet.

In *Visiting Emily* (2000) editors Sheila Coghill and Thom Tammaro have collected Dickinson-related poems by eighty poets from across the decades, including John Berryman, Billy Collins, Hart Crane, Alice Fulton, Donald Hall, Galway Kinnell, Maxine Kumin, Joyce Carol Oates, Sharon Olds, Alicia Ostriker, Linda Pastan, Adrienne Rich, and William Stafford. Most of the poems are "serious" in the sense that they grapple with the paradoxical and elusive aspects of Emily Dickinson's life and artistry. As the editors state in their introduction, "The intellectual range and thematic focus, the unbounded center of her images simultaneously haunt and elude us. Of course this makes her American muse par excellence" (xiv). A few of the poets, such as X. J. Kennedy, opt for buffoonery as a way of deconstructing Dickinson's mythic allure. Kennedy parodies her condensed syntax in a poem titled "Emily Dickinson Leaves a Message to the World, Now That Her Homestead in Amherst Has an Answering Machine."

One of the most intriguing poems in the collection is a monologue, "Emily Dickinson's Sestina for Molly Bloom," by Barbara F. Lefcowitz. Here are its opening lines:

> At times I almost believed it: madness
> the only way to say yes,

to stumble into shapes of night
that gape open
like abandoned wells —

Like Molly Bloom, Lefcowitz's Emily Dickinson is aroused by the possibilities of night, paradoxically disclosing as it conceals. Poems of imaginative power such as those by Lefcowitz have the capacity to deepen our insight into Dickinson's complex interior life. Conventional criticism, even of a postmodern stripe, can only go so far in capturing the genius of a poet like Emily Dickinson. One must either fuse criticism with poetry, as Susan Howe manages to do, or be a highly accomplished poet oneself in order to venture deeper.

Profiles of poets influenced by Dickinson are a regular feature of *The Emily Dickinson International Society Bulletin*. Under the banner of "Poet to Poet," some of the profiles include (together with examples of their Dickinson-inspired poems) Stephanie A. Tingley's "Sandra Gilbert and Emily Dickinson" (6.1; May/June 1994); Jonnie Guerra's "Marianne Boruch and Emily Dickinson" (11.1; May/June 1999); Elizabeth M. Mills, "Punishment and Poetry: Emily Dickinson Shares with Sharon Olds" (14.1; May/June 2002); and Erika Scheurer, "From the Prairie to the World: Patricia Hampl and Emily Dickinson" (14.2; November-December 2002).

Works of Prose Fiction

For sheer audacity of speculation, writers of prose fiction take the prize. At least seven novels about Emily Dickinson have appeared in the last thirty-five years:[5] Anne Edwards' *The Hesitant Heart* (1974) focuses on the poet's love affair with Judge Otis Lord. Jane Langton's mystery novel and academic satire, *Emily Dickinson is Dead* (1984), features the amiable detective and Thoreau scholar Homer Kelly, who works closely with English professor Owen Kraznik in helping to solve the murder of an Emily Dickinson look-alike murdered while attending a conference in Amherst on the centennial of Dickinson's death.

In Joanne Dobson's mystery novel *Quieter than Sleep* (1997) Dickinson *scholars* get murdered one by one once they discover some amazing secret about Emily Dickinson's life. Like Langton's Homer Kelly, Dobson's Karen Pelletier is an academic sleuth — an Emily Dickinson specialist. One evening at a cocktail party, Pelletier discovers one of her colleagues strangled to death in a closet. "His handsome face was contorted and

---

[5] Novels of earlier origin include, in addition to Helen Hunt Jackson's *Mercy Philbrick's Choice* (mentioned above), MacGregor Jenkins's *Emily* (1930) and Laura Benet's *Come Slowly, Eden* (1942).

swollen.... Whoever had killed him had turned his whimsical necktie into a ... lethal weapon" (24–25).

A very different kind of novel, Jamie Fuller's *The Diary of Emily Dickinson* (1993), conjures up a fictitious diary of the poet. Many of the entries have a Dickinsonian feel to them, and are quite comical. For example:

> *Thursday, May 23.* Tonight while clearing the table I dropped a dish half full of gravy — and some splashed upon Father. For several moments Christian charity departed — and I was severely upbraided for my carelessness. "Daughter, does your mind always reside in separate quarters from the task at hand?" I could not think his anger unjust — he trades in justice all the day! (54–55)

Fuller occasionally intersperses these imaginary entries with straightforward commentary. Following an entry in which Dickinson expresses uncertainty over what Thomas Wentworth Higginson thinks of her and her work ("Does he think me worthy of his mighty efforts — or am I only Curiosity? I am not bold enough to ask"), Fuller writes:

> The student of Dickinson might well ask the same question . . . since the reason for the attraction between Higginson and his pupil is no clearer from his perspective than from hers. As we have seen, he advised her against publication and had no real appreciation of her work until after her death. (91)

Fuller's commentary is useful for readers who do not know the details of Dickinson's life; on the other hand, it continually interrupts the fictive universe generated by the diaries — rather like adding footnotes to a poem.

Somewhat more somber in tone is Judith Farr's *I Never Came to You in White* (1996), a novel that opens an unusual perspective into the poet's nature by way of imaginary letters written by Dickinson, together with imaginary letters written by Dickinson's friends and relatives after her death. In one of them, Lavinia is sitting in her sister's bedroom a few days after her death, writing to her cousin Clara Newman Green about an almost unbearable task she must carry out:

> Today, before sunset, I must put her personal letters in the fire. Our New England custom. Oh, Clary, it is sad to burn so many letters! She kept hundreds of them, all bound up with different colored ribbons and stacked in that antique chest of Mother's. (198)

To be sure, every student of Emily Dickinson has felt the pain brought on by this actual event. Farr not only brings the moment to life in this fictive rendering; she also implicitly reminds us that despite the allegiance to custom as well as to her sister's wishes, Lavinia too felt pain, but only after the deed was done.

Lavinia is the narrator in *The Sister: A Novel of Emily Dickinson* (English trans. 2007[6]) by the Argentine novelist Paola Kaufmann (who died in 2006). Although Kaufmann dramatizes key moments in the lives of the family members, those moments are perfunctorily presented, more like Martha Dickinson Bianchi's early reminiscences than the dramatic rendering we expect from a novel. Nevertheless, Kaufmann does manage to engross us with the climactic courtroom drama in which Lavinia vents her frustration and hatred toward the woman she is suing for fraud: Mabel Loomis Todd, the editor of her sister's poems, but also the mistress of her brother, who had, before his death, promised Mabel a parcel of land, which Lavinia is now contesting on grounds that she was duped into signing the deed.

Whereas Kaufmann's novel seems insubstantial as fiction because she restricts her story almost exclusively to known historical or biographical events in the poet's life, Rose MacMurray's novel, *Afternoons with Emily* (2007), also published posthumously, takes the opposite course. MacMurray creates a completely fictional narrator, Miranda Chase, a precocious ten-year-old whose professor-mythologist father has steeped her in the classics and encouraged in her a love for innovative thinking. We become thoroughly acquainted with her before she ever encounters Emily Dickinson, thirteen years her senior. All the reader needs is a walloping ability to suspend disbelief: shortly after arriving in Amherst and becoming part of Amherst social life, Miranda receives the following invitation:

My dear Miss Chase,
    A rumor flew and lit at my window. Do you too refuse Salvation?
Let us then consider Perdition together — here on Monday, at four o'clock.
    Your unprofessed friend,
                      Emily E. Dickinson (86)

The challenge to the suspension of disbelief lies not in the wording of the letter — it's amazing to see MacMurray emulate Dickinson's language so well — but with the fact that Emily Dickinson, even in 1857, would ever extend such an invitation to a stranger. But once readers tackle that hurdle, they will find the friendship between Miranda and Emily intrinsically believable and intellectually fascinating, even as Miranda finds herself becoming enmeshed in Dickinson family crises.

On a lighter note, you know that someone has entered the pantheon of myth and legend when fantasy and science-fiction writers start to weave yarns about that individual. I have thus far chanced upon three stories involving the poet — in bizarre ways, as you might expect. Jane Yolen, a fantasist, folklorist, and prolific author of children's books, in her Nebula-

---

[6] Published in Spanish in 2003 under the title *La Hermana*.

Award-winning short story, "Sister Emily's Lightship" (1996), has the poet confront alien beings who visit her late at night and take her into space to view the world as she had already imagined it in her poetry. Connie Willis, in her satiric "The Soul Selects Her Own Society: Invasion and Repulsion: A Chronological Reinterpretation of Two of Emily Dickinson's Poems: A Wellsian Perspective" (1996) seems more intent on ridiculing arcane academic writing (fine by me!) — as one can infer from the title — than she does on commemorating the centennial of H. G. Wells's *War of the Worlds*. Willis has Emily Dickinson writing poems that chronicle the Martians' invasion of earth ten years after her death. And in Paul DiFilippo's novella, "Walt and Emily" (1995), Walt Whitman seduces the poet and then travels with her into a parallel universe to meet Allen Ginsberg. So much for realistic extrapolation.

In assessing the impact that a great writer has upon our culture, we would do well to give serious attention to how that writer has influenced other creative writers. Harold Bloom has famously explored this in the context of what he calls "the anxiety of influence"[7] And, most recently, Thomas Gardner, in *A Door Ajar: Contemporary Writers and Emily Dickinson* (2006) has perceptively described the strategies by which several contemporary writers (Lucie Brock-Broido, Jorie Graham, Robert Hass, Susan Howe, Marilynne Robinson) have reconceptualized Dickinsonian tropes in the modern idiom.[8]

Gardner begins with Brock-Broido's eerie fusion of Dickinson's original Master Letter with her own Master Letter. Dickinson's "You asked me what my flowers said — then they were disobedient — I gave them messages" — becomes Brock-Broido's "You say I Misenveloped & sent you something Else. In the middle of it all, my mind went blank, all the red notes of terror blinking. Please to tell me — have I unsettled you by this?" (3). Brock-Broido's rendering enables the reader to see Dickinson's speakers anguish in a new context. Gardner writes, "Working with its [Dickinson's Master Letter language], Brock-Broido re-experiences . . . Dickinson's confrontation with human limits" (5). Gardner thus explores how the contemporary writers he has interviewed,[9] through their own

---

[7] "Poetic history . . . is held to be indistinguishable from poetic influence, since strong poets make that history by misreading one another, so as to clear imaginative space for themselves" *(The Anxiety of Influence: A Theory of Poetry,* 2nd edition (1997), 5.

[8] Cf. Michael Hofmann and James Lasdun's *After Ovid: New Metamorphoses* (1994), an anthology of poems by forty-two contemporary poets who "metamorphose" themes in Ovid's masterpiece. The anthology, however, other than a brief introduction, lacks commentary.

[9] Graham, Howe, Robinson, and Wright. Gardner includes the texts of these interviews in the book.

poetry and prose, enact "in their own terms, some aspect of the broken responsiveness before a world that can no longer be held in place that Dickinson puts into play" (6). Ruth, the narrator of Marilynne Robinson's novel *Housekeeping* (1980), "left on her own to make sense of the world around her by a series of deaths and losses, picks up on a series of images and situations first put into play by Emily Dickinson and speculatively recreates her world through them" (25).

Anyone interested in a dramatization of the scandalous love affair between Emily Dickinson's brother Austin and Mabel Loomis Todd, Dickinson's first editor (the affair was first brought to light by Richard B. Sewall in his 1974 biography and popularized by Polly Longsworth's 1984 publication of the lovers' impassioned correspondence under the title *Austin and Mabel*), might enjoy Candace Ridington's well-researched novel, *Rubicon* (1997).[10] "Rubicon" was the word Austin scribbled in his diary when he and Mabel divulged their amorous commitment to each other — a commitment that lasted from late 1882 (the year after she arrived in Amherst with her astronomer husband David) until Austin's death in 1895. Did Emily know about the affair? There is indirect evidence that she not only knew about it but helped it along, together with her sister Lavinia. The story that Ridington dramatizes in her novel thus has plausible grounding.[11]

Musical Compositions

Not even the novelists have been as productive as the composers. Dickinson bibliographer Carlton Lowenberg, in his *Musicians Wrestle Everywhere: Emily Dickinson and Music* (1992), inventories documents relating to Dickinson's own involvement in music as well as cataloguing more than 1600 musical compositions based on Dickinson texts, the earliest being "Have You Got a Brook in Your Little Heart," composed by Etta Parker in 1896, based on an early poem (Fr94; J136). The first stanza reads as follows:

> Have you got a Brook in your little heart,
> Where bashful flowers blow,
> And blushing birds go down to drink —
> And shadows tremble so —

Lowenberg also cross-references the poems to the musical compositions based on them and includes an index by performance medium (solo

---

[10] Ridington includes a three-page "List of Works Consulted" (494–96).
[11] For more background on the impact of the affair on the lives of all involved, see John Evangelist Walsh's *This Brief Tragedy: Unraveling the Todd-Dickinson Affair* (1991).

voice, soprano; solo voice, contralto; violin, viola, vocal ensemble, orchestra, instrumental works, and so on). Here is a representative sampling:

- John Adams. *Harmonium, for Mixed Chorus and Orchestra* (1981)
- Gloria Coates. *In Search of Something* (voice, percussion, piano; 1972); based on "I've Seen a Dying Eye" (Fr648; Fr547); many other songs based on Dickinson poems.
- Aaron Copland, *Twelve Poems of Emily Dickinson, Set to Music* (1951); *Eight Poems of Emily Dickinson for Voice and Chamber Orchestra* (1981)
- Arthur Farwell, "Sea of Sunset" (voice, piano), based on Fr297; J266, "This is the land that Sunset washes —" Farwell composed thirty-nine songs based on Dickinson's poems between 1928 and 1949.
- Henry Mollicone, "Five Poems of Love" (chorus, piano, harp); 1966, 1988; based on "Have you got a Brook in your little heart" (Fr94; J136); "Did the Harebell loose her girdle" (Fr134; J213); "I held a Jewel in my fingers" (Fr261; J245); "A solemn thing — it was — I said —" (Fr307; J271); "I envy Seas, whereon He rides —" (Fr368; J498).
- Alice Parker, "Commentaries: A Cantata for Two Choruses of Women's Voices and Full Orchestra, Based on Five Poems of Emily Dickinson and Southern Folksongs, Hymns, and Spirituals," 1978.

Another noteworthy feature of this bibliography is the inclusion of several profiles of contemporary composers, who explain their reasons for setting Dickinson's work to music. Ragtime pianist and entertainer Max Morath, for example, explains that he experiences "A light, nearly humorous quality to Dickinson, extremely subtle and often obscured. 'I Never Saw a Moor' (Fr800; J1052) begins like a plaint, but spins lightly around as it sets its terms and develops its analogy. The rag tune and rhythm work seamlessly with such word play" (73).

Visual Interpretations of Dickinson's Life and Work

"What is it about Dickinson's poetry," Maryanne M. Garbowsky wonders, "that has the power to inspire artists to create?" In *Double Vision: Contemporary Artists Look at the Poetry of Emily Dickinson* (2002), Garbowsky profiles seventeen painters, calligraphers, sculptors, and mixed media artists who transform Emily Dickinson's poetry into visual works of art. "Reading and rereading poems," these artists "found that certain words struck them physically . . . wedging themselves in their consciousness, urging them to make art" (vii–viii).

Another resource for artwork based on Dickinson's poetry is *Language as Object: Emily Dickinson and Contemporary Art* (1997), edited by Susan Danly. This book, covering the exhibition organized by the Mead Art Museum at Amherst College, features thirteen artists and a portfolio of poems about Emily Dickinson by ten poets. The book also includes three essays that discuss contemporary artists' reception of Dickinson (Karen Sánchez-Eppler), the popularization of Emily Dickinson's face (Polly Longsworth), and Dickinson's impact on American poetry (Christopher Benfey). In her essay, "Exhibiting Sheets of Place: Seeing Emily Dickinson through Contemporary Art," Sánchez-Eppler explains how the artists avoid "the sweet and sentimental" but reveal the iconoclastic (15). The artists, Sánchez-Eppler explains, "do not illustrate Dickinson's poems" but attempt to "collaborate" with them, or "translate" them (16).

One of the most provocative works in the exhibit was Judy Chicago's installation *The Dinner Party*, which "consists of a triangular table with place settings for thirty-nine women, chosen because of their historical accomplishments or legendary powers." One of the reasons Chicago included Dickinson is that she regards her poetry as socially "dangerous" (70). The item from the installation that is depicted in the catalogue is a ceramic plate bearing a lace butterfly-shaped design "surrounding a red, vulva-shaped center [that] visually extends the notion of liberation into the sexual realm" (70).[12] Also provocative and startlingly original are Lesley Dill's "Poem Hands," twin banners depicting arms, the open hands of which are covered with the words of Dickinson's "I felt my life with both my hands / To see if it was there —" (Fr357; J351).

The artists in this exhibition, Susan Danly explains, rather than attempting to translate Dickinson's language directly into visual representations, "convey more generalized feelings of ambiguity, contradiction, and a heightened sense of visceral perception — the same characteristics that define Dickinson's peculiar mode of poetic expression" (67). As with the poetic, fictive, dramatic, and musical responses to Dickinson's life and work, these visual renderings demonstrate the power this poet has in artistically transforming our perceptions of the world. For me, such artistic endeavors reveal a societal impulse to bring one of the most brilliant poets — and *thinkers* — in American history into closer relation to our own world, the spiritual life, and in the end, to ourselves.

---

[12] See also Jonnie Guerra's reflections on Chicago's installation in "Dickinson Adaptations in the Arts and the Theater." (1998), 398–99.

10: Concluding Reflections

> *And now, among Circumference —*
> *Her steady Boat be seen —*
> *At home — among the Billows — As*
> *The Bough where she was born —*
> (Fr853; J798)

EMILY DICKINSON, LIKE OTHER MAJOR AUTHORS, produced a body of work that has commanded many critical approaches and has inspired creative artists the world over. With its seemingly unfathomable riches, this body of work constitutes a "compound vision" of philosophical, spiritual, psychological, historical, and aesthetic power — or simply "poetic" power, as I think Emily Dickinson conceived of that word. The themes and critical or artistic perspectives I have brought into focus by way of an examination of the work of dozens of exemplary Dickinson scholars may not quite form a coherent vision of the poet's life and work, but they do illuminate, through their various critical lenses, the many facets of her genius. Moreover, having these diverse critical and artistic voices gathered together under one tent should facilitate in-depth study of the poet by students, professional scholars, and literary enthusiasts alike. Scrutinizing Dickinson through different critical approaches should prove rewarding for several reasons:

- *The greater the diversity of opinion, the richer the artistic experience.* Necessary though it may be for a critic regardless of "school" to regard his or her approach (think "paradigm") as the most useful for fully understanding the author's intentions — similar to Thomas Kuhn's premise in *The Structure of Scientific Revolutions* (1970) that scientific work can advance only if one assumes the operational paradigm to be true (or at least beyond question for the moment). I, for one, while working on this book, have been continually reminded of the wealth of insights each critical approach offers, including approaches held to be old-fashioned by the mainstream of academic scholarship, and of how each approach reveals a new facet that permits additional light to shine forth from Dickinson's art.
- *The mutual compatibilities between one critical perspective and another outweigh the differences.* By mutual compatibilities I mean not only their ability to help us read Dickinson, to appreciate her innovative

artistry, but their ability to help us better understand the poet in the context of her culture, including understanding the connections between her Biblical and literary motifs and the importance of these motifs in her day.

- *Contemplating Dickinson from a multitude of critical perspectives enriches any single perspective by calling attention to the blind spots of any one of them.* For example, a feminist perspective on a given poem might illuminate feminist elements already inherent in the poem — in its imagery or word choice or tone of voice. Similarly, a psychoanalytic perspective might highlight spiritual or cultural-context concerns, such as Dickinson's simultaneous resistance to and embrace of Calvinist Christianity. Such perspectives, we might say, supplement and amplify the concerns of those critics interested in investigating the more traditionally aesthetic aspects of the work.

The wealth of Dickinson studies produced during the past half century has helped me personally acquire a deeper appreciation for the interplay of artistic, biographical, and cultural elements in Dickinson's poems. For example, my study of Dickinson as a nineteenth-century New England woman poet, not just as a poet whose genius transcended gender and historical or geographical circumstance, did not require me to privilege sociology or psychology over literature, as some formalist critics would assert; rather, it broadened for me the very idea of literature or the experience of literature, including what is meant by textual explication. A case in point: in the lines "Without the Snow's Tableau / Winter, were lie — to me — / Because I see — New Englandly —" (Fr256; J285), the "I" may well be a persona, a fictive construct — but that simply means the "I" is not *necessarily* the poet. It means that the "I" can be both the poet and anyone else. To put it another way, the strictly biographical "I" is perforce universalized in poetic utterance, but that universalized "I" may still embody the personal "I." This simple insight alone legitimizes the use of biographical and cultural-context criticism.

Literature is by its very nature interdisciplinary, and a good deal of recent scholarship demonstrates the fruitfulness of this fact. Judith Farr's research into the visual arts of Dickinson's day in *The Passion of Emily Dickinson* has yielded wonderful insights into the poet's cultural awareness as well as her aesthetic sensibility. James Guthrie's medical research into Dickinson's eye problems in *Emily Dickinson's Vision* helps us better understand her visual metaphors. Virginia Jackson's study of Dickinson's lyricism, which is also a study of the history of lyric reading, incorporates the history of the book and of reading — relatively new approaches to literary studies, not just to Dickinson criticism.[1]

Another potential germinator of future scholarly methodologies is the Dickinson Electronic Archives (www.emilydickinson.org) where many disciplinary conventions ranging from comparative studies of writings from various Dickinson family members (including those of Emily's sister-in-law Susan Gilbert Dickinson) to creative responses to Dickinson's writing. There is also an open forum for critical commentary.

Immersing oneself in critical polyvocality should also diminish, not intensify, contentiousness among critics. Border skirmishes are understandable (if deplorable) in military contexts; they should not undermine the intellectual pursuits of humanist scholars. Ridicule is easy and intellectually purposeless. One critic, for example, likened formalist criticism to a t-shirt caricature of Emily Dickinson confined to a room no larger than the size of her crouched body. Yes, it is true that formalists exclude "external" matters like the poet's personal life; but they do so because their interests lie with textual complexity and they would not be able to include all they wished to say about that complexity if they were obliged to speculate on biographical, psychological, or cultural influences. So to call formalism "confining" is like calling writing sonnets confining — or, for that matter, writing in slant-rhyme common meter confining. Limitations can liberate, as Emily Dickinson herself has demonstrated in so many ways.

The rapid growth of feminist literary criticism in the 1970s marked the beginning of an Emily Dickinson renaissance; it also marked the freedom to choose between traditional formalist or psychoanalytic criticism (which, despite their efforts to bring us closer to the "true" Emily Dickinson, sometimes ironically took us farther afield), and more inclusive approaches. Suzanne Juhasz's *Naked and Fiery Forms: Modern American Poetry by Women* (1976) initiated the renaissance by focusing on Dickinson the woman artist in full control of her innovative art even as she strove to "dissolve her self in the pure abstractness of timelessness," as Gudrun Grabher expressed it in her essay "Dickinson's Lyrical Self" (225).

Another area of rapid growth in Dickinson studies, and one that effectively interacts with feminist and cultural-historical criticism, is that of manuscript research. Thanks to Franklin's ingenious reconstruction of the fascicle sequences, scholars are now shedding light on one of the greatest mysteries in Dickinson's poetic project: the meanings generated by the poems in *sequence*. This is not to imply that manuscript scholars are

---

[1] See the January 2006 issue of *PMLA*, whose special topic was "The History of the Book and the Idea of Literature."

reaching consensus — not by any means; but every theory adds a new dimension of poetic possibility. Many more monographs on Dickinson's bound and unbound fascicles and especially on the worksheet drafts are sure to appear in the near future. Thus far, the output has been quite remarkable.

In a mere six-year period following the rise of feminist literary scholarship in the late 1970s the following studies of Dickinson with a feminist emphasis (exclusively or in part; not counting bibliographies) were published:

- Sharon Cameron, *Lyric Time: Dickinson and the Limits of Genre* (1979)
- Sandra Gilbert and Susan Gubar, *The Madwoman in the Attic* (1979)
- Karl Keller, *The Only Kangaroo among the Beauty* (1979)
- Rebecca Patterson, *Emily Dickinson's Imagery* (1979)
- Margaret Homans, *Women Writers and Poetic Identity* (1980)
- Joanne Feit Diehl, *Dickinson and the Romantic Imagination* (1981)
- Barbara Antonina Clarke Mossberg, *Emily Dickinson: When a Writer Is a Daughter* (1982)
- Suzanne Juhasz, *The Undiscovered Continent: Emily Dickinson and the Space of Mind* (1983)
- Suzanne Juhasz, ed. *Feminist Critics Read Emily Dickinson* (1983)
- Christopher E. G. Benfey, *Emily Dickinson and the Problem of Others* (1984)
- Wendy Martin, *An American Triptych: Anne Bradstreet, Emily Dickinson, Adrienne Rich* (1984)
- Vivian R. Pollak, *Dickinson: The Anxiety of Gender* (1984)
- Shira Wolosky, *Emily Dickinson: A Voice of War* (1984)
- Susan Howe, *My Emily Dickinson* (1985)

In addition to feminist scholarship on the poet more formalist or cultural/biographical studies were also being published during this period:

- Ben Kimpel, *Emily Dickinson as Philosopher* (1981)
- David Porter, *Dickinson: The Modern Idiom* (1981)
- William H. Shurr, *The Marriage of Emily Dickinson* (1983)
- Paul J. Ferlazzo, ed. *Critical Essays on Emily Dickinson* (1984)
- Barton Levi St. Armand, *Emily Dickinson and Her Culture* (1984)
- E. Miller Budick, *Emily Dickinson and the Life of Language* (1985)
- Agnieszka Salska, *Walt Whitman and Emily Dickinson: Poetry of the Central Consciousness* (1985)

The next ten years saw just as rich a critical outpouring, but one that exhibited a broader spectrum of topics and methods. Highlights include Cynthia Griffin Wolff's intellectual biography of the poet, *Emily Dickinson* (1986); Cristanne Miller's analysis of Dickinson's stylistic techniques, *Emily Dickinson: A Poet's Grammar* (1987); Paula Bennet's examination of Dickinson's sexual (more specifically, homoerotic) motifs, *Emily Dickinson: Woman Poet* (1990); Judy Jo Small's thorough analysis of the poet's complex rhyming techniques, and their relationship to music and to poetic meaning, *Positive as Sound: Emily Dickinson's Rhyme* (1990); Camille Paglia's *Sexual Personae* and Gary Lee Stonum's *The Dickinson Sublime,* both published in 1990 and both fascinating explorations of Dickinson's archetypal motifs; and two in-depth studies of Dickinson's poetry from the perspective of her manuscripts — Martha Nell Smith's *Rowing in Eden: Rereading Emily Dickinson* (1995), and Dorothy Huff Oberhaus's *Emily Dickinson's Fascicles: Method and Meaning* (1995).

Feminists, joining ranks with cultural critics and textual scholars, with no small assistance from the postmodernists, seemed for a while to have laid formalism to rest once and for all — but that has not been the case. Formalism seems to have acquired new life via textual/manuscript criticism, whose proponents are working happily alongside feminists, cultural critics, and historians of the book, as well as within the parameters of other methodologies (the "Chinese boxes" phenomenon I mentioned in the introduction). Formalism has taught everyone enduringly good habits of reading that are easily adaptable to any critical philosophy. Indeed, some of the finest formalist explications of individual poems I have come upon have been written by feminist and postmodernist Dickinsonians.

Dickinson scholarship in the twenty-first century has become more varied than ever. Twenty-two works have been published thus far:

- Angela Conrad, *The Wayward Nun of Amherst: Emily Dickinson and Medieval Mystical Women* (2000)
- Cynthia MacKenzie, *A Concordance to the Letters of Emily Dickinson* (2000)
- James McIntosh, *Nimble Believing: Dickinson and the Unknown* (2000)
- Domhnall Mitchell, *Emily Dickinson: Monarch of Perception* (2000)
- Alfred Habegger, *My Wars Are Laid Away in Books: The Life of Emily Dickinson* (2001)
- Jerome Liebling, with Christopher Benfey, Polly Longsworth, and Barton Levi St. Armand, *The Dickinsons of Amherst* (2001)
- John Delli Carpini, *Poetry as Prayer: Emily Dickinson* (2002)
- Graham Clarke, ed. *Emily Dickinson: Critical Assessments* (2002)

- Wendy Martin, ed. *The Cambridge Companion to Emily Dickinson* (2002)
- Eleanor Heginbotham, *Reading the Fascicles of Emily Dickinson* (2003)
- Richard E. Brantley, *Experience and Faith: The Late-Romantic Imagination of Emily Dickinson* (2004)
- Vivian R. Pollak, ed. *A Historical Guide to Emily Dickinson* (2004)
- Judith Farr, *The Gardens of Emily Dickinson* (2004)
- Helen Vendler, *Poets Thinking: Pope, Whitman, Dickinson, Yeats* (2004)
- Virginia Jackson, *Dickinson's Misery: A Theory of Lyric Reading* (2005)
- Domhnall Mitchell, *Measures of Possibility: Emily Dickinson's Manuscripts* (2005)
- Aliki Barnstone, *Changing Rapture: Emily Dickinson's Poetic Development* (2006)
- Páriac Finnerty, *Emily Dickinson's Shakespeare* (2006)
- Thomas Gardner, *A Door Ajar: Contemporary Writers and Emily Dickinson* (2006)
- Sharon Leiter, *Critical Companion to Emily Dickinson* (2007)
- Wendy Martin, *The Cambridge Introduction to Emily Dickinson* (2007)
- Lena Christensen, *Editing Emily Dickinson: The Production of an Author* (2008)

One of these books — *The Dickinsons of Amherst* — is a stunning photographic introduction to Dickinson family portraits and interiors: the furnishings of the Homestead (where Emily Dickinson lived out her life), and the Evergreens (the Italianate Villa next door — well, sixty yards to the west at any rate — where Emily's brother Austin and his wife Susan raised a family. A third house and family is also represented: the Dells — home of the Todds — Mabel Loomis and her astronomer husband, David. I dwell on this book with its haunting and somber photographs and lucid essays by three notable Dickinsonians because it tells me that Emily Dickinson is finally emerging from her myth to begin penetrating the soul of literate mainstream America. Like William Shakespeare, Emily Dickinson is a poet for the ages; but unlike Shakespeare, as Helen McNeil prophesied in 1986, "Dickinson's impact has yet to be felt."

Selected Editions of Emily Dickinson's Poems and Letters

Note: All volumes of Dickinson's poems were published posthumously. Only one of her poems, "Success is counted sweetest," appeared anonymously in book form in her lifetime — in an anthology titled *A Masque of Poets,* edited by Helen Hunt Jackson (Boston: Roberts Brothers, 1878).

Nineteenth-Century Editions

Poems. Edited by T. W. Higginson and Mabel Loomis Todd. Boston: Roberts Brothers, 1890.

Poems. Second Series, edited by T. W. Higginson and Mabel Loomis Todd. Boston: Roberts Brothers, 1891.

Poems. Third Series, ed. Mabel Loomis Todd. Boston: Roberts Brothers, 1896.

Letters of Emily Dickinson. 2 vols., ed. Mabel Loomis Todd. Boston: Roberts Brothers, 1894.

Twentieth-Century Editions

The Single Hound: Poems of a Lifetime. Ed. Martha Dickinson Bianchi. Boston: Little, Brown, 1914.

The Life and Letters of Emily Dickinson. Ed. Martha Dickinson Bianchi. Boston 1924.

Further Poems of Emily Dickinson. Ed. Martha Dickinson Bianchi and Alfred Leete Hampson. Boston: Little, Brown, 1929.

Unpublished Poems of Emily Dickinson. Ed. Martha Dickinson Bianchi and Alfred Leete Hampson. Boston: Little, Brown, 1936.

The Poems of Emily Dickinson. Ed. Martha Dickinson Bianchi and Alfred Leete Hampson. Boston: Little, Brown, 1937.

Bolts of Melody: New Poems of Emily Dickinson. Ed. Mabel Loomis Todd and Millicent. Todd Bingham. New York and London: Harper and Brothers, 1945.

Selected Editions of Emily Dickinson's Poems and Letters

The Poems of Emily Dickinson. 3 vols., ed. Thomas H. Johnson. Cambridge, MA and London: Belknap Press of Harvard UP, 1955.

The Letters of Emily Dickinson. 3 vols., ed Thomas H. Johnson and Theodora Ward. Cambridge, MA and London: Belknap Press of Harvard UP, 1958.

Acts of Light. With paintings by Nancy Ekholm Burkert and commentary by Jane Langton. Boston: New York Graphic Society, 1980.

The Manuscript Books of Emily Dickinson. 2 vols., ed. R. W. Franklin. Cambridge, MA: Belknap Press of Harvard UP, 1981.

The Master Letters of Emily Dickinson. Ed. R. W. Franklin. Amherst: Amherst College P, 1986.

The Poems of Emily Dickinson. 3 vols., ed. R. W. Franklin. Cambridge, MA: Belknap Press of Harvard UP, 1998.

Open Me Carefully: Emily Dickinson's Intimate Letters to Susan Huntington Dickinson. Ed. Ellen Louise Hart and Martha Nell Smith. Ashfield, MA: Paris Press, 1998.

Works Cited

Ackmann, Martha. "Biographical Studies of Dickinson." In *The Emily Dickinson Handbook*, ed. Gudrun Grabher, Roland Hagenbüchle, and Cristanne Miller, 11–23. Amherst: U of Massachusetts P, 1998.

———. "'I'm Glad I Finally Surfaced'": A Norcross Descendent Remembers Emily Dickinson." *The Emily Dickinson Journal* 5.2 (1996): 120–26.

Aiken, Conrad. "Emily Dickinson." *Dial* 76 (April 1924): 301–8. Reprinted in *Emily Dickinson: A Collection of Critical Essays*, ed. Richard B. Sewall, 9–15. Englewood Cliffs, NJ: Prentice-Hall, Inc., 1963.

Anderson, Charles R. *Emily Dickinson's Poetry: Stairway of Surprise*. New York: Holt, Rinehart and Winston, 1960.

Aristotle. *Poetics*. Trans. Francis Fergusson. New York: Hill and Wang, 1961.

Banzer, Judith. "Compound Manner: Emily Dickinson and the Metaphysical Poets." *American Literature* 32 (Jan. 1961): 417–33.

Barker, Wendy. *Lunacy of Light: Emily Dickinson and the Experience of Metaphor*. Carbondale and Edwardsville: Southern Illinois UP, 1987.

Barnes, Daniel R. "Telling It Slant: Emily Dickinson and the Proverb." *Genre* 12 (1979): 219–41.

Barnstone, Aliki. *Changing Rapture: Emily Dickinson's Poetic Development*. Hanover, NH, and London: UP of New England, 2006.

Beauvoir, Simone de. *The Second Sex*. New York: Alfred A. Knopf, 1953.

Benfey, Christopher E. G. *Emily Dickinson and the Problem of Others*. Amherst: U of Massachusetts P, 1984.

Bennett, Paula. *Emily Dickinson: Woman Poet*. Iowa City: U of Iowa P, 1990.

Benvenuto, Richard. "Words within Words: Dickinson's Use of the Dictionary." *Emerson Society Quarterly* 29 (1983): 46–55.

Bercovich, Sacvan. *The Puritan Origins of the American Self*. New Haven: Yale UP, 1975.

Bingham, Millicent Todd, ed. *Emily Dickinson's Home: Letters of Edward Dickinson and His Family*. New York: Harper & Bros. Publishers, 1955.

Blake, Caesar R., and Carleton F. Wells, eds. *The Recognition of Emily Dickinson: Selected Criticism since 1890*. Ann Arbor: U of Michigan P, 1968.

Blasing, Mutlu Konuk. *American Poetry: The Rhetoric of Its Forms*. New Haven and London: Yale UP, 1987.

Bloom, Harold. *The Anxiety of Influence: A Theory of Poetry*. 2nd ed. New York and Oxford: Oxford UP, 1997.

———. *A Map of Misreading*. Oxford, New York: Oxford UP, 1975.

———, ed. *Modern Critical Views: Emily Dickinson*. New York: Chelsea House Publishers, 1985.

———. *The Western Canon: The Books and School of the Ages*. New York, San Diego, and London: Harcourt Brace and Company, 1994.

Bogan, Louise. "A Mystical Poet." In *Emily Dickinson: A Collection of Critical Essays*, ed. Richard B. Sewall, 137–43. Englewood Cliffs, NJ: Prentice-Hall, 1963.

Boswell, Jeanetta. *Emily Dickinson: A Bibliography of Secondary Sources, with Selective Annotations, 1890 through 1987*. Jefferson, NC, and London: McFarland, 1989.

Brantley, Richard E. *Experience and Faith: The Late-Romantic Imagination of Emily Dickinson*. London: Palgrave Macmillan, 2004.

Brégy, Kathérine. "Emily Dickinson: A New England Anchoress." *The Catholic World* 120 (Dec. 1924): 344–54.

Brock-Broido, Lucie. *The Master Letters: Poems*. New York: Alfred A. Knopf, 1997.

Brooks, Cleanth. *The Well-Wrought Urn: Studies in the Structure of Poetry*. New York: Harcourt, Brace, 1947.

Browning, Elizabeth Barrett. *Aurora Leigh*. 1857; reprint, Oxford and New York: Oxford UP, 1993.

Buckingham, Willis J. *Emily Dickinson: An Annotated Bibliography: Writings, Scholarship, and Ana, 1850–1968*. Bloomington and London: Indiana UP, 1970.

———. "Emily Dickinson and the Reading Life." In *Dickinson and Audience*, ed. Martin Orzeck and Robert Weisbuch, 233–54. Ann Arbor: U of Michigan P, 1996.

———. "Emily Dickinson's Dictionary." *Harvard Library Bulletin* 25 (1977): 489–92.

———, ed. *Emily Dickinson's Reception in the 1890s: A Documentary History*. Pittsburgh: U of Pittsburgh P, 1989.

Budick, E. Miller. *Emily Dickinson and the Life of Language: A Study in Symbolic Poetics*. Baton Rouge and London: Louisiana State UP, 1985.

Burbick, Joan. "'One Unbroken Company': Religion and Emily Dickinson." *New England Quarterly* 53 (1980): 62–75.

Burke, Kenneth. *Language as Symbolic Action: Essays on Life, Literature, and Action.* Berkeley: U of California P, 1966.

———. *Philosophy of Literary Form: Studies in Symbolic Action.* Rev. ed. New York: Vintage Books, 1957.

Bushell, Sally. "Meaning in Dickinson's Manuscripts: Intending the Unintentional." *The Emily Dickinson Journal* 14.1 (2005): 24–61.

Bushnell, Horace. "Preliminary Dissertation on the Nature of Language as Related to Thought and Spirit" In *Horace Bushnell: Selected Writings on Language, Religion, and American Culture,* ed. David L. Smith. Chico, CA: Scholars Press, 1984. (Originally published in *God in Christ,* 1849.)

Cameron, Sharon. *Choosing Not Choosing: Dickinson's Fascicles.* Chicago and London: U of Chicago P, 1992.

———. "Dickinson's Fascicles." *The Emily Dickinson Handbook,* ed. Gudrun Grabher, Roland Hagenbüchle, and Cristanne Miller, 138–60. Amherst: U of Massachusetts P, 1998.

———. *Lyric Time: Dickinson and the Limits of Genre.* Baltimore and London: Johns Hopkins UP, 1979.

Capps, Jack L. *Emily Dickinson's Reading.* Cambridge, MA: Harvard UP, 1966.

Carpini, John Delli. *Poetry as Prayer: Emily Dickinson.* Boston: Pauline Books & Media, 2002.

Carlyle, Thomas. *On Heroes, Hero-Worship and the Heroic in History.* 1841; reprint, Oxford: Geoffrey Cumberlege, 1904.

Carton, Evan. *The Rhetoric of American Romance: Dialectic and Identity in Emerson, Dickinson, Poe, and Hawthorne.* Baltimore and London: Johns Hopkins UP, 1985.

Channing, William Ellery. "Likeness to God." In *Selected Writings of the American Transcendentalists,* ed. George Hochfield, 54–66. New York and Toronto: New American Library, 1966.

———. "Unitarian Christianity." In *Selected Writings of the American Transcendentalists,* ed. George Hochfield, 33–44. New York and Toronto: New American Library, 1966.

Chase, Richard. *Emily Dickinson.* New York: William Sloane Associates, Inc., 1951.

Christensen, Lena. *Editing Emily Dickinson: The Production of an Author.* New York and London: Routledge, 2008.

Clarke, Graham, ed. *Emily Dickinson: Critical Assessments.* 4 vols. Mountfield, East Essex, UK: Helm Information Ltd., 2002.

Cody, John. *After Great Pain: The Inner Life of Emily Dickinson*. Cambridge, MA: Belknap Press of Harvard UP, 1971.

Coghill, Sheila, and Thom Tammaro, eds. *Visiting Emily: Poems Inspired by the Life and Work of Emily Dickinson*. Iowa City: U of Iowa P, 2000.

Conrad, Angela. *The Wayward Nun: Emily Dickinson and Medieval Mystical Women*. New York and London: Garland Publishing, Inc., 2000.

Corbett, Edward P. J. *Rhetorical Analyses of Literary Works*. New York, London, Toronto: Oxford UP, 1969.

Crumbley, Paul. *Inflections of the Pen: Dash and Voice in Emily Dickinson*. Lexington, KY: UP of Kentucky, 1997.

Danly, Susan, ed. *Language as Object: Emily Dickinson and Contemporary Art*. Amherst: Mead Art Museum, Amherst College, 1997.

Denman, Kamilla. "Dickinson's Volcanic Punctuation." *The Emily Dickinson Journal* 2.1 (1993): 22–46.

Deppman, Jed. "To Own the Art within the Soul: Emily Dickinson and Creative Writing." *EDIS Bulletin* 17.1 (May/June 2005): 1–2.

Derrida, Jacques. "Structure, Sign, and Play in the Discourse of the Human Sciences." In *Writing and Difference,* trans. Alan Bass, 178–93. Chicago: U of Chicago P, 1978.

Dickenson, Donna. *Emily Dickinson*. Leamington Spa, UK, Dover, NH, and Heidelberg: Berg, 1985.

Dickie, Margaret. "Feminist Conceptions of Dickinson." *The Emily Dickinson Handbook,* ed. Gudrun Grabher, Roland Hagenbüchle, and Cristanne Miller, 342–55. Amherst: U of Massachusetts P, 1998.

———. *Lyric Contingencies: Emily Dickinson and Wallace Stevens*. Philadelphia: U of Pennsylvania P, 1991.

Diehl, Joanne Feit. *Dickinson and the Romantic Imagination*. Princeton: Princeton UP, 1981.

Di Filippo, Paul. "Walt and Emily." In *The Steampunk Trilogy,* 237–352. New York and London: Four Walls Eight Windows, 1995.

Dobson, Joanne A. "'Oh, Susie, it is dangerous': Emily Dickinson and the Archetype of the Masculine." In *Feminist Critics Read Emily Dickinson,* ed. Suzanne Juhasz, 80–97. Bloomington: Indiana UP, 1983.

———. *Dickinson and the Strategies of Reticence: The Woman Writer in Nineteenth-Century America*. Bloomington: Indiana UP, 1989.

———. *Quieter than Sleep: A Modern Mystery of Emily Dickinson*. New York: Doubleday, 1997.

Donoghue, Denis. *Emily Dickinson*. Pamphlets on American Writers #81. Minneapolis: U of Minnesota P, 1969.

Doriani, Beth Maclay. *Emily Dickinson, Daughter of Prophecy.* Amherst: U of Massachusetts P, 1996.

Duchac, Joseph. *The Poems of Emily Dickinson: An Annotated Guide to Commentary Published in English, 1890–1977.* New York and Toronto: G. K. Hall, 1979.

———. *The Poems of Emily Dickinson: An Annotated Guide to Commentary Published in English, 1978–1989.* Boson: G. K. Hall, 1993.

Eaves, Morris. "'Why Don't They Leave It Alone?' Speculations on the Authority of the Audience in Editorial Theory." In *Cultural Artifacts and the Production of Meaning: The Page, the Image, and the Body*, ed. Margaret J. M. Ezell and Katherine O'Brien O'Keeffe, 85–99. Ann Arbor: U of Michigan P, 1994.

Eberwein, Jane Donahue. *Dickinson: Strategies of Limitation.* Amherst: U of Massachusetts P, 1985.

———. "Dickinson's Local, Global, and Cosmic Perspectives." *The Emily Dickinson Handbook,* ed. Gudrun Grabher, Roland Hagenbüchle, and Cristanne Miller, 27–43. Amherst: U of Massachusetts P, 1998.

———, ed. *An Emily Dickinson Encyclopedia.* Westport, CT: Greenwood Press, 1998.

———. "'Is Immortality True?': Salvaging Faith in an Age of Upheavals." *A Historical Guide to Emily Dickinson,* ed. Vivian R. Pollak, 67–102. Oxford and New York: Oxford UP, 2004.

———. "'Where — Omnipresence — fly'? Calvinism as Impetus to Spiritual Amplitude." *The Emily Dickinson Journal* 13.2 (2005): 12–23.

Edwards, Anne. *The Hesitant Heart: A Love Story Based on the Life of Emily Dickinson.* New York: Random House, 1974.

Ellis, Richard S. "'A Little East of Jordan': Human-Divine Encounters in Dickinson and the Hebrew Bible." *The Emily Dickinson Journal* 8.1 (1999): 36–58.

Emerson, Ralph Waldo. "Circles." In *Essays, First Series* (1841). *Selected Writings of Ralph Waldo Emerson,* ed. William H. Gilman, 295–306. New York: New American Library, 1965.

———. *Nature* (1836). *Selected Writings of Ralph Waldo Emerson,* ed. William H. Gilman, 186–223. New York: New American Library, 1965.

Emily Dickinson Electronic Archives. www.emilydickinson.org.

England, Martha Winburn, and John Sparrow. *Hymns Unbidden: Donne, Herbert, Blake, Emily Dickinson and the Hymnographers.* New York: New York Public Library, 1966.

Erkkila, Betsy. "Dickinson and the Art of Politics." In *A Historical Guide to Emily Dickinson,* ed. Vivian R. Pollak, 133–74. Oxford and New York: Oxford UP, 2004.

———. "Emily Dickinson and Class." *American Literary History* 4 (Spring 1992): 1–27.

Ezell, Margaret J. M., and Katherine O'Brien O'Keeffe, eds. *Cultural Artifacts and the Production of Meaning: The Page, the Image, and the Body.* Ann Arbor: U of Michigan P, 1994.

Farr, Judith. "Dickinson and the Visual Arts." In *The Emily Dickinson Handbook,* ed. Gudrun Grabher, Roland Hagenbüchle, and Cristanne Miller, 61–92. Amherst: U of Massachusetts P, 1998.

———. *I Never Came to You in White.* Boston: Houghton Mifflin, 1996.

———. *The Passion of Emily Dickinson.* Cambridge, MA and London, England: Harvard UP, 1992.

Farr, Judith, with Louise Carter. *The Gardens of Emily Dickinson.* Cambridge, MA, and London: Harvard UP, 2004.

Fast, Robin Riley, and Christine Mack Gordon, eds. *Approaches to Teaching Emily Dickinson's Poetry.* New York: Modern Language Association of America, 1989.

Ferlazzo, Paul J., ed. *Critical Essays on Emily Dickinson.* Boston: G. K. Hall, 1984.

———. *Emily Dickinson.* Twayne United States Authors Series. Indianapolis: Bobbs-Merrill Educational Publishing, 1976.

Fiedelson, Charles Jr. *Symbolism and American Literature.* Chicago: U of Chicago P, 1965.

Finnerty, Páraic. *Emily Dickinson's Shakespeare.* Amherst and Boston: U of Massachusetts P, 2006.

Ford, Thomas W. *Heaven Beguiles the Tired: Death in the Poetry of Emily Dickinson.* University, AL: U of Alabama P, 1966.

Foster, Richard. *The New Romantics: A Reappraisal of the New Criticism.* Bloomington: Indiana UP, 1962.

Foucault, Michel. *The Archaeology of Knowledge.* Trans A. M. Sheridan Smith. New York: Harper & Row, 1976.

Fraiberg, Louis. *Psychoanalysis & American Literary Criticism.* Detroit: Wayne State UP, 1960.

Franklin, R. W. *The Editing of Emily Dickinson.* Madison, Milwaukee, and London: U of Wisconsin P, 1967.

Freeman, Margaret H. Introduction to *Emily Dickinson's Imagery* by Rebecca Patterson, v–xviii. Amherst: U of Massachusetts P, 1979.

Friends of the Amherst College Library. *Emily Dickinson: A Letter.* With a Note by Polly Longsworth. The Friends of the Amherst College Library, 1992.

Freud, Sigmund. *The Interpretation of Dreams.* Trans. James Strachey. Originally published 1900; translation published New York: Avon Books,; 1965.

———. "The Relation of the Poet to Day-Dreaming." In *On Creativity and the Unconscious: Papers on the Psychology of Art, Literature, Love, Religion,* 44–54. New York: Harper & Row, Publishers, 1958.

———. "The Uncanny." In *On Creativity and the Unconscious: Papers on the Psychology of Art, Literature, Love, Religion,* 122–61. New York: Harper & Row, Publishers, 1958.

Frye, Northrop. *Anatomy of Criticism: Four Essays.* Princeton: Princeton UP, 1957.

———. *Fables of Identity.* San Diego, New York: Harcourt, Brace, 1963.

Fuller, Jamie. *The Diary of Emily Dickinson.* San Francisco: Mercury House, 1993.

Fuller, Margaret. *Woman in the Nineteenth Century.* 1845; reprint, New York: Norton, 1971.

Furey, Martha. "Tea with Emily." Unpublished play. 2002.

Garbowsky, Maryanne M. *Double Vision: Contemporary Artists Look at the Poetry of Emily Dickinson.* Chester, VT: Putnam Hill Press, 2002.

———. *The House without the Door: A Study of Emily Dickinson and the Illness of Agoraphobia.* Rutherford, NJ: Fairleigh Dickinson UP, 1989.

Gardner, Thomas. *A Door Ajar: Contemporary Writers and Emily Dickinson.* Oxford and New York: Oxford UP, 2006.

Gelpi, Albert. "Emily Dickinson and the Deerslayer: The Dilemma of the Woman Poet in America." In *Shakespeare's Sisters: Feminist Essays on Woman Poets,* ed. Sandra M. Gilbert and Susan Gubar, 122–50. Bloomington: Indiana UP, 1979.

———. *Emily Dickinson: The Mind of the Poet.* Cambridge, MA: Harvard UP, 1965.

———. *The Tenth Muse.* Cambridge, MA: Harvard UP, 1975.

Gilbert, Sandra M., and Susan Gubar. *The Madwoman in the Attic: The Woman Writer and the Nineteenth Century Literary Imagination.* New Haven and London: Yale UP, 1979.

Grabher, Gudrun. "Dickinson's Lyrical Self." In *The Emily Dickinson Handbook,* ed. Gudrun Grabher, Roland Hagenbüchle, and Cristanne Miller, 224–39. Amherst: U of Massachusetts P, 1998.

Grabher, Gudrun, Roland Hagenbüchle, and Cristanne Miller, eds. *The Emily Dickinson Handbook.* Amherst: U of Massachusetts P, 1998.

Green, Daniel. "Literature Itself: The New Criticism and Aesthetic Experience." *Philosophy and Literature* 27.1 (2003): 62–79.

Griffith, Clark. *The Long Shadow: Emily Dickinson's Tragic Poetry*. Princeton: Princeton UP, 1964.

Guerra, Jonnie. "Dickinson Adaptations in the Arts and the Theater." *The Emily Dickinson Handbook*, ed. Gudrun Grabher, Roland Hagenbüchle, and Cristanne Miller, 385–407. Amherst: U of Massachusetts P, 1998.

———. "Marianne Boruch and Emily Dickinson." *EDIS Bulletin* 11.1 (May/June 1999: 4–5; 24.

———. "Reflections on EDIS — Past, Present, and Future." *EDIS Bulletin* 10.2 (Nov.–Dec. 1998): 16–18.

Guides at the Dickinson Homestead. *Emily Dickinson: Profile of the Poet as Cook, with Selected Recipes*. Amherst, MA: Hamilton I. Newell, Inc., 1976.

Gura, Philip F. *The Wisdom of Words: Language, Theology, and Literature in the New England Renaissance*. Middletown, CT: Wesleyan UP, 1981.

Guthrie, James R. *Emily Dickinson's Vision: Illness and Identity in Her Poetry*. Gainesville: UP of Florida, 1998.

Habegger, Alfred. *My Wars Are Laid Away in Books: The Life of Emily Dickinson*. New York: Random House, 2001.

Hagenbüchle, Roland. "Dickinson and Literary Theory." In *The Emily Dickinson Handbook*, ed. Gudrun Grabher, Roland Hagenbüchle, and Cristanne Miller, 356–84. Amherst: U of Massachusetts P, 1998.

———. "Emily Dickinson's Poetic Covenant." *The Emily Dickinson Journal* 2.1 (1993): 14–39.

Hart, Ellen Louise. "The Elizabeth Whitney Putnam Manuscripts and New Strategies for Editing Emily Dickinson's Letters." *The Emily Dickinson Journal* 4.1 (1995): 44–74.

———. Review of *Measures of Possibility: Emily Dickinson's Manuscripts*, by Domhnall Mitchell. *EDIS Bulletin* 18.2 (November–December 2006): 11–14.

Heginbotham, Eleanor Elson. *Reading the Fascicles of Emily Dickinson: Dwelling in Possibilities*. Columbus: Ohio State UP, 2003.

Henneberg, Sylvia. "Neither Lesbian nor Straight: Multiple Eroticisms in Emily Dickinson's Love Poetry." *The Emily Dickinson Journal* 4.2 (1995): 1–19.

Higgins, David. *Portrait of Emily Dickinson: The Poet and Her Prose*. New Brunswick: Rutgers UP, 1967.

Higginson, Thomas Wentworth. "Emily Dickinson's Letters." *The Atlantic Monthly* 68 (Nov. 1891); reprinted in *Emily Dickinson's Reception in the 1890s: A Documentary History*, ed. Willis J. Buckingham, 182–99. Pittsburgh: U of Pittsburgh P, 1989.

———. "An Open Portfolio." *Christian Union* 42 (Sept. 25, 1890). Reprinted in *Emily Dickinson's Reception in the 1890s: A Documentary History*, ed. Willis J. Buckingham, 3–9. Pittsburgh: U of Pittsburgh P, 1989.

Hitchcock, Edward. *The Religion of Geology and Its Connected Sciences*. Boston: Phillips, Sampson, and Company, 1851.

Hofmann, Michael, and James Lasdun, eds. *After Ovid: New Metamorphoses*. New York: Farrar, Straus and Giroux, 1994.

Holland, Jeanne. "Scraps, Stamps, and Cutouts: Emily Dickinson's Domestic Technologies of Publication." *Cultural Artifacts and the Production of Meaning: The Page, the Image, and the Body*, ed. Margaret J. M. Ezell and Katherine O'Brien O'Keeffe, 139–82. Ann Arbor: U of Michigan P, 1994.

Homans, Margaret. "'Oh, Vision of Language!': Dickinson's Poems of Love and Death." *Feminist Critics Read Emily Dickinson*, ed. Suzanne Juhasz, 114–33. Bloomington: Indiana UP, 1983.

———. *Women Writers and Poetic Identity: Dorothy Wordsworth, Emily Bronte, and Emily Dickinson*. Princeton: Princeton UP, 1980.

Howard, Richard. "A Consideration of the Writings of Emily Dickinson." *Prose* 6 (Spring 1973): 67–97.

Howard, William. "Emily Dickinson's Poetic Vocabulary." *PMLA* 72 (March 1957): 225–48.

Howe, Susan. *The Birth-Mark: Unsettling the Wilderness in American Literary History*. Hanover, NH, and London: Wesleyan UP, 1993.

———. *My Emily Dickinson*. Berkeley: North Atlantic Books, 1985.

Irigaray, Luce. *Speculum of the Other Woman*. Ithaca, NY and London: Cornell UP, 1985.

Jackson, Helen Hunt, ed. *A Masque of Poets*. Boston: Roberts Brothers, 1878.

———. *Mercy Philbrick's Choice*. Boston: Roberts Brothers, 1876.

Jackson, Virginia. "Dickinson's Figure of Address." In *Dickinson and Audience*, ed. Martin Orzeck and Robert Weisbuch, 77–103. Ann Arbor: U of Michigan P, 1996.

———. *Dickinson's Misery: A Theory of Lyric Reading*. Princeton and Oxford: Princeton UP, 2005.

Jancovich, Mark. *The Cultural Politics of the New Criticism*. Cambridge: Cambridge UP, 1993.

Johnson, Greg. *Emily Dickinson: Perception and the Poet's Quest*. University, AL: U of Alabama P, 1985

Johnson, Thomas H. *Emily Dickinson: An Interpretive Biography*. Cambridge: Belknap Press of Harvard UP, 1955.

Jones, Rowena Revis. "Emily Dickinson's 'Flood Subject': Immortality." Unpublished Ph.D. Dissertation, Northwestern University, 1960: *Dissertation Abstracts* 21 (1960): 1554–55.

———. "The Preparation of a Poet: Puritan Directions in Emily Dickinson's Education." In *Studies in the American Renaissance,* ed. Joel Myerson, 285–324. Boston: Twayne Publishers, 1982.

———. "A Taste for 'Poison': Dickinson's Departure from Orthodoxy." *The Emily Dickinson Journal* 11.1 (1993): 47–64.

Juhasz, Suzanne, ed. *Feminist Critics Read Emily Dickinson.* Bloomington: Indiana UP, 1983.

———. "Materiality and the Poet." *The Emily Dickinson Handbook,* ed. Gudrun Grabher, Roland Hagenbüchle, and Cristanne Miller, 427–39. Amherst: U of Massachusetts P, 1998.

———. *Naked and Fiery Forms: Modern American Poetry by Women: A New Tradition.* New York: Harper & Row, 1976.

———. *The Undiscovered Continent: Emily Dickinson and the Space of the Mind.* Bloomington: Indiana UP, 1983.

Juhasz, Suzanne, Cristanne Miller, and Martha Nell Smith. *Comic Power in Emily Dickinson.* Austin: U of Texas P, 1993.

Jung, C. G. "Psychological Aspects of the Mother Archetype." *Four Archetypes: Mother/Rebirth/Spirit/Trickster.* Trans. R. F. C. Hull. Princeton: Princeton UP, 1969: 9–44.

Kames, Lord (Henry Home). *Elements of Criticism.* New York: Huntington & Savage, 1833.

Kant, Immanuel. *Critique of Pure Reason.* 2nd rev. ed., 1787. Trans. F. Max Müller. New York: Macmillan, 1925.

Kaufmann, Paola. *The Sister: A Novel of Emily Dickinson* (2003). Translated by William Rowlandson. New York: Overlook/Rookery, 2007.

Keller, Karl. *The Only Kangaroo among the Beauty: Emily Dickinson and America.* Baltimore and London: Johns Hopkins UP, 1979.

Kher, Inder Nath. *The Landscape of Absence: Emily Dickinson's Poetry.* New Haven and London: Yale UP, 1974.

Kierkegaard, Soren. *Fear and Trembling* and *The Sickness Unto Death.* Trans. Walter Lowrie. Garden City, NY: Doubleday Anchor Books, 1954.

Kimpel, Ben. *Emily Dickinson as Philosopher.* New York and Toronto: Edwin Mellen Press, 1981.

Kirk, Connie Ann. "'The distance would not haunt me so —': Teaching Dickinson's Poetry through Distance Education." *EDIS Bulletin* 14.1 (May/June 2002): 8–10.

Kirkby, Joan. *Emily Dickinson*. London: Macmillan Education Ltd, 1991.

Knapp, Bettina L. *Emily Dickinson*. New York: Continuum, 1991.

Kristeva, Julia. *Revolution in Poetic Language*. Trans. Margaret Walker. New York: Columbia UP, 1984.

Kuhn, Thomas S. *The Structure of Scientific Revolutions*. 2nd ed. Chicago: U of Chicago P, 1970.

Ladin, Jay. "'Goblin with a Gauge': Teaching Emily Dickinson." *The Emily Dickinson Journal* 9.2 (2000): 32–41.

Langton, Jane. *Emily Dickinson is Dead*. New York: St. Martin's, 1984.

Lease, Benjamin. *Emily Dickinson's Readings of Men and Books: Sacred Soundings*. New York: St. Martin's, 1990.

Leiter, Sharon. *Critical Companion to Emily Dickinson*. New York: Facts on File, 2007.

Lentricchia, Frank. *After the New Criticism*. Chicago: U of Chicago P, 1980.

Leonard, Douglas Novich. "Certain Slants of Light: Exploring the Art of Dickinson's Fascicle 13. In *Approaches to Teaching Dickinson's Poetry*, ed. Robin Riley Fast and Christine Mack Gordon, 124–33. New York: Modern Language Association of America, 1989.

Leyda, Jay. *The Years and Hours of Emily Dickinson*. 2 vols. New Haven: Yale UP, 1960.

Liebling, Jerome, with Christopher Benfey, Polly Longsworth, and Barton Levi St. Armand. *The Dickinsons of Amherst*. Hanover, NH, and London: UP of New England, 2001.

Lilliedahl, Ann. *Emily Dickinson in Europe: Her Literary Reputation in Selected Countries*. Washington, DC: UP of America, 1981.

Lindberg-Seyersted, Brita. *The Voice of the Poet: Aspects of Style in the Poetry of Emily Dickinson*. Cambridge, MA: Harvard UP, 1968.

Loeffelholz, Mary. *Dickinson and the Boundaries of Feminist Theory*. Urbana and Chicago: U of Illinois P, 1991.

Lombardo, Daniel. Review of *Emily Dickinson: Critical Assessments*, ed. Graham Clarke. *The EDIS Bulletin* (Nov.–Dec. 2003): 23–26.

Longfellow, Henry Wadsworth. *Kavanagh*. 1849; reprint, Boston: Houghton Mifflin, 1886.

Longsworth, Polly, ed. *Austin and Mabel: The Amherst Affair and Love Letters of Austin Dickinson and Mabel Loomis Todd*. New York: Farrar Straus Giroux, 1984.

———. *The World of Emily Dickinson*. New York: Norton, 1990.

Loving, Jerome. *Emily Dickinson: The Poet on the Second Story*. Cambridge: Cambridge UP, 1986.

Lowenberg, Carlton. *Emily Dickinson's Textbooks*. Lafayette, CA: Carlton Lowenberg, 1986.

———. *Musicians Wrestle Everywhere: Emily Dickinson and Music*. Berkeley: Fallen Leaf Press, 1992.

Lubbers, Klaus. *Emily Dickinson: The Critical Revolution*. Ann Arbor: U of Michigan P, 1968.

Lucas, Dolores Dyer. *Emily Dickinson and Riddle*. DeKalb: Northern Illinois UP, 1969.

Luce, William. *The Belle of Amherst: A Play Based on the Life of Emily Dickinson*. Boston: Houghton Mifflin Company, 1976.

Lundin, Roger. *Emily Dickinson and the Art of Belief*. Grand Rapids, MI and Cambridge, UK: William B. Eerdmans Publishing Co., 1998.

MacKenzie, Cynthia, ed. *Concordance to the Letters of Emily Dickinson*. Boulder: UP of Colorado, 2000.

Machor, James L. "Emily Dickinson and Feminine Rhetoric." *Arizona Quarterly* 36 (1980): 131–46.

MacLeish, Archibald. *Poetry and Experience*. Baltimore: Penguin Books, 1964.

MacMurray, Rose. *Afternoons with Emily*. New York, Boston, London: Little, Brown and Company, 2007.

Mann, John S. "Dream in Emily Dickinson's Poetry." *Dickinson Studies* 34 (2nd Half, 1978): 19–26.

Marsh, Brian. *The Search for Emily: A Play in Two Acts*. Belchertown, MA: Brian R. Marsh, 1988.

Martin, Wendy. *An American Triptych: Anne Bradstreet, Emily Dickinson, Adrienne Rich*. Chapel Hill and London: U of North Carolina P, 1984.

———. *The Cambridge Introduction to Emily Dickinson*. Cambridge: Cambridge UP, 2007.

———. "Emily Dickinson." *The Columbia Literary History of the United States*. New York: Columbia UP, 1988.

McGann, Jerome. "Emily Dickinson's Visible Language." In *Emily Dickinson: A Collection of Critical Essays*, ed. Judith Farr, 248–59. Upper Saddle River, NJ: Prentice-Hall, 1996.

McIntosh, James. *Nimble Believing: Dickinson and the Unknown*. Ann Arbor: U of Michigan P, 2000.

McNeil, Helen. *Emily Dickinson*. New York: Virago Pantheon Pioneers, 1986.

Messmer, Marietta. "Dickinson's Critical Reception." In *The Emily Dickinson Handbook,* ed. Gudrun Grabher, Roland Hagenbüchle, and Cristanne Miller, 299–322. Amherst: U of Massachusetts P, 1998.

———. *A Vice for Voices: Reading Emily Dickinson's Correspondence.* Amherst: U of Massachusetts P, 2001.

Miller, Cristanne. "Dickinson's Language: Interpreting Truth Told Slant. *Approaches to Teaching Dickinson's Poetry,* ed. Robin Riley Fast and Christine Mack Gordon, 78–84. New York: MLA, 1989.

———. *Emily Dickinson: A Poet's Grammar.* Cambridge: Harvard UP, 1987.

———. "The Sound of Shifting Paradigms, or Hearing Dickinson in the Twenty-First Century." *A Historical Guide to Emily Dickinson,* ed. Vivian R. Pollak, 201–34. Oxford and New York: Oxford UP, 2004.

Miller, Ruth. *The Poetry of Emily Dickinson.* Middletown, CT: Wesleyan UP, 1968.

Mills, Elizabeth M. "Punishment and Poetry: Emily Dickinson Shares with Sharon Olds." *EDIS Bulletin* 14.1 (May/June 2002): 4–5; 25.

Mitchell, Domhnall. *Emily Dickinson: Monarch of Perception.* Amherst: U of Massachusetts P, 2000.

———. *Measures of Possibility: Emily Dickinson's Manuscripts.* Amherst and Boston: U of Massachusetts P, 2005.

Moore, Hastings. "Emily Dickinson and Orthothanasia." *Dickinson Studies* 32 (1979): 110–18.

Mossberg, Barbara Antonina Clarke. "Emily Dickinson's Nursery Rhymes." *Feminist Critics Read Emily Dickinson,* ed. Suzanne Juhasz, 45–66. Bloomington: Indiana UP, 1983.

———. *Emily Dickinson: When the Writer Is a Daughter.* Bloomington: Indiana UP, 1982.

Mudge, Jean McClure. *Emily Dickinson and the Image of Home.* Amherst: U of Massachusetts P, 1975.

New, Elisa. *The Regenerate Lyric: Theology and Innovation in American Poetry.* Cambridge: Cambridge UP, 1993.

Nietzsche, Friedrich. *The Genealogy of Morals.* 1887; reprint, Garden City: Doubleday Anchor Books, 1956.

———. *The Will to Power.* 1884; reprint, New York: Vintage Books, 1968.

Novak, Barbara. *Voyages of the Self: Pairs, Parallels, and Patterns in American Art and Literature.* Oxford and New York: Oxford UP, 2007.

Oberhaus, Dorothy Huff. *Emily Dickinson's Fascicles: Method & Meaning.* University Park, PA: Pennsylvania State UP, 1995.

Orzeck, Martin, and Robert Weisbuch. *Dickinson and Audience*. Ann Arbor: U of Michigan P, 1996.

Paglia, Camille. *Sexual Personae: Art and Decadence from Nefertiti to Emily Dickinson*. New Haven: Yale UP, 1990.

Parker, Theodore. *The Two Christmas Celebrations*. Boston: Rufus Leighton, Jr., 1859.

Patterson, Rebecca. *Emily Dickinson's Imagery*. Amherst: U of Massachusetts P, 1979.

———. *The Riddle of Emily Dickinson*. Boston: Houghton Mifflin, 1951.

Peeples, Scott. *The Afterlife of Edgar Allan Poe*. Rochester, NY: Camden House, 2004.

Petrino, Elizabeth A. *Emily Dickinson and Her Contemporaries: Women's Verse in America, 1820–1885*. Hanover, NH and London: UP of New England, 1998.

Phillips, Elizabeth. *Emily Dickinson: Personae and Performance*. University Park and London: Pennsylvania State UP, 1988.

Plato. *The Republic*. In *Great Dialogues of Plato*. Translated by W. H. D. Rouse. New York: New American Library, 1956.

Polk, Mary Lynn Cooper. "Emily Dickinson: A Survey of the Criticism and Selective Annotated Bibliography." Ph.D. Diss., University of South Carolina, 1984.

Pollak, Vivian R. *Dickinson: The Anxiety of Gender*. Ithaca, NY: Cornell UP, 1984.

———, ed. *A Historical Guide to Emily Dickinson*. Oxford and New York: Oxford UP, 2004.

———, ed. *A Poet's Parents: The Courtship Letters of Emily Norcross and Edward Dickinson*. Chapel Hill and London: U of North Carolina P, 1988.

Pollitt, Josephine. *Emily Dickinson: The Human Background of Her Poetry*. New York and London: Harper & Brothers Publishers, 1930.

Porter, David T. *The Art of Emily Dickinson's Early Poetry*. Cambridge, MA: Harvard UP, 1966.

———. *Emily Dickinson: The Modern Idiom*. Cambridge, MA, and London, England: Harvard UP, 1981.

Porter, Ebenezer. *The Rhetorical Reader*. Andover: Gould and Newman, 1832.

Power, Sister Mary James. *In the Name of the Bee: The Significance of Emily Dickinson*. New York: Sheed & Ward, 1943.

Ransom, John Crowe. "Emily Dickinson: A Poet Restored." In *Emily Dickinson: A Collection of Critical Essays*, ed. Richard B. Sewall, 88–100. Englewood Cliffs, NJ: Prentice-Hall, Inc., 1963.

———. *The New Criticism*. Norfolk, CT: New Directions, 1941.

Reynolds, David S. *Beneath the American Renaissance: The Subversive Imagination in the Age of Emerson and Melville*. Cambridge, MA and London, England: Harvard UP, 1988.

Rich, Adrienne. "Vesuvius at Home: The Power of Emily Dickinson." *Parnassus* 5 (1976): 49–74.

Ridington, Candace. *Rubicon*. Birmingham, AL: Arlington Press, 1997.

Robinson, John. *Emily Dickinson: Looking to Canaan*. London and Boston: Faber and Faber Ltd., 1986.

Robinson, Marilynne. *Housekeeping*. New York: Farrar, Straus and Giroux, 1980.

Rosenbaum, S. P. *A Concordance to the Poems of Emily Dickinson*. Ithaca, NY: Cornell UP, 1964.

Rosenthal, M. L., and Sally M. Gall. *The Modern Poetic Sequence: The Genius of Modern Poetry*. New York and Oxford: Oxford UP, 1983.

Rotella, Guy. *Reading and Writing Nature: The Poetry of Robert Frost, Wallace Stevens, Marianne Moore, and Elizabeth Bishop*. Boston: Northeastern UP, 1991.

Rothberg, Morey. "A New Emily Dickinson Letter from the Library of Congress." *Dickinson Studies* 78 (1991): 20–21.

Rothberg, Morey, and Vivian Pollak. "An Emily Dickinson Manuscript (Re)Identified at the Library of Congress." *The Emily Dickinson Journal* 10.2 (2001): 453–51.

Runzo, Sandra. "Dickinson's Transgressive Body." *The Emily Dickinson Journal* 8.1 (1999): 59–72.

St. Armand, Barton Levi. *Emily Dickinson and Her Culture: The Soul's Society*. Cambridge: Cambridge UP, 1984.

Salska, Agnieszka. *Walt Whitman and Emily Dickinson: Poetry of the Central Consciousness*. Philadelphia: U of Pennsylvania P, 1985.

Sánchez-Eppler, Karen. "Exhibiting Sheets of Place: Seeing Emily Dickinson through Contemporary Art." In *Language as Object: Emily Dickinson and Contemporary Art*, ed. Susan Danly, 15–33. Amherst: Mead Art Museum in association with the of Massachusetts P, 1997.

Sato, Tomoko. *Emily Dickinson's Poems: Bulletins from Immortality*. Tokyo: Shinzansha Publishing Co., Ltd., 1999.

Saussure, Ferdinand de. *Course in General Linguistics*. New York: Philosophical Library, 1959.

Scheurer, Erika. "From the Prairie to the World: Patricia Hampl and Emily Dickinson." *EDIS Bulletin* 14.2 (November/December 2002): 4–5; 13.

Scholl, Diane Gabrielson. "From Aaron 'Drest' to Dickinson's 'Queen': Protestant Typology in Herbert and Dickinson." *The Emily Dickinson Journal* 3.1 (1994): 1–23.

Sewall, Richard. "The Continuing Presence of Emily Dickinson." *The Emily Dickinson Handbook*, ed. Gudrun Grabher, Roland Hagenbüchle, and Cristanne Miller, 3–7. Amherst: U of Massachusetts P, 1998.

Sewall, Richard B., ed. *Emily Dickinson: A Collection of Critical Essays*. Englewood Cliffs, NJ: Prentice-Hall, 1963.

———. "In Search of Emily Dickinson." In *Extraordinary Lives: The Art and Craft of American Biography*, ed. William Zinsser, 65–90. Boston: Houghton Mifflin Company, 1986.

———. *The Life of Emily Dickinson*. One-volume edition. New York: Farrar, Straus and Giroux, 1974.

———. *The Lyman Letters: New Light on Emily Dickinson and Her Family*. Amherst: U of Massachusetts P, 1965.

———. "Teaching Dickinson: Testimony of a Veteran." In *Approaches to Teaching Emily Dickinson*, ed. Robin Riley Fast and Christine Mack Gordon, 30–38. New York: MLA, 1989.

Shackford, Martha Hale. "The Poetry of Emily Dickinson." *The Atlantic Monthly*, January 1913, 93–97. Reprinted in *The Recognition of Emily Dickinson*, ed. Caesar R. Blake and Carlton F. Wells, 79–88.

Shakinovsky, Lynn. "No Frame of Reference: The Absence of Context in Emily Dickinson's Poetry." *The Emily Dickinson Journal* 3.2 (1994): 19–37.

Shapiro, Karl. *Beyond Criticism*. Lincoln: U of Nebraska P, 1953.

Sherwood, William R. *Circumference and Circumstance: Stages in the Mind and Art of Emily Dickinson*. New York and London: Columbia UP, 1968.

Shoobridge, Helen. "'Reverence for each Other Being the Sweet Aim': Dickinson Face to Face with the Masculine." *The Emily Dickinson Journal* 9.1 (2000): 87–111.

Short, Bryan C. "Emily Dickinson and the Scottish New Rhetoric. *The Emily Dickinson Journal* 5.2 (1996): 261–66.

Shurr, William H. *The Marriage of Emily Dickinson: A Study of the Fascicles*. 1983.

Sinclair, Andrew. *The Emancipation of the American Woman*. New York: Harper and Row, 1965.

Small, Judy Jo. *Positive as Sound: Emily Dickinson's Rhyme*. Athens, GA, and London, England: U of Georgia P, 1990.

Smith, Martha Nell. "Dickinson's Manuscripts." In *The Emily Dickinson Handbook,* ed. Gudrun Grabher, Roland Hagenbüchle, and Cristanne Miller, 113–37. Amherst: U of Massachusetts P, 1998.

———. "The Poet as Cartoonist: Pictures Sewed to Words." In *Comic Power in Emily Dickinson,* by Suzanne Juhasz, Cristanne Miller, and Martha Nell Smith, 63–102. Austin: U of Texas P, 1993.

———. *Rowing in Eden: Rereading Emily Dickinson.* Austin: U of Texas P, 1992.

Smith, Robert McClure. *The Seductions of Emily Dickinson.* Tuscaloosa and London: U of Alabama P, 1996.

Spencer, Theodore. "Concentration and Intensity." *New England Quarterly* 2 (July 1929); reprinted in *The Recognition of Emily Dickinson,* ed. Caesar R. Blake and Carlton F. Wells, 131–33. Ann Arbor: U of Michigan P, 1968.

Stonum, Gary Lee. *The Dickinson Sublime.* Madison: U of Wisconsin P, 1990.

Taggard, Genevieve. *The Life and Mind of Emily Dickinson.* London and New York: Alfred A. Knopf, 1930.

Tate, Allen. "Emily Dickinson." In *Emily Dickinson: A Collection of Critical Essays,* ed. Richard B. Sewall, 16–27. Englewood Cliffs, NJ: Prentice Hall, 1963.

Thompson, G. R., ed. *The Gothic Imagination: Essays in Dark Romanticism.* Pullman: Washington State UP, 1974.

Tingley, Stephanie A. "Sandra Gilbert and Emily Dickinson." *EDIS Bulletin* 6.1 (May/June 1994): 1–3.

Todd, John Emerson. *Emily Dickinson's Use of the Persona.* The Hague and Paris: Mouton, 1973.

Urban, Wilbur. *Language and Reality.* London: Allen & Unwin, Ltd., 1939.

Vendler, Helen. *Poets Thinking: Pope, Whitman, Dickinson, Yeats.* Cambridge, MA, and London, England: Harvard UP, 2004.

Wadsworth, Charles. *Sermons.* 1869. New York and San Francisco: A. Roman, 1869.

Walker, Cheryl. "Dickinson in Context: Nineteenth-Century American Women Poets." In *A Historical Guide to Emily Dickinson,* ed. Vivian R. Pollak, 175–200. Oxford and New York: Oxford UP, 2004.

———. *The Nightingale's Burden: Women Poets and American Culture before 1900.* Bloomington: Indiana UP, 1982.

Walsh, John Evangelist. *The Hidden Life of Emily Dickinson.* New York: Simon and Schuster, 1971.

———. *This Brief Tragedy: Unraveling the Todd-Dickinson Affair.* New York: Gove Weidenfeld, 1991.

Wand, Martin, and Richard B. Sewall. "'Eyes Be Blind, Heart Be Still': A New Perspective on Emily Dickinson's Eye Problem." *The New England Quarterly* 52 (Sept. 1979): 400–406.

Ward, Theodora. *Emily Dickinson's Letters to Dr. and Mrs. Josiah Holland.* Cambridge, MA: Harvard UP, 1951,

———. *The Capsule of the Mind: Chapters in the Life of Emily Dickinson.* Cambridge: Belknap Press of Harvard UP, 1961.

Wardrop, Daneen. "Emily Dickinson and the Gothic in Fascicle 16." *The Cambridge Companion to Emily Dickinson,* ed. Wendy Martin, 142–64. Cambridge: Cambridge UP, 2002.

———. *Emily Dickinson's Gothic: Goblin with a Gauge.* Iowa City: U of Iowa P, 1996.

Warren, Austin. "Emily Dickinson." In *Emily Dickinson: A Collection of Critical Essays,* ed. Richard B. Sewall, 101–16. Englewood Cliffs, NJ: Prentice-Hall, 1963.

Watts, Isaac. *The Psalms, Hymns, and Spiritual Songs of the Rev. Isaac Watts, D.D.* Edited by Samuel N. Worcester. Boston: Crocker and Brewster, 1834.

Webster, Grant. *The Republic of Letters: A History of Postwar American Literary Opinion.* Baltimore and London: Johns Hopkins UP, 1979.

Weisbuch, Robert. *Emily Dickinson's Poetry.* Chicago and London: U of Chicago P, 1975.

Weisbuch, Robert. "Nobody's Business: Dickinson's Dissolving Audience." In *Dickinson and Audience,* ed. Martin Orzeck and Robert Weisbuch, 57–76. Ann Arbor: U of Michigan P, 1996.

Weisbuch, Robert. "Whitman and Dickinson." In *American Literary Scholarship: An Annual, 1983,* ed. David J. Nordloh, 79–96. Durham, NC: Duke UP, 1985.

Wellek, René, and Austin Warren. *Theory of Literature.* 3rd ed. New York: Harcourt, Brace & World, 1956.

Werner, Marta L. *Emily Dickinson's Open Folios: Scenes of Reading, Surfaces of Writing.* Ann Arbor: U of Michigan P, 1995.

Whicher, George Frisbie. *This Was a Poet: A Critical Biography of Emily Dickinson.* New York and London: Charles Scribner's Sons, 1938.

White, Fred D. "Dickinson's Existential Dramas." In *The Cambridge Companion to Emily Dickinson,* ed. Wendy Martin, 91–106. Cambridge: Cambridge UP, 2002.

Whitman, Walt. "Song of Myself." In *Leaves of Grass* (1891 edition). *Complete Poetry and Selected Prose*, ed. James E. Miller, Jr., 25–68. Boston: Houghton Mifflin Company, 1959.

Wilbur, Richard. "'Sumptuous Destitution.'" In *Emily Dickinson: A Collection of Critical Essays*, ed. Richard B. Sewall, 127–36. Englewood Cliffs, NJ: Prentice-Hall, 1963.

Willis, Connie. "The Soul Selects Her Own Society: Invasion and Repulsion: A Chronological Reinterpretation of Two of Emily Dickinson's Poems: A Wellsian Perspective." *Asimov's Science Fiction*, April 1996: 20–27.

Willis, Laurette. "Emily Dickinson: The Soul's Society." Unpublished play, 1995.

Winhusen, Steven. "Emily Dickinson and Schizotypy." *The Emily Dickinson Journal* 13.1 (2004): 77–96.

Winters, Yvor. "Emily Dickinson and the Limits of Judgment." (1938) In *Emily Dickinson: A Collection of Critical Essays*, ed. Richard B. Sewall, 28–40. Englewood Cliffs, NJ: Prentice-Hall, 1963.

Wolosky, Shira. *Emily Dickinson: A Voice of War*. New Haven and London: Yale UP, 1984.

———. "Rhetoric or Not: Hymnal Tropes in Emily Dickinson and Isaac Watts." *New England Quarterly* 61 (1988): 214–32.

———. "Public and Private in Dickinson's War Poetry." In *A Historical Guide to Emily Dickinson*, ed. Vivian R. Pollak, 103–74. Oxford and New York: Oxford UP, 2004.

Woodress, James. "Emily Dickinson." In *Fifteen American Authors before 1900*, 139–68. Madison: U of Wisconsin P, 1971.

Wollf, Cynthia Griffin. *Emily Dickinson*. New York: Knopf, 1986.

Wright, Elizabeth. *Psychoanalytic Criticism: A Reappraisal*. 2nd ed. New York: Routledge, 1998.

Wylder, Edith. *The Last Face: Emily Dickinson's Manuscripts*. Albuquerque: U of New Mexico P, 1971.

Yamakawa, Tamaaki. "Emily Dickinson's Mystic Well — an Aspect of Fascicle 14." In *After a Hundred Years: Essays on Emily Dickinson*, ed. The Emily Dickinson Society of Japan, 67–85. Kyoto: Apollon-sha, 1988.

Yin, Joanna. "'Arguments of Pearl': Dickinson's Response to Puritan Semiology." *The Emily Dickinson Journal* 11.1 (1993): 65–83.

Yolen, Jane. "Sister Emily's Lightship." In *Starlight 1*, ed. Patrick Nielsen Hayden, 57–70. New York: Tor, 1996:.

Zinsser, William, ed. *Extraordinary Lives: The Art and Craft of American Biography*. Boston: Houghton Mifflin Company, 1986.

General Index

Ackmann, Martha, 2, 91–92
Adams, John, 185
Aiken, Conrad, 5
Alger, William R., 55
allegorical poetry, 16
Amherst, MA, 49, 107
Amherst Academy, 54, 91, 96, 135
Amherst College, 2, 105, 133n, 186
amplified contexts, 98–99, 102
anagogical poetry, 16
analogical imagery, 147
Anderson, Charles, 29–31, 33, 34, 66, 132, 158
Anthon, Catherine (Kate) Scott, 29, 47, 74
aphoristic elements in Dickinson's poetry, 76
apocalyptic imagery, 147
archetypal criticism of Dickinson, 114, 146–58
archetypes, 70, 114, 150–51, 157
Archives, Emily Dickinson Electronic, 9, 11, 105, 176, 189
Aristotle, 12, 13, 60
Auden, W. H., 97
audience in Dickinson's poetry, 15

Bakhtin, Mikhail, 83, 92
Banzer, Judith, 50
Barker, Wendy, 67, 74–75, 79
Barnes, Daniel, 16
Barnstone, Aliki, 121–22, 192
Bates, Arlo, 5
Beauvoir, Simone de, 65
Beecher, Henry Ward, 135
Beethoven, Ludwig van, 27
Benet, Laura, 180n

Benfey, Christopher E. G., 9, 156, 158–59, 186, 190, 191
Bennett, Paula, 80–82, 89, 191
Benvenuto, Richard, 23
Bercovich, Sacvan, 169
Bernhard, Mary Elizabeth Kromer, 10n
Berryman, John, 19, 179
Bianchi, Martha Dickinson, 4, 6, 73, 182
Biblical allusions in Dickinson's poetry, 99, 103, 153, 166
Bingham, Millicent Todd, 20, 55n
biographical criticism of Dickinson, 29, 34, 40–64, 77
biographical fallacy, 42, 76–77
biography, intellectual, 42, 53
Blackmur, R. P., 5, 29
Blair, Hugh, 13
Blake, Caesar R., 5, 130n
Blake, William, 102, 112, 130
Blasing, Mutlu Konuk, 16–17
Bloom, Harold, 77–78, 119n, 151–52, 183
Bogan, Louise, 130
Bonaparte, Marie, 56
Boruch, Marianne, 180
Boswell, Jeanetta, 6, 176
Bowles, Mary (Mrs. Samuel), 55, 140
Bowles, Samuel, 4, 9, 42, 46, 77, 108, 114, 140
Bradstreet, Anne, 108, 130
Brantley, Richard E., 133n, 144, 192
Brégy, Kathérine, 127
Brock-Broido, Lucie, 183
Brooklyn Daily Union, 119n

Brooks, Cleanth, 28, 29, 39, 170
Browne, Emma Alice, 117
Browning, Elizabeth Barrett, 68, 77, 104
Browning, Robert, 51
Buckingham, Willis J., 5, 6, 22, 96n
Budick, E. Miller, 18, 66, 169, 190
Burbick, Joan, 124
Burgum, Edwin Berry, 27n
Burke, Kenneth, 16
Bushell, Sally, 95, 104
Bushnell, Horace, 126

Calvin, John, 141
Cameron, Sharon, 98–99, 105, 166–67, 190
Campbell, George, 13
Capps, Jack L., 106, 107
Carlyle, Thomas, 25, 150, 172
Carpini, John Delli, 138, 139–40
Carter, Louise, 115–16
Carton, Evan, 18
catharsis, 60
Catherine of Siena, 128
"centripetal" vs. "centrifugal" criticism, 147
Channing, William Ellery, 135
Chase, Richard, 29, 67n, 129, 158
Chicago, Judy, 186
Chicago School of Criticism, 27
Chickering, Joseph A., 78n
Christensen, Lena, 90n, 192
Christian Union, 4
chromatic progression in Dickinson's poetry, 76
Cicero, 13
Cixous, Helen, 56
Clarke, Graham, 6, 191
Clendenning, Sheila T., 6–7
Coates, Gloria, 185
Cody, John, 52, 56–60, 63, 71, 73, 75, 76, 164, 167n, 175
Coghill, Sheila, 179
Cole, Thomas, 108, 113–14, 115
Coleman, Lyman, 135

Coleridge, Samuel Taylor, 60
Collins, Billy, 179
Columbus, Christopher, 148
comedic elements in Dickinson's poetry, 82, 95
compression in Dickinson's poetry, 11, 20, 23, 83
Connecticut Valley, 43, 107, 145
Conrad, Angela, 128, 191
Cooper, James Fenimore, 75
Copland, Aaron, 185
Corbett, Edward P. J., 14
Cranach, Lucas, 115n
Crane, Hart, 176, 179
Croce, Benedetto, 27n
Crumbley, Paul, 92–93
cultural criticism of Dickinson, 106–24
culture of reading in Dickinson's day, 122–24

Danly, Susan, 186
Darwin, Charles, 138
dash, 86, 89, 91, 92–93, 105
death and dying in Dickinson's poetry, 18, 32, 39, 60, 103
deconstruction, 175
Dells (home of David and Mabel Todd), 192
demonic imagery, 147
Denman, Kamilla, 92n
Deppman, Jed, 11
Der Westen, 5
Derrida, Jacques, 162, 170
dialectic, Dickinson's use of, 17, 18, 167
Dickens, Charles, 95
Dickenson, Donna, 8
Dickie, Margaret, 2, 170–71
Dickinson, Austin, 9, 44, 50, 55–56, 134, 135, 184, 192
Dickinson, Cindy, 10n
Dickinson, Edward, 50, 58, 73, 94, 136

Dickinson, Emily:
  agoraphobia in, 60–62, 88
  audience awareness of, 20
  attitude toward books, 123
  attitude toward death, 59–60
  attitude toward publishing, 42, 85
  biblical allusions in poems of, 99, 142–43, 148, 150, 151–52
  botanical knowledge of, 116
  "Brother Pegasus" letter of, 44
  and Christianity, 17, 99–100, 122, 128–32, 133, 134, 136–40, 143–44, 155
  and the Civil War, 107, 119–20
  as cultural critic, 120–22
  dictionary used by, 22–23, 121
  in drama, 177–78
  education of, 95
  as existentialist, 139
  eye problems of, 40n, 62–63, 72n, 188
  fascicles (manuscript booklets) of, 3, 36, 51, 86, 87, 95–103
  as the female Sade, 79, 150
  in fiction, 180–84
  "flood subjects" of, 125, 148
  handwriting (chirography) of, 85–93
  iconographic imagination of, 115
  legal vocabulary of, 42
  letter-poems of, 104, 105, 122
  letters of, 34, 46–47, 83, 103–4
  lineation in poems and letters of, 2, 103
  manuscripts of, 85–105
  and metaphysical poets, 142
  in music, 184–85
  as philosopher, 156–61
  in poetry, 178–80
  political awareness of, 107
  and Puritan culture, 60, 68, 107, 108–10
  as Puritan rebel, 128
  and Shakespeare, 123
  skepticism of, 158–59
  theological vocabulary of, 129, 143, 144
  and Transcendentalism, 132–34
  and Victorian culture, 110–12
  white dress of, 41
  worksheet drafts of, 94–95
Dickinson, Emily Norcross, 9, 58, 59, 115
Dickinson, Gilbert ("Gib"), 9, 47
Dickinson, Lavinia, 9, 49, 50, 181–82
Dickinson, Ned, 51
Dickinson, Samuel Fowler, 49, 50
Dickinson, Susan (Sue) Huntington Gilbert, 4, 29, 41, 50, 60, 71, 74, 77, 80, 90, 104, 105, 108, 189, 192
Diehl, Joanne Feit, 77–78, 159, 190
DiFilippo, Paul, 183
Dill, Leslie, 186
Dobson, Joanne A., 70–71, 180–81
Donne, John, 14, 51
Doriani, Beth Maclay, 79
Duchac, Joseph, 5, 6
Durand, Asher, 108, 112

Eaves, Morris, 88
Eberwein, Jane Donahue, 7, 54n, 107, 124, 132, 137, 143–45
EDIS Bulletin, 10, 11, 180
Editing Collective, Emily Dickinson, 9, 105
Edwards, Anne, 180
Edwards, Jonathan, 108, 112, 127, 145
Eissler, K. R., 60n
Eliot, T. S., 97
Ellis, Richard S., 143
elocutionary marks, Dickinson's use of, 86, 91
Emerson, Ralph Waldo, 16, 18, 20, 43, 79, 96, 108, 112, 132, 133–34, 137, 149, 150, 152, 158, 159, 162, 164, 170, 171

Emily Dickinson Editing Collective. *See* Editing Collective, Emily Dickinson
Emily Dickinson Electronic Archives. *See* Archives, Emily Dickinson Electronic
Emily Dickinson International Society (EDIS), 10
Emily Dickinson Journal, The, 10, 11
Emmons, Henry Vaughan, 46, 96
England, Martha Winburn, 17n
Erikson, Erik, 71
Erkkila, Betsy, 107, 174
erotic elements in Dickinson's poetry, 48–49, 77, 153, 191
Evergreens (home of Austin and Susan Dickinson), 9, 48, 192

Farr, Judith, 10n, 108, 113–17, 120, 167n, 181, 188
Farwell, Arthur, 185
Fast, Robin Riley, 10
feminist literary criticism of Dickinson, 1, 24, 59–60, 65–84, 108
Ferlazzo, Paul J., 8, 177, 190
Fiedelson, Charles, Jr., 169
Fish, Stanley, 11
Finnerty, Páriac, 122–24, 192
Flynt, Eudocia Converse, 54
Ford, Emily Fowler, 178–79
Ford, Thomas W., 158
formalism, Russian, 27n
formalist, criticism of Dickinson, 27–37, 66, 67, 146–47, 166, 189
Foster, Richard, 29
Foucault, Michel, 141, 170
Fowler, Emily. *See* Ford, Emily Fowler
Fowler, William, 178
Franklin, R. W., 2, 3, 44n, 47n, 48n, 78n, 86, 87, 88, 90, 96, 102n, 163n

Franklin and Johnson variorum editions of Dickinson's poems compared, 90
Freeman, Margaret, 10, 60, 73
Freud, Sigmund, 41, 56, 71, 152, 153, 175
Friedan, Betty, 65
Friends of the Amherst College Library, 47
Frost, Robert, 109
Frye, Northrop, 146, 148–50
Fuller, Jamie, 181
Fuller, Margaret, 65, 79, 109
Fulton, Alice, 179
Furey, Martha, 178
Furukawa, Takao, 10n

Gall, Sally M., 97
Garbowsky, Maryanne, 60–62, 185
Gardner, Dorothy, 177
Gardner, Thomas, 183, 192
Gelpi, Albert, 43–44, 129, 138, 149, 150, 156, 167n
Gilbert, Sandra M., 66, 67–78, 113, 190
Gilbert, Susan. *See* Dickinson, Susan Gilbert
Glaspell, Susan, 177
Gordon, Christine Mack, 10
gothicism, 100–101, 152–54
Gould, George, 42
Gould, Hannah, 117
Grabher, Gudrun, 2, 7, 10n
Graham, Jorie, 183
grammar in Dickinson's poetry, 23–24
Green, Clara Newman, 181
Green, Daniel, 28n
Griffith, Clark, 14, 31–33, 66, 67n, 168
Gubar, Susan, 66, 67–68, 71, 113, 190
Guerra, Jonnie, 2, 10, 176, 178, 180, 186n
Gura, Philip F., 126

guides at the Dickinson Homestead, 177n
Guthrie, James R., 41n, 62–63, 188

Habegger, Alfred, 4, 53–56, 125, 176n, 191
Hagenbüchle, Roland, 2, 7, 18, 148–49
Hall, Donald, 179
Hampl, Patricia, 180
Harris, Julie, 177
Hart, Ellen Louise, 71n, 87n, 103–4, 105
Harvard University, 105
Hass, Robert, 183
hauntedness as Dickinson's artistic ideal, 153
Hawthorne, Nathaniel, 108, 109
Heginbotham, Eleanor Elson, 100, 102, 103n, 192
Henneberg, Sylvia, 77
Herbert, George, 142
Herrick, Robert, 28
heteroglossia in Dickinson's poetry, 92
Higgins, David, 46–47
Higginson, Thomas Wentworth, 4, 5, 6, 9, 16, 22, 28, 40–41, 50, 63n, 73, 76, 80, 85, 86, 91, 96, 108, 109, 112, 115n, 136, 140, 158, 170, 181
Hildegard of Bingen, 128
history of the book and of reading, 188–89
Hitchcock, Edward, 133n
Hoffman, E. T. A., 153
Hofmann, Michael, 183n
Holland, Elizabeth, 50, 177
Holland, Jeanne, 94
Holland, Josiah, 4, 50, 108, 130
Holcomb, Timothy, 178n
Homans, Margaret, 66, 68, 84, 190
Homestead (Emily Dickinson's home), 9, 11, 121, 192
Hopkins, Gerard Manley, 128

Howard, Richard, 117n
Howard, William, 22
Howe, Julia Ward, 120
Howe, Susan, 2, 81–82, 139n, 172–73, 180, 190
Howells, William Dean, 5
Howitt, Mary, 112
Hudson River School, 112
Hume, David, 13
Humphrey, Jane, 43
Hunt, Lieutenant Edward, 42
hymnal meter, 23, 17n, 36, 131

Irigaray, Luce, 73
intertextuality, 102
irony in Dickinson's poetry, 17, 57

Jackson, Helen Hunt, 4, 29, 42, 117, 119n, 176, 180
Jackson, Virginia, 21, 169–70, 188, 192
Jakobson, Roman, 27n
James, Henry, 75
Jameson, John Franklin, 47n
Jancovich, Mark, 28
Jenkins, Macgregor, 180n
Johnson, Greg, 156–57
Johnson, Thomas H., 1, 3, 30, 42–43, 87, 90, 104, 128–29
Jones, Ernest, 56
Jones, Rowena Revis, 140–41
Jordan, Mary Augusta, 5
Juhasz, Suzanne, 59–60, 65n, 67, 68, 70, 72, 82, 105, 189, 190
Jung, Carl, 56, 148n

Kames, Lord, 13
Kant, Immanuel, 13, 159
Kaufmann, Paola, 182
Keats, John, 51
Keller, Karl, 108–10, 130, 190
Kennedy, X. J., 179
Kher, Inder Nath, 66–67, 108, 156–57
Kierkegaard, Soren, 139

Kimpel, Ben, 159–61, 190
Kinnell, Galway, 179
Kirk, Connie Ann, 11
Kirkby, Joan, 8–9
Knapp, Bettina L., 8, 30, 144
Kristeva, Julia, 92, 101
Kuhn, Thomas, 187
Kumin, Maxine, 179

Lacan, Jacques, 56, 164–66
Ladin, Jay, 11
Langton, Jane, 180
Lasdun, James, 183n
Lawrence, D. H., 81, 172
Lease, Benjamin, 10n, 135
Lefcowitz, Barbara F., 179–80
Leiter, Sharon, 9, 192
Lentricchia, Frank, 146, 170
Leonard, Douglas Novich, 102
Lewis, Matthew Gregory, 152
Leyda, Jay, 7–8, 53
Liebling, Jerome, 9, 191
Lilliedahl, Ann, 5
Lindberg-Seyersted, Brita, 12n, 21–23
linguistic disruption in Dickinson's poetry, 24
Loeffelholz, Mary, 72, 164–66
Lombardo, Daniel, 6
Longfellow, Henry Wadsworth, 108, 134
Longsworth, Polly, 9, 10n, 184, 191
Lord, Otis, 9, 104, 180
Loving, Jerome, 30, 51–52, 167n
Lowell, Robert, 19
Lowenberg, Carlton, 13, 176, 184
Lubbers, Klaus, 1, 2, 4, 127, 176
Lucas, Dorothy Dyer, 14
Luce, William, 177
Lundin, Roger, 138
Lyell, Charles, 138
Lyman, Joseph, 40n, 47n
Lyman letters, 41n, 47n
Lyon, Mary, 9, 136, 174

lyricism in Dickinson's poetry, 21, 170–72

Machor, James L., 65, 66n
MacKenzie, Cynthia, 7, 191
MacLeish, Archibald, 12, 92
MacMurray, Rose, 182
Mann, John S., 41n
Marsh, Brian, 178
Martin, Wendy, 133–34, 144, 190, 192
"Master" letters, 73, 114
Mather, Cotton, 127
McGann, Jerome, 86
McIntosh, James, 17, 138, 139, 191
McNeil, Helen, 9, 13, 19, 77, 83, 92, 192
Melville, Herman, 75, 120
Merriam, George, 140n
Messmer, Marietta, 2, 15n, 83, 103
military analogies in Dickinson's poetry, 35
Miller, Cristanne, 2, 7, 11, 21, 23–25, 76n, 82, 107, 108, 167n, 191
Miller, J. Hillis, 162
Miller, Ruth, 96–97
Millett, Kate, 65n
Mills, Elizabeth M., 180
Milton, John, 174
Mitchell, Domhnall, 86, 90–91, 120–21, 191, 192
Mollicone, Henry, 185
Montaigne, Michel de, 158
Moore, Hastings, 60n
Morath, Max, 185
Morse, Jonathan, 108
Moses, 165
Mossberg, Barbara Antonina Clarke, 69–70, 72–73, 167n, 190
Mount Holyoke, 50
Mt. Holyoke College, 11. *See also* Mt. Holyoke Seminary for Women
Mt. Holyoke Seminary for Women, 9, 54, 113, 136, 174

Mudge, Jean McClure, 71–72, 121
Myerson, Joel, 7

Nabokov, Vladimir, 108
negative capability, 60
New, Elisa, 125, 129
New Criticism. *See* formalist approaches to Dickinson's poetry
Newman, Clara. *See* Green, Clara Newman
Newman, Samuel P., 13
Newton, Benjamin, 22, 43, 49
Nietzsche, Friedrich, 129, 141
Niles, Thomas, 87
Noah, 148
Norcross, Fanny, 115, 163
Norcross, Louisa ("Loo"), 92, 115, 163
Novak, Barbara, 114n

Oates, Joyce Carol, 179
Oberhaus, Dorothy Huff, 99, 100, 102, 191
Olds, Sharon, 179
"omitted center" theory of Dickinson's poetry, 8, 53
Ostricker, Alicia, 179
Orzeck, Martin, 20

Paglia, Camille, 79, 150–51, 152, 191
paradox in Dickinson's poetry, 18, 143, 171
Parley's Magazine, 112
Park, Edwards A., 126, 135
Parker, Alice, 185
Parker, Etta, 184
Parker, Theodore, 140
Pastan, Linda, 179
Patterson, Rebecca, 29, 37n, 47, 49, 73, 190
Peeples, Scott, 56n
persona, Emily Dickinson's use of, 19, 28, 37–39, 54n, 66, 68, 70, 188

Petrino, Elizabeth A., 117–18
Phillips, Elizabeth, 38
philosophical approaches to Dickinson's poetry, 158–61
Plath, Sylvia, 19
Plato, 18, 160, 169, 170
Plotinus, 130
Poe, Edgar Allan, 16, 25
poetics of seduction, 174–75
poetry of the portfolio, 96
Pohl, Frederick J., 4, 177
Polk, Mary Lynn Cooper, 2–3, 5
Pollak, Vivian R., 7, 47n, 58n, 66, 67, 78, 107, 108, 190, 192
Pollitt, Josephine, 6, 42
Porter, David T., 33–34, 66, 130–31, 150, 163–64, 167n, 190
Porter, Ebenezer, 13n, 89, 91
postmodern approaches to Dickinson's poetry, 162–75
Pound, Ezra, 97
Power, Sister Mary James, 127–28
Prague Linguistic Circle, 27n
private publishing. *See* poetry of the portfolio
proverb in Dickinson's poetry, 16
psychoanalytic approaches to Dickinson's poetry, 41, 56–62, 63, 175

Quintilian, 13

Radcliffe, Anne, 152
Ransom, John Crowe, 27n, 39
reader-response theory, 11
reference tools in Dickinson scholarship, 3
regionalisms in Dickinson's poetry, 22
Reilly, Charles Nelson, 177
Reynolds, David S., 134
rhetoric, 13–21, 83, 163
rhyme, Dickinson's use of, 23, 25–27
Rich, Adrienne, 167n, 179
Richards, I. A., 29

riddle, Emily Dickinson's use of, 15
Ridington, Candace, 184
Robinson, John, 9, 35–36, 125
Robinson, Marilynne, 184
Romanticism, 34, 72, 77, 79, 133, 138, 151, 153, 156, 169, 170, 171
Root, Abiah, 46
Rosenbaum, S. P., 3
Rosenthal, M. L., 97
Rossetti, Christina, 68
Rotella, Guy, 164
Rothberg, Morey, 47n
Runzo, Sandra, 70n
Ruskin, John, 82, 112
Ryder, Albert Pinkham, 114

Salska, Agnieszka, 155, 190
Sanborn, Franklin Benjamin, 123
Sánchez-Eppler, Karen, 186
Sand, George, 94
Sato, Tomoko, 101–2
Saussure, Ferdinand de, 162
Scheurer, Erika, 180
Scholl, Diane Gabrielson, 142
Scott, Kate. *See* Anthon, Kate Scott
Sewall, Richard B., 4, 7, 10–11, 40n, 49–51, 56, 137, 178, 179
Shackford, Martha Hale, 5, 130
Shakespeare, William, 63, 122–23, 192
Shakinovsky, Lynn, 83
Shapiro, Karl, 123
Sherwood, William R., 132, 136, 137
Shoobridge, Helen, 73,
Short, Bryan C., 13
Showalter, Elaine, 66
Shurr, William H., 30, 51, 97–98, 153, 190
Sigourney, Lydia, 111, 117, 119n
Sinclair, Andrew, 65
Small, Judy Jo, 25–27, 191
Smith, Martha Nell, 9, 71n, 82, 86, 89, 95, 104, 105, 191

Smith, Robert McClure, 174–75
Sparrow, John, 17n
speech elements in Dickinson's poetry, 91–92
Spingarn, Joel, 27n
spiritual approaches to Dickinson's poetry, 125–45
Springfield Republican, 4, 52, 85, 123, 179
St. Armand, Barton Levi, 9, 110–13, 117, 120, 122, 190, 191
Stafford, William, 179
stages of development in Dickinson's poetry, 122
Stein, Gertrude, 89, 172
Stevens, Wallace, 97,
Stonum, Gary Lee, 61, 149–50, 155, 191
Stowe, Harriet Beecher, 108
structuralism, 27n
stylistic elements in Dickinson's poetry, 21–27, 83
sublime, the, in Dickinson's poetry, 150
Sweet, Anna Jones Norcross, 91–92
Sweetser, Catherine Dickinson, 18, 76n
syntactic elements in Dickinson's poetry, 23–24

Taggard, Genevieve, 6, 42
Tammaro, Thom, 179
Tate, Allen, 5, 29, 39, 126, 127, 128, 129
Taylor, Edward, 112, 144
teaching Emily Dickinson, 10–11, 102–3
textual scholarship of Dickinson's poetry, 85–105
Thompson, G. R., 153
Thompson, Maurice, 5
Thoreau, Henry David, 150, 178
Tingley, Stephanie A., 180
Titanic Operas, 176
Todd, David Peck, 184, 192

Todd-Dickinson affair, 50, 184
Todd, John Emerson, 28, 37–38
Todd, Mabel Loomis, 4, 5, 20, 87, 96, 115n, 163n, 182, 184, 192
Transcendentalism, 79, 132–34, 169
Twain, Mark, 178

Urban, Wilbur, 169

Vedder, Elihu, 114
Vendler, Helen, 39, 76, 192
Virgil, 54, 92n
voice in Dickinson's poetry, 15, 22, 52–53, 68

Wadsworth, Charles, 47, 51, 108, 134–35
Walker, Cheryl, 66n, 74, 106
Walsh, John Evangelist, 77, 184n
Wand, Martin, 62
Ward, A. C., 5
Ward, Theodora, 3, 30, 44–46
Wardrop, Daneen, 41n, 100–101, 152–54, 167n
Warner, Mary, 111, 112
Warren, Austin, 5, 29
Warren, Robert Penn, 28n, 39, 170
Watts, Isaac, 131–32
Webster, Grant, 27n
Webster, Noah, 22, 92, 121, 178
Weisbuch, Robert, 20–21, 34–35, 97, 98
Wellek, René, 29
Wells, Carleton, 5, 130n
Wells, H. G., 183
Werner, Marta, 104
Whicher, George F., 5, 6, 29, 43, 70, 129, 158
White, Fred D., 159n
Whitman, Walt, 13, 16, 97, 102, 109, 155, 170, 171
Whitney, Maria, 121
Wilbur, Richard, 119, 176
Wilde, Oscar, 172
Williams, William Carlos, 81, 97
Willis, Connie, 183
Willis, Laurette, 178
Winhusen, Steven, 63
Winters, Yvor, 19, 125
Wolff, Cynthia Griffin, 17n, 52–53, 133, 166n, 191
Wolosky, Shira, 17n, 107, 119–20, 124, 130–31, 167n, 190
Wollstonecraft, Mary, 65
Wood, Abby, 54
Woodress, James, 2
wordplay in Dickinson's poetry, 30, 143
Wordsworth, William, 72
Wright, Elizabeth, 41
Wylder, Edith, 86, 91–92, 105

Yamakawa, Tamasaki, 97n
Yeats, William Butler, 97
Yin, Joanna, 141–42
Yolen, Jane, 182–83
York, Vincent, 4, 177

Index of First Lines of Poems Discussed

All Dickinson poems cited in this book are from the Franklin variorum edition (Belknap/Harvard, 1998). Numbers in parentheses refer to the Franklin and Johnson variorum editions respectively.

After great pain, a formal feeling comes — (Fr372; J341), 57, 58, 122
A little East of Jordan (Fr145B; J59), 78, 143
All the letters I could write, (Fr380A; J334), 55, 77
Alone and in a Circumstance (Fr1174; J1167), 94
A loss of something ever felt I — (Fr1072; J959), 58
A narrow Fellow in the Grass (Fr1096B; J986), 85, 89
A nearness to Tremendousness — (Fr824; J963), 118
A science — so the Savants say (Fr147; J100), 122
At least — to pray — is left — is left (Fr377; J502), 70
A Wife — at Daybreak I shall be — (Fr185B; J461), 142
A word is dead when it is said, (Fr278A.1; J1212), 162, 163

Because I could not stop for Death — (Fr479; J712), 163, 164
Because that you are going (Fr1314A; J1260), 148
Bees are Black, with Gilt Surcingles — (Fr1426A; J1405), 30–31
Before I got my eye put out (Fr336A; J327), 62–63, 101, 157
Behind Me — dips Eternity (Fr743; J721), 144
Better — than Music! (Fr378; J503), 25–26
Blazing in Gold and quenching in Purple (Fr321C; J228), 103, 169
By my Window have I for Scenery (Fr849; J797), 144

Come slowly — Eden! (Fr205; J211), 80–81, 114

Death's Waylaying not the sharpest (Fr1315; J1296), 18
Did the Harebell loose her girdle (Fr134; J213), 21, 81, 185
Distrustful of the Gentian (Fr26; J20), 114
Dying! Dying in the night! (Fr222; J158), 37

Essential oils are wrung — (Fr772; J675), 132
Estranged from Beauty — none can be — (Fr1515; J1474), 93
Experiment to me (Fr1081C; J1073), 38

Faith is the Pierless Bridge (Fr978; J915), 131–32
Far from Love the Heavenly Father (Fr1032; J1021), 128

Four trees — upon a solitary Acre — (Fr778; J742), 23, 164n
From Blank to Blank (Fr484; J761), 151

Glory is that bright tragic thing (Fr1700; J1660), 129, 144
God is a distant — stately Lover — (Fr615; J357), 140, 145
Going to Him! Happy letter! (Fr278; J494), 77
Good Morning — Midnight — (Fr382; J425), 22, 75
Good night, because we must, (Fr97A; J114), 36
Good Night! Which put the Candle out? (Fr322; J259), 103

Had I presumed to hope — (Fr634; J522), 157
Have you got a Brook in your little heart, (Fr94; J136), 184, 185
He ate and drank the precious Words — (Fr1593; J1587), 143, 155
"Heaven" — is what I cannot reach! (Fr310; J239), 155
Her breast was fit for pearls (Fr121B; J84), 114
He strained my faith — (Fr366; J497), 145
He was weak, and I was strong — then — (Fr221; J190), 98
How happy is the little Stone (Fr1570B; J1510), 128, 155
How the old Mountains drip with Sunset (Fr327; J291), 103

I am alive — I guess — (Fr605; J470), 71
I breathed enough to take the Trick — (Fr308; J272), 154
I cannot live with You (Fr706; J640), 21
I died for beauty — but was scarce (Fr448; J449), 37
I felt a Cleaving in my Mind (Fr867B; J937), 76
I felt a Funeral, in my Brain (Fr340; J280), 101, 114, 163
If ever the lid gets off my head (Fr585; J1727), 151
If this is "fading" (Fr119; J120), 112
I gave myself to Him (Fr426; J580), 97, 145
I got so I could hear his name (Fr292; J293), 54, 167
I heard a Fly buzz when I died (Fr591; J465), 33, 53
I know that He exists (Fr365; J338), 19, 129
I like to see it lap the Miles — (Fr383; J585), 120–21
I'm ceded — I've stopped being Their's — (Fr353; J508), 38, 142
I'm saying every day (Fr575; J373), 38
I'm "wife" — I've finished that — (Fr225; J199), 22, 97
I never felt at Home — Below — (Fr437; J413), 171
I never lost as much but twice — (Fr39; J49), 66
In many and reportless places (Fr1404; J1382), 18, 139, 172–73
I prayed at first, a little Girl (Fr546; J576), 137
I shall know why — when Time is over — (Fr215; J193), 24
I shall not murmur if at last (Fr1429; Fr1410), 48
I should have been too glad, I see — (Fr283B; J313), 110, 167
I should not dare to leave my friend (Fr234; J205), 37
I started early — took my Dog (Fr620; J520), 31–32, 168

It always felt to me — a wrong (Fr521; J597), 164–65
I taste a liquor never brewed (Fr207; J214), 82
It bloomed and dropt, a Single Noon — (Fr843; J978), 116–17
It dropped so low — in my regard — (Fr785; J747), 98
It's like the Light — (Fr302; J297), 99
It was a quiet way — (Fr573B; J1053), 174–75
It was too late for Man — (Fr689; J623), 127

Like Flowers, that heard the news of Dews (Fr361; J513), 136
Love — is anterior to Life — (Fr980; J917), 44, 127
Love is done when Love's begun, (Fr1526; J1485), 16

Many cross the Rhine (Fr107; J123), 37
Me — come! My dazzled face (Fr381; J431), 135
Mine — by the Right of the White Election! (Fr411; J528), 70n
More than the Grave is closed to me — (Fr1532; J1503), 19
My Cocoon tightens — Colors teaze — (Fr1107; J1099), 141–42
My faith is larger than the Hills (Fr489; J766), 140
My Life had stood — a Loaded Gun — (Fr764; J754), 23, 52, 167–68, 173
My Maker — let me be (Fr1463; J1403), 137
My Triumph lasted till the Drums (Fr1212; J1227), 120

No matter — now — Sweet — (Fr734; J704), 22
No Rack can torture me — (Fr649; J384), 156

Of nearness to her sundered Things (Fr337; J607), 101
Of this is Day composed (Fr1692; J1675), 74
Oh give it motion — deck it sweet (Fr1550; J1527), 39
On a Columnar Self — (Fr740; J789), 62
Once more, my now bewildered Dove (Fr65; J48), 148
One Anguish — in a Crowd — (Fr527; J565), 79
One Joy of so much anguish (Fr1450; J1420), 160–61
One need not be a Chamber — to be Haunted — (Fr407; J670), 72, 156

Papa above! (Fr151B; J61), 38, 137
Paradise is that old mansion (Fr1144; J1119), 121
Perhaps I asked too large — (Fr358; J352), 19–20
Publication — is the Auction (Fr788; J709), 87, 88

Remorse — is Memory — awake — (Fr781; J744), 166–67

Satisfaction — is the Agent (Fr984; J1036), 129
She lay as if at play (Fr412; J369), 15
She rose to His Requirement — dropt (Fr857; J732), 25–26
She sweeps with many-colored Brooms — (Fr318A; J219), 75, 103

Sleep is supposed to be (Fr35; J13), 34
Some keep the Sabbath going to Church (Fr236; J324), 61
Some things that fly there be — (Fr68; J89), 133
So much of Heaven has gone from Earth (Fr1240; J1228), 138
Split the lark — and you'll find the Music — (Fr905; J861), 158
Still own thee — still thou art (Fr1654; J1633), 23
Success is counted sweetest (Fr112C; J67), 119
Summer for thee, grant I may be (Fr7; J31), 97, 102
Sunset at Night — is natural — (Fr427; J415), 69
Superiority to Fate (Fr1043; J1081), 36

That sacred Closet when you sweep (Fr1385; J1273), 95
The daisy follows soft the Sun — (Fr161; J106), 69
The dandelion's pallid tube (Fr1565; J1519), 156
The definition of Beauty is (Fr797B; J988), 18, 126
The Fact that Earth is Heaven — (Fr1435; J1408), 19
The first Day's Night had come — (Fr423; J410), 61, 97, 99
The Gentian weaves her fringes — (Fr21; J18), 102, 97
The last Night that She lived (Fr1100; J1100), 32, 33
The Love a Life can show Below (Fr285B; J673), 110
The Months have ends — the Years — a knot — (Fr416; J423), 26
There came a Day at Summer's full (Fr325; J322), 98
There is a Zone whose even Years (Fr1020; J1056), 122
There's a certain Slant of light (Fr320; J258), 122, 164
There's been a death in the opposite House (Fr547; J389), 33
The Robin's my Criterion for Tune — (Fr256; J285), 22, 106, 188
The Soul selects her own society (Fr409A; J303), 72, 110
The Soul's Superior instants (Fr630B; J306), 98
The Spider as an Artist (Fr1373; J1275), 111–12
The spider Holds a Silver Ball (Fr513; J605), 112
The sun kept stooping — stooping — low! (Fr182; J152), 112
The Tint I cannot take — is best — (Fr696; J627), 152
They shut me up in Prose — (Fr445; J613), 70, 72, 100
This is my letter to the World (Fr519; J441), 15, 92
This was a Poet — (Fr446; J448), 100
This World is not Conclusion (Fr373; J501), 27, 138, 144
Those — dying then, (Fr1581; J1551), 17
Three times — we parted — Breath — and I — (Fr514; J598), 45
Time feels so vast that were it not (Fr858; J802), 149
'Tis Opposites — entice — (Fr612; J355), 109
'Tis so appalling — it exhilarates — (Fr341; J281), 101
Title divine — is mine! (Fr194A; J1072), 77, 114
"Tomorrow" — whose location (Fr1417; J1367), 159
To my small Hearth His fire came — (Fr703; J638), 137

'Twas just this time, last year, I died. (Fr344; J445), 118
'Twas my one Glory (Fr1040; J1028), 109

We like a Hairbreadth 'scape (Fr1247; J1175), 123
We lose — because we win — (Fr28; J21), 102
We met as Sparks — Diverging Flints (Fr918; J958), 160
We play at paste — (Fr282A; J320), 118–19
Were it to be the last (Fr1165; J1164), 76
We shun it ere it comes (Fr1595; J1580), 78
Who never lost, are unprepared (Fr136B; J73), 35
Wild nights — wild nights! (Fr269; J249), 37

You'll know Her — by Her Foot — (Fr604; J634), 142, 171–72
You'll know it — as you know 'tis Noon — (Fr429; J420), 144
You see I cannot see — your lifetime — (Fr313; J253), 98

When Klaus Lubbers's meticulously detailed *Emily Dickinson: The Critical Revolution* appeared in 1968, examining Dickinson criticism from 1886 to 1962, a second revolution in Dickinson criticism was already gathering force. Enabled by Thomas H. Johnson's variorum edition of the *Poems* (1955), the Johnson/Theodora Ward edition of the *Letters* (1958), Richard B. Sewall's document-rich, definitive *Life of Emily Dickinson* (1974), and R. W. Franklin's reassembled *Manuscript Books of Emily Dickinson* (1981), a new generation of scholars representing a wide spectrum of critical perspectives began reassessing the poet's life and work. In the nearly forty years since Lubbers's survey, approximately one hundred books — monographs, bibliographies, biographies, essay collections — about Dickinson and her oeuvre have appeared, making her one of the most extensively studied poets in American history. *Approaching Emily Dickinson* provides an objective examination of that vast body of scholarship.

The book gives detailed attention to the principal trends in Dickinson scholarship during the past half-century: rhetorical and stylistic analysis of the poems and letters; biographical studies informed by theories of gender, sexuality, and by medical history; feminist studies of the poet's life and work; textual studies of the bound and unbound fascicles and the so-called worksheet drafts (or "scraps"); new assessments of the poet's social and cultural milieu, including influences on her spiritual sensibility, and of her theories of poetry, including lyricism. Fred White also examines Dickinson's artistic reception over the past half-century — an area of ever-growing fascination, not only among Dickinson scholars but among artists, creative writers, dramatists, and musicians for whom Dickinson's genius has proven to be a powerful conduit for insights into the human condition.

A fundamental research tool for both scholars and students in the way it clearly identifies the lines of inquiry during the past half century, *Approaching Emily Dickinson* also enables fruitful comparisons both among and within different critical and artistic perspectives.

FRED D. WHITE is professor of English at Santa Clara University. His studies of Emily Dickinson have been published in *College Literature* and in the *Cambridge Companion to Emily Dickinson*. He has also edited *Essential Muir: A Selection of John Muir's Best Writings* (Heyday Books, 2006), and is the co-author (with Simone Billings) of The Well-Crafted Argument, the third edition of which was published by Houghton Mifflin in 2008.

Fred White's survey of Dickinson scholarship since 1960 is an essential resource for both long-term readers of Dickinson and those coming to her work for the first time. Readers interested in knowing how Dickinson criticism developed from 1960 to the present will find this book a highly informative and stimulating read.

                                              THE EMILY DICKINSON JOURNAL

www.ingramcontent.com/pod-product-compliance
Lightning Source LLC
Chambersburg PA
CBHW020650230426
43665CB00008B/376